RUTH DAVIDSON

RUTH DAVIDSON

AND THE

Resurgence

OF THE

Scottish Tories

ANDREW LIDDLE

Biteback Publishing

First published in Great Britain in 2018 by
Biteback Publishing Ltd
Westminster Tower
3 Albert Embankment
London SE1 7SP
Copyright © Andrew Liddle 2018

ISBN 978-1-78590-174-4

10 9 8 7 6 5 4 3 2 1

A CIP catalogue record for this book is available from the British Library.

Set in Adobe Caslon Pro and Bodoni Oldstyle

Printed and bound in Great Britain by
CPI Group (UK) Ltd, Croydon CR0 4YY

MIX
Paper from
responsible sources
FSC
www.fsc.org   FSC® C020471

For Chris and Freddie, sorry about the Bush

CONTENTS

CONTENTS

ACKNOWLEDGEMENTS

R uth Davidson's rise to political prominence has been short and stratospheric. She has lived through – and helped shape – some of the most politically turbulent times in Scottish – and British – politics.

The aim of this book is to consider Ruth's role in recent political history – particularly the independence referendum, the EU referendum and, most importantly, the 2016 Scottish election.

Naturally, such important political events are discussed in detail, but the focus is on Ruth's role in them. The work assumes some knowledge of Scottish and UK politics, but I hope it remains accessible and readable.

Written when Ruth is only thirty-nine years old – and when she has been directly involved in politics for less than seven years – it cannot be and is not a complete account of her political career. However, I hope the final chapters offer some analysis and insight into her prospects – and those of the Scottish Conservatives.

As a political biography, this book does not aim to answer key questions over the future of the Union, the rights and wrong of independence or the UK's relationship with Europe. Others, far more qualified than I, will undoubtedly address those in detail elsewhere.

It does, of course, aim to put the Scottish Conservatives' 2016 result in its historical context – but it does not strive to provide a complete history of the Tories in Scotland. I would hope, however, that it provides a useful introduction for those looking to understand more about the history of the Conservatives in Scotland, as well as some refreshing ideas for those who may have studied the subject in more detail.

It should be noted that this is an unauthorised political biography. I know Ruth professionally, and I therefore only delve into personal aspects of her story where necessary. While she herself declined to cooperate, she has not attempted in any way to stop me speaking to those around her. As such, I have had access to her inner circle of advisers, former and present, Tory MSPs and their staff, as well as others who knew her well during her earlier career before politics. Many of those I have spoken to have, given the contemporary nature of the events discussed, asked to remain anonymous or not be quoted directly.

Some of those I can name and who have been particularly helpful are listed in no particular order, but I am grateful to them all.

Ruth's directory of strategy, Eddie Barnes, gave up a considerable amount of his time and was extremely good at elucidating the inner workings of his leader's office.

I am also grateful to Steve Bargeton, who provided some extremely useful information on Ruth's time in the army and her leadership style.

Elsewhere, David Torrance and Chris Land proved both amiable dinner companions and fine sources of ideas and inspiration. David's erudite works on the history of the Scottish Conservatives – a good place for those wishing to explore this subject further – have also been an invaluable source of information and background.

Gareth McPherson has been not just a good friend throughout the months of writing, but also a source of good humour and bonhomie. Fellow journalists in the Holyrood lobby – particularly Andy Picken – deserve thanks for providing first-hand accounts of events I could not witness myself.

The staff at my former newspaper, the *Press and Journal*, and Damian Bates, my former editor, also have my gratitude for letting me pursue this project and putting up with me while I was doing it (and always).

Lindsay Razaq in particular has been a great bastion of support and advice.

A special thanks too must go to Connor McCann, who helped me enormously in digging out archive material and preparing well-written notes on various key points in Ruth's life.

The staff at the National Library of Scotland also deserve recognition for their patience in dealing with my obscure requests.

I am indebted to Olivia Beattie and Victoria Godden at Biteback, who had to put up with me – not always an easy task. Iain Dale, too, deserves thanks for agreeing the project.

Finally, my parents Caroline and Roger have been as supportive as ever.

And, of course, any and all mistakes are my own.

A NIGHT TO REMEMBER

The Royal Highland Showground is an unlikely place for an unprecedented victory.

Nestled between Edinburgh Airport and one of Scotland's busiest roads, the cavernous hall is better known for hosting car boot sales than political turning points.

Yet, at 4.20 a.m. on 6 May 2016, as Ruth Davidson took the stage, which that weekend would play host to the capital's antiques fair, she was celebrating not just a personal but also a party triumph.

As the cameras flashed and the film rolled, all eyes were on this stocky, gay ex-soldier who had confounded her critics and defied expectation. Nails bitten to the quick, she had earlier woken to day three of a gruelling tension headache. Though her skin was tarred by a rash – she was closing in on a forty-hour shift at the end of six weeks on the campaign trail, her third in less than two years – she was brimming with delight. Not only had she defeated the SNP in her seat of Edinburgh Central – where her party had previously come fourth – she had also led the Tories back to the front line of Scottish politics.

The scale of the victory is perhaps best confirmed by Ruth herself, who, despite striding onto the stage with her trademark confidence, had prepared no victory speech. Instead, she was left to swiftly adapt her notes conceding defeat to the SNP candidate, Alison Dickie, who had been the favourite in the Edinburgh Central contest.

Always superstitious – she wears the same pair of Tory-blue pants emblazoned with the words 'election night' for every count – Ruth was perhaps wary of jinxing what was clearly becoming a sensational result for her party as she spoke. But, having been shunted between media interviews throughout the night, sweating under her black trouser suit, she also had a more fractured picture of how her party were performing than the close aides at her side. 'One thing we're learning as tonight goes on is that there are people right across the country who are sending the SNP a message,' she told a cocktail of cheering party activists, journalists and glum rivals. 'The voices and the decision we made as a country will not be ignored.' Somewhat gingerly, she added: 'If I am by any small measure elected to be the leader of the opposition party, I promise I will serve to the best of my abilities – and it is a role I will take seriously.'

Her caution is intriguing, if surprising. Throughout the campaign, polls had suggested Ruth's Tories were on the brink of replacing Labour as the party of opposition, although none had predicted the scale of the victory. Of course, her language had been puckered with characteristic boisterousness over the previous six weeks, regularly insisting – rightly, it emerged – that her party was on course for its best ever result in a Scottish Parliament election. The 37-year-old's entire campaign had been based around the slogan 'Strong Opposition' – which must make the

Scottish Conservatives one of the very few major mainstream parties in history to go into an election categorically saying they did not want to win it. If she was embarrassed when a copy of her manifesto was discovered containing the emphatic statement 'This is not a plan for government', she need not have worried.

By the close of the night, Ruth's party would count thirty-one MSPs – more than double the number they had started with in the morning – while Labour had collapsed, retaining just twenty-four of their thirty-eight seats. It was her party's best performance since devolution in 1999, gaining 22 per cent or more on both the constituency and the regional list vote. By pushing Labour into third place north of the border, the Scottish Conservatives re-formed a political landscape not seen in Scotland since 1918.

By the close of the election, back home with her partner Jen, snuggled in her pyjamas, glass of rum in hand, Ruth was certainly the Leader of the Opposition – and by a large measure. It was, as Prime Minister David Cameron would tell Ruth, 'a historic result'.

There is no doubt that Ruth is central to understanding and explaining the Tory resurgence in Scotland. Without her, it never would have happened.

However, as she alluded to in her hastily prepared victory speech, the context of Scottish post-referendum politics is also important. Despite the defeat of the Yes campaign – driven by the SNP – in 2014's Scottish independence referendum, the question of the future of the United Kingdom remained far from answered, as demonstrated by the subsequent surge in support for Nicola Sturgeon's Nationalists. Just days after the vote, thousands of Scots would start joining the party, leading membership to top more than 100,000 by March 2015. Ms Sturgeon herself attracted such large crowds during a speaking tour of Scotland that she was likened more to a pop star than a politician. Come the general election in May, that support would translate into a near total wipe-out of other parties in Scotland, with the SNP taking fifty-six of the fifty-nine seats available and Labour, the Liberal Democrats and the Tories left with just a seat apiece north of the border.

That surge in support, coupled with Ms Sturgeon's rhetoric, made supporters of the Union increasingly anxious about a possible rerun of the 2014 contest that had at the time been branded a 'once in a generation' vote. Concern among those opposed to independence only grew as the SNP talked up the possibility of a Brexit vote triggering another referendum on the future of the Union. Even now, despite the SNP losing six of their seats in the 2016 Scottish Parliament election, the constitutional question remains at the forefront of politics.

With that context, Ruth made opposition to a second referendum one of her key messages ahead of the 2016 vote. There were no ifs or buts. The Tories under Ruth would not countenance even the slightest whisper of a second vote in any circumstance. In contrast to then Scottish Labour leader Kezia Dugdale, who appeared to flip-flop on her support for the Union, Ruth had a coherent message that clearly resonated with voters. While Labour – and to a lesser extent the Liberal Democrats – went fishing for pro-independence voters they could never catch, Ruth was able to launch a strong appeal to the 55 per cent of the population who voted No in 2014.

It was a strategy with strong echoes of Lynton Crosby's campaign for the Tories in the 2015 general election, which featured the now notorious image of former SNP leader Alex Salmond with then Labour leader Ed Miliband in his top pocket. Some commentators, notably Aidan Kerr and David Torrance, have suggested this strategy – and the resulting success for the Tories – represents the beginning of the 'Ulsterisation' of Scottish politics: that is, the notion that voters will pick their parties based on allegiance to, or disdain for, the Union above all else. Yet while some voters clearly made their choice based on fear of or support for a second independence referendum, such an argument largely ignores the role Ruth played in the contest.

Like Margaret Thatcher, Ruth Davidson does not look like a Tory leader.

Yet, like the Iron Lady, she understands the strengths of honing her image in synthesis with her policies.

Gone are the handbags and pearls. Aquascutum skirts have been replaced by dark trouser suits. Standing at just over five foot, Ruth's hair is cut short over her shoulders. Her face has a remarkable ability to be both stern and cheery, often simultaneously. Her personality, too, is one of contrast. As a devout Christian but also a lesbian, she struggled for much of her early life with her sexuality. Despite being a former signaller in the Territorial Army, she is quite the opposite of military stuffiness, being famed for her great bonhomie, particularly on the campaign trail. Ruth has, for instance, been pictured riding a buffalo and driving a tank – photo calls most modern politicians would run a mile from. Her performances on such hit TV shows as *Have I Got News For You* have helped reinforce her reputation – particularly in Westminster – as a gregarious, 'normal' person. She is charming, but also notably ruthless, showing no mercy to her political opponents, most especially those in her own party.

More remarkably, of course, this unconventional, adventurous young politician is a Tory, but one who appears to have a greater sense of social justice than her Etonian compatriots south of the border. But most importantly, she is Scottish – not just in nationality, but in outlook and persona.

It was this character that was centrally responsible for revitalising the Tories in Scotland by shaking off the image of the Conservatives as an English party representing English interests.

While it may be difficult for younger generations to imagine, Scotland was not always a Tory wasteland. On the contrary, in the early part of the twentieth century the land north of Hadrian's Wall was, to a large extent, a Conservative stronghold. In 1955, the party would secure a majority of votes and seats in Scotland – a landslide that would only be surpassed in scope and scale by the SNP in 2015. Following that result, however, the party began a slow decline.

The Unionist Party, as it was known pre-1965, merged with the Conservative Party in England, becoming the Scottish Conservative and Unionist Party – ceding control to London Central Office with it. While there was still an appetite for centre-right politics in Scotland, following the merger the Tories steadily lost support to parties perceived to have Scots' interests closer at heart.

Mrs Thatcher, of course, is often – inaccurately – viewed as the bogeywoman for the decline. In fact, on her election in 1979, the Tories received their first bump in support for several decades. Indeed, before she was leader, Thatcher was actually moderately supportive of devolution, although that quickly changed once she gained the keys to Downing Street. As her reign went on, she became increasingly – and combatively – opposed to devolution in any form. That opposition, coupled with her decision to introduce the notorious poll tax a year earlier in Scotland than in England, as an ill-fated experiment, confirmed to Scots that the Tories were primarily an English-centric party.

Thatcher did not start the decline of the Tories in Scotland, but she delivered the *coup de grâce*. Matters failed to improve as successive Tory leaders railed against devolution, including leaders of the party in Scotland after the establishment of the Scottish Parliament in 1999. In the 1997 devolution referendum – which would eventually deliver the Holyrood chamber – the Tories backed the No campaign, supported by only a fifth of Scots. Following its establishment, Holyrood continued to be viewed as a kind of inconvenience by the Conservatives. And with Ruth's election to the leadership in November 2011, it looked like matters were unlikely to improve.

A favourite of David Cameron's, Ruth was thrust into the leadership after her preferred candidate, John Lamont, imploded after making what was branded a sectarian attack on Catholic schools. In truth, she was wholly unprepared for the challenge, having only been elected for the first time just three months before, but she gained strong allies with her platform of a 'line in the sand' against further devolution. Indeed, the chain-smoking, long-serving Tory spinner Ramsay Jones was suspended from the party for 'inappropriately supporting' Ruth's candidacy after party staff had been instructed to remain neutral, while Scotland's only Tory MP, David Mundell – an ally of Cameron's – also backed her.

The young, inexperienced and pugnacious Ruth eventually won the bitter leadership battle against the odds, running on an uncontroversial platform that included opposition to further Scottish devolution – a conservative platform.

Had she continued with that policy – especially in the face of the 2014 independence referendum – there is no doubt her party would not have enjoyed the surge in support it now does. But, despite increasing opposition from within her own party, Ruth launched a dramatic about-turn in 2013.

The advantage of a line in the sand, of course, is that it is easily washed away.

Ahead of the party conference at Stirling in June, she outlined her plans for more powers for Scotland. It was a courageous move – a decision that very nearly cost her the leadership amid the Machiavellian intrigue and smoke-filled rooms of party politics – largely because Ruth's early years in the leadership had been unhappy and ineffective. The SNP First Minister, Alex Salmond, regularly trounced her in Parliament, and she faced powerful rivals within her own party, who disagreed with her leadership style and tactics.

With her establishment of the Strathclyde Commission, however – named after its author, the Scottish peer Lord Strathclyde – the Tory leader regained the initiative, not just within her own party, but in Scotland.

In June 2014, the commission concluded that control over income tax and benefit spending should be devolved. Published just four months before the independence referendum, the report argued that the devolution of such powers was 'required for a sustained relationship' between Scotland and the rest of the UK.

In both asking for the review and embracing its proposed changes, Ruth achieved her Clause Four moment, the point when the Scottish Conservative and Unionist Party finally became Scottish again.

Ruth's rise cannot, of course, be seen without the context of the Scottish independence referendum in 2014. While she played a more minor role than, for instance, Scottish Labour figures – most notably Alistair Darling and Gordon Brown – the ballot would nevertheless be the catalyst for Ruth and the Scottish Conservatives to grow. Ideologically, it helped the Scottish Tory leader continue to redefine her party's attitude to Scotland. She would make a deeply personal argument in favour of the UK – one built around patriotism and public service. The Union, she would declare in 2013, is 'in our DNA'.

As with much of Ruth's life and work, the armed forces would also play a prominent role. 'We are a responsible nation in the world and we are not afraid to help shoulder the burden of a persecuted people,' she would declare in the same speech, drawing on her experiences as a reporter in Kosovo. 'And we're only able to do so because we have the integrated armed forces we do – pulling together from every part of the UK to keep our people safe at home and to work for peace abroad.'

These appeals – which could be summed up as Britishness – were matched with the more pragmatic arguments of the Better Together campaign. Ruth was a clear advocate of the 'broad shoulders' theory – namely, that Scotland is better off with the support of the wider UK economy. Such arguments would be lambasted as overly negative, with the Better Together campaign gaining the unenviable nickname of Project Fear. Scots were warned of tax hikes, spending cuts and pension deficits if they voted Yes. Questions of currency and EU membership would also dominate the pro-UK campaign's rhetoric. As the campaign moved into its final weeks, there were fears that these arguments had turned off voters who viewed them as overly negative.

Yet Ruth was a keen supporter of the message that would, in September 2014, deliver a No vote.

Politically speaking, the referendum helped galvanise the Scottish Conservatives' ailing support base. Throughout the campaign, it would acquire the contact details of around 70,000 pro-Union supporters – a database that would prove crucial for the coming Holyrood election. It was Ruth, however, who truly flourished, growing into her leadership role throughout the referendum campaign as she gained an exposure previously unknown to leaders of Scotland's then third party. As well as giving public speeches, she proved a passionate debater, notably succeeding in navigating a question-and-answer session with thousands of sixteen- and seventeen-year-old voters at Glasgow's SSE Hydro. Her growth in confidence and stature was matched by an improved reception among the Scottish public, some of whom – but by no means all – were struck by her bonhomie and boisterousness.

When it came to the Holyrood election, strategists played to these strengths from the outset. From leaflets to ballot papers, the Tories emphasised not just 'Strong Opposition', but 'Ruth Davidson for a Strong Opposition'. This may in part have been to assuage fears that the toxic Tory brand would damage their chances, but it was also an overt acknowledgement that Ruth – and her Scottishness – was popular with voters.

Indeed, while everyone involved will loathe the comparison, her campaign was not dissimilar to the SNP's in its 2015 triumph. Nicola Sturgeon used the slogan 'Stronger for Scotland' – another clear example of how voters north of the border pick their party based on its perceived strength to stand up for the country's interests. Before and during the 2016 campaign, Ruth also made much of her opposition to Tory austerity politics, challenging the then Chancellor, George Osborne, on his plan to scrap tax credits. And it was no accident that David Cameron – who was not just Prime Minister but effectively Ruth's boss – was conspicuously absent from the campaign trail, not visiting Scotland once. While Scottish Labour juggled with how to handle the ideological Rubik's cube of Jeremy Corbyn's UK-wide leadership, Ruth was clear – in Scotland, this was her party.

She describes herself in US political terms as a Democrat – and suggested she would back any candidate over the Republican, Donald Trump.

In the aftermath of her election triumph at the Royal Highland Showground, Ruth suggested that Scotland had reached what she described as 'peak Nat'. With Nicola Sturgeon failing to repeat the SNP's unprecedented majority of 2011, Ruth argued the only way was down for the Nationalists.

Yet, she conspicuously ignored articulating what the result meant for her own party – and for her. Both George Osborne and David Cameron have suggested she would make a 'fantastic' leader of the national Tory Party. A poll on the Conservative Home website suggested that members also overwhelmingly backed this view. Ruth has persistently suggested there is 'no chance' of such a move – but as with the 'line in the sand' and her Scottish leadership bid itself, she is nothing if not flexible.

On 6 May 2016, the day after the election, a buoyant if tired Ruth told journalists the SNP, as a minority government, now had 'no mandate' for a second vote. 'There has been a material change,' she said, echoing Ms Sturgeon's much-touted potential trigger for re-raising the constitutional question. 'As she starts her new term of office, I hope Nicola Sturgeon makes it clear that she will now focus entirely on what she was elected to do – lead a devolved administration.'

Such hopes would prove premature. The question of independence would continue to dominate.

With the coming of the EU referendum, Ruth would be once again thrust into the limelight, this time in a bid to dodge Brexit and save her chief ally, Cameron. In many ways, the EU referendum – and Ruth's role in it – cemented her position as a national political figure. She had already received some prominence in the 2014 independence vote, and her quirky campaign photo calls in the 2015 general election had kept her on the radar of much of the press lobby outside Scotland. Her triumph at Holyrood had established her as a politician of the future – one to watch, as it were – but the EU referendum was the first time she entered the consciousness of the general public south of the border. Ruth, unlike many in her own party, is a passionate pro-European, for much the same reasons she is a supporter of the UK. Her performance in the national debate at Wembley – where she took on Boris Johnson and Andrea Leadsom – was widely praised and must be one of the most remembered parts of an otherwise often dreary Remain campaign. Her ferocious attacks on members of her own party ignited the campaign in its final stages, with many of her predictions of there being no Brexit plan proving prophetic.

Fiery though it was, it was not, of course, enough to halt a Leave vote. Just weeks after her triumph at Holyrood, Ruth was facing political oblivion following the EU referendum. Her allies in Westminster had resigned. Her party was in chaos. Ruth's relationship with Cameron – which had been so crucial to her rise, but was also a genuine friendship – was now politically worthless. No. 10 was vacant. The Scottish Tory leader – who is no fan of Boris Johnson – would have to carefully navigate the intrigues of a Conservative leadership election for the first time.

With May's victory, she would have to fight to preserve her access in Westminster. While insiders insist her relationship with the new Prime Minister is close, there is no doubt it is less warm than her friendship with Cameron and Osborne. Ruth is uncomfortable with much of the more hard-line post-Brexit rhetoric flooding out of Westminster. Indeed, she would feel strongly enough about the proposal to get firms to list foreign workers to publicly distance herself from it in her conference speech introducing May.

Most importantly, the threat of independence – which she had so played up in the Holyrood election – was now back on the table, thanks to her own party.

Of course, it helps Ruth's often expedient political rhetoric on the Union for the spectre of independence to linger. In many ways, the Brexit vote has given Ruth's Holyrood campaign more resonance, even though the resurgence of separatism is a self-inflicted wound. A second ballot remains, in the First Minister's words, 'highly likely'. A generally peripheral player in the first referendum campaign, occasionally moving into the limelight, Ruth would undoubtedly now play a much more central role in opposing any future referendum.

Nicola Sturgeon, of course, stayed true to her word and, relatively promptly, began preparations for a second ballot on independence. This was the situation Ruth and the Tories most feared and yet also had directly contributed to. After a brief flirtation with blocking a second referendum, what was hoped would be a more long-term solution was reached – a snap general election. Of course, Theresa May pitched the 2017 general election to the country as a chance to endorse her vision of Brexit. Riding high in the polls and facing an apparently terminally ill Labour Party,

May took a political gamble. But a secondary objective was to force the SNP into an election it was unprepared for and – largely because of its enormous success in 2015 – unlikely to succeed in. Sturgeon had won so many seats in 2015, it would be unlikely she would hold them all again.

The backdrop to the 2017 general election in Scotland was undoubtedly the question of independence and, once again, it played a key part in Ruth's electoral strategy. While the Holyrood victory of 2016 was more unexpected, it would be this campaign that would entrench Ruth as a national political figure and a genuine force within the Conservative Party, if not national politics as well. In that snap contest, the Tories under Ruth garnered an impressive thirteen seats, an increase of twelve from their showing just two years earlier. More significantly, the increase in the number of Scottish Conservative seats allowed Theresa May – who lost her majority in a reversal of fortunes unthinkable at the start of the campaign – to stay in government with the help of the DUP.

As a result, Ruth now wields considerable political power not just in Scotland but nationally. Amid the confusion of Brexit negotiations, she and her Scottish Conservative MPs are a serious force that command significant influence in No. 10 and in Parliament. They could, if Ruth so wished, even bring down the government.

There is no doubt that Ruth has lived through – and in some ways helped form – politically turbulent times.

She has, by returning the Tories to the front line of Scottish politics, achieved what no one thought possible. She did this by making the Tories the opposition *for* Scotland, not *against* Scotland – a situation that had not existed for almost fifty years.

Ruth's star has risen stratospherically and many are – rightly – considering her wider political future.

Yet she also played up the threat of the SNP and kept constitutional politics at the fore. Such political expediency could not only cost her party dearly, but her much-loved country too.

As her political career unfolds, there are many challenges ahead. But she is nothing if not determined.

CHAPTER 1

THE LONG DECLINE

When Ruth was born in Edinburgh, on 10 November 1978, the Conservatives were in the midst of a great decline in Scotland. Yet they were not always political pariahs in the north – in fact, for much of the twentieth century they were the natural party of government. The 'toxic Tories' won the largest number of seats north of the border in 1918, 1924, 1931 and 1935. In 1955, they would win more than 50 per cent of the vote across Scotland – a feat only matched by the SNP in the 2015 general election.

The key to this success was a unique sense of Scottish identity, a policy not of devolution but certainly of decentralising. Tories favoured the Union, of course, but it was not an overtly political issue for the party for much of the twentieth century. Above all, they were a pragmatic party, with a separate political establishment, outwith Westminster control, which was able to tailor its views to a Scottish audience.

They were, of course, not even known as the Conservative Party in Scotland until 1965. Before then, from the beginning of the twentieth century, they were simply the Unionist Party, with a separate leadership and administration to the Tories in England, albeit taking the Conservative whip in Westminster. The Unionist Party in Scotland emerged from the split in the Liberal Party resulting from Irish Home Rule in 1886. The Liberal Unionists, as they became known, formed an electoral pact with the Conservative Party, which would greatly improve Tory fortunes north of the border. The two parties remained officially separate until they merged in 1912, into the Conservative and Unionist Party in England and Wales – and the Unionist Party in Scotland.

The influence of the Liberals – the former dominant political force in Scotland – helped give the Unionist Party a decidedly Scottish outlook throughout much of the early twentieth century. The attitude of the party was not nationalist, but rather patriotic – with an emphasis on a love of Scotland, Britain and Empire. Unionists therefore enjoyed a cross-section of support – not just from landed aristocracy, but also from working-class, particularly Protestant, communities. What would become 'Red' Clydeside, for instance, voted for the Unionist Party throughout much of the 1920s and 1930s. Times may have changed, but Ruth has embraced much of this rhetoric that the Tories in Scotland would lose over the ensuing decades.

The unique Unionist Party attitude is perhaps best emphasised by their MP Robert – better known as Bob – Boothby. Representing Aberdeenshire, Bob Boothby was fiercely upper-class in both his background and his prejudices. The son of an Edinburgh stockbroker, he was educated at Eton and graduated from Oxford, himself working in financial services before moving into politics. Dressed in well-cut three-piece suits, he enjoyed a reputation as a high-society bon vivant. Yet he also epitomised the appeal of the Unionist Party in Scotland that would be lost in later years. In his first election in victory in 1924, a baby-faced but handsome Boothby ran under the slogan 'A friend for all'. His service as Parliamentary Private Secretary to the ardently imperial Winston Churchill emphasises his fondness for the empire. Boothby would join with the future Prime Minister in vehemently opposing disarmament and Adolf Hitler. But he was also a patriotic Scot – and emphasised Scottish interests to his mentor.

In one letter, written after Churchill's accession to power in 1940, the Aberdeenshire MP lambasts the Prime Minister over the lack of Scottish representation in the new government at Westminster. 'I cannot conceal from you the deep distress I feel at the series of "sabotaging" political appointments that have been made,' he wrote to the Prime Minister in May.

> I met my Unionist colleagues in Scotland at the Carlton Club this evening, and their indignation at the appointment of an Englishman as Secretary of State [for Scotland] – for the first, and it is to be hoped the last, time in history – knows no bounds. They take the view, unanimously, that it is nothing short of a public insult to Scotland at the most critical moment in her proud history.

Such records reflect the attitude of Unionist politics more generally – patriotic, to both Scotland and Britain.

These views, however, did not stray into support for devolution, even in those early days. Boothby was scathing about a trial meeting of the 'Scottish National Parliament' – not SNP for short – branding it a 'dismal fiasco' that he met with 'horrified dismay'. These views would be the dominant discourse among the Scottish centre-right in the pre-1950s period. The emerging Labour Party, meanwhile, tended to favour nationwide initiatives delivered from central government. The great achievements of the 1945 Clement Attlee administration, for instance – the NHS, the welfare state – were all delivered with a broad brush from Whitehall.

Indeed, as the historian Richard J. Finlay suggests, the separation of parties in Scotland and England allowed the Unionist party to forge a 'middle way' that appealed to a cross-section of Scottish society. The party were happy to bolster the free market, but the emergence of a fully fledged welfare state also allowed them to tailor a unique message to Scots voters. That the Unionist party vote in Scotland was higher than that in England in the 1940s and early 1950s emphasises the success of this approach – but it was the electoral triumph in 1955 typified it. Winning more than 50 per cent for the first – and, so far, only – time in Scotland helped return a Tory government to Westminster. The Tory Party election handbook that year quoted future leader Harold Macmillan as saying the UK Union must be 'the wedding ring (and) not the handcuff'. (The SNP at this point, according to the historian Tom Devine, were an 'irrelevant and eccentric sect rather than a mainstream political party'.)

This, however, would turn out to be the high point of the Unionist Party. While support initially remained strong despite government debacles – most notably the Suez Crisis – it would begin a slow decline, as the loss of empire coupled with a sapping of sectarian tensions drew support away from the Tories in Scotland. From the 1955 high point, Tory vote share in Scotland would fall to 47 per cent in the 1959 general election. While this narrowly beat Labour's 46 per cent, handing the Tories the largest share of the popular vote, it would translate to a total of only thirty-one of the seventy-one seats north of the border, seeing the Unionists beaten into second place by Labour. Tory leader Harold Macmillan would, of course, be returned to office in a remarkable turnaround. In the aftermath of Suez, Labour had enjoyed a thirteen-point lead over the Conservatives, but that evaporated as voters seemingly lacked confidence in Labour's tax-and-spend plans.

Yet while 1959 was not a disaster for the Tories, the vote-share data clearly reflects a definite and continuing decline in support for the government in Scotland. By 1964, the party would poll 41 per cent of the vote. By most measures, it was a decent showing, but it still represented a decline of almost 10 per cent in as many years. It would also lead to a significant drop in seats – seven in total – leaving the Unionists with just twenty-four MPs in Scotland, well behind Labour's forty-three. This result was all the more remarkable given Alec Douglas-Home, a Scot, was now the Conservative candidate for Prime Minister.

It was not until the Unionist Party merged with the Conservative Party in England in 1965, however, that the decline would really gather pace. The brainchild of Edward Heath, who had taken over the party leadership from Douglas-Home, the rebranding would lead to the growing perception in Scotland that the Tories – as they now were – no longer had Scottish interests at heart. Party management and control were now ceded entirely to Westminster – a takeover that commentator Colin Sutherland believes would ultimately bear responsibility for the Tories' failure to recover their 1955 levels of support.

Of course, the Tories – and Heath in particular – were strong on Scottish rhetoric, if not policy, beyond the merger. Heath, elected Prime Minister in 1970, was from the moderate branch of the Conservative Party. Indeed, Thatcher would later brand him a 'wet' for his reluctance to go along with her liberalising economic agenda. One of his chief aims on ascending to No. 10 was to try to boost economic growth in regional areas. Scotland, understandably, featured heavily in this.

In the snap 1966 election – Heath's first as leader – the Tory vote share in Scotland would fall to a new low of 38 per cent as they failed to win a UK majority. To put that figure in context, the Tory vote share in the rest of the UK was 43 per cent, down just one point from 1964. It was now increasingly clear – even to the most stubborn – that the Tories had a growing problem in Scotland, and Heath was increasingly anxious to be perceived as being on the right side of the Scots.

The Declaration of Perth, delivered in 1968 when Heath was Leader of the Opposition, promised the first devolved Scottish assembly. While the assembly was set to be limited in power and scope – particularly compared to the post-1997 devolution settlement – Mr Heath's statement echoed the historic attitudes of Tories in Scotland. 'Let there be no doubt about this: the Conservative Party is determined to effect a real improvement in the machinery of government in Scotland,' he told his startled party conference in Perth in 1968. 'It is pledged to give the people of Scotland genuine participation in the making of decisions that affect them – all within the historic unity of the United Kingdom.' Of course, much of this statement may have been born of pragmatism rather than ideology.

Falling support for his party in Scotland, coupled with the rise of nationalist sentiment, forced Heath to act. One survey at the time suggested Labour and the SNP were both polling at 30 per cent in Scotland – the same level as the Tories – while a year earlier the SNP's Winnie Ewing had won a surprise victory in the Hamilton by-election. As David Torrance points out, it was in the face of SNP extremism that Heath's shadow Cabinet – including future Scottish Secretary George Younger – approved the speech promising devolution. Heath himself would later write: 'In the light of the evident shift in opinion since that election [1966], it would have been politically suicidal to stick to our guns.'

Yet that does not detract from the fact that Heath was merely echoing long-held sentiments among Tories north of the border – that decentralising control to Scotland was a good thing. While Conservative members and MPs were split on the proposals, they were the logical extension of Scottish Tory attitudes that had gained the party such electoral success in the early part of the century.

The now famous Declaration of Perth did help arrest the decline of the Tories in Scotland somewhat. In the 1970 general election, they would poll 38 per cent – the same share they received four years earlier. That, however, must be viewed in contrast to the Tory vote share in the rest of the UK, which rose by almost 5 per cent on 1966 and helped return Edward Heath as Prime Minister. In Scotland, while they gained three additional seats on 1966, they were still significantly behind Labour, who controlled forty-four of Scotland's seats, compared to the Tories' twenty-three.

Now in office and with the firing gun very much started with the Declaration of Perth, Heath, a Conservative leader, had begun the long and slow process that would lead to the creation of the Scottish Parliament some thirty years later. Alec Douglas-Home

– the Scottish Tory MP and former Prime Minister – was tasked with formalising Heath's proposals. His report, entitled 'Scotland's Government', recommended the formation of a 120-strong Scottish Assembly to oversee laws affecting Scots. Heath's initial enthusiasm, however, soon waned as bigger decisions got in the way – most notably the decision to enter the European Community in 1973, which, coincidentally, helped erode the importance of the UK single market to Scotland. Douglas-Home's recommendations would gather dust until, in 1975, Heath was ousted by Margaret Thatcher.

Meanwhile, the Tories would continue to suffer from a lack of progress in Scotland as devolution stalled. The two elections of 1974 provide further evidence of the declining support for the party in Scotland. In February, their share dropped to 33 per cent, down 5 per cent from 1970, as Edward Heath lost control of No. 10. By the second election of 1974, in October, the Tory vote share in Scotland would fall to just 25 per cent. With the Conservatives out of office, Thatcher would secure the leadership of the party.

If Heath was inactive on devolution, the Iron Lady would be positively opposed.

Contrary to popular belief, Thatcher did not kill the Tories in Scotland. As we have seen, that decline began some years before, with the loss of a Scottish identity following the merger of the Unionist Party with the English Conservatives, as well as a faltering electoral base. On her first visit, a crowd of 3,000 came to see Thatcher tour the St James shopping centre in Edinburgh, with three people fainting from excitement.

Indeed, the Conservatives actually picked up support in Scotland in the 1979 election – the first Thatcher fought – gaining 31 per cent of the vote, an increase of 6 per cent on five years earlier.

That vote came in the wake of a Labour-initiated referendum on a devolved Scottish chamber. While a narrow majority voted for the legislation, this amounted to less than 40 per cent of the Scottish electorate voting in favour, rendering the result invalid.

While Thatcher herself opposed the proposed devolution, Douglas-Home told Scottish voters to reject it in favour of a better deal from the next Tory administration. Not only was a better deal not forthcoming, but Thatcher, who had already been sceptical, became increasingly opposed to any form of devolution.

She was not alone in her party in holding such views. As her archive notes: 'Many in the parliamentary party were privately lukewarm, dubious or downright hostile. They feared devolution might damage or lead to the break-up [of] the United Kingdom, [and] foresaw a backlash against the policy in England.' Before she even took office, Thatcher was said to like the idea of the UK as a whole having a say in any devolution settlement – a view that was hardly palatable in Scotland.

The direction of travel was not wholly welcome. Heath, who claimed to have 'seen more of Scotland over the past seventeen years than any other national political figure', came to regret his lack of action on devolution and the Douglas-Home recommendations. The former Prime Minister, now in the political wilderness, became increasingly agitated by the reluctance of his fellow Conservatives to support new powers for Scotland. In 1976, for instance, Heath would abstain on a three-line-whip for the first time in his life as Thatcher attempted to block Labour's referendum on devolution.

Thatcher's continued opposition to devolution would see Tory support begin to decline again as a consequence. However, she was not always so opposed to ceding power to Scotland, declaring on a 1975 visit to Edinburgh that a Scottish Assembly should be a 'top priority'. Such views shifted as she came closer to political office herself. By 1988 she would declare: 'As long as I am leader of this party, we shall defend the Union and reject legislative devolution unequivocally.'

This opposition would further accelerate as a 'democratic deficit' emerged, with the Iron Lady's government in Westminster looking increasingly unlike the MPs Scots were voting for. In the 1983 and 1987 elections, around 20 per cent fewer Scots would vote Tory than their – increasingly separate – compatriots in England. This divergence of opinion saw Scots increasingly backing parties they believed held their interests closer to heart – Labour and the SNP – than the prim, pearled Thatcher.

If Bob Boothby epitomised the Unionist Party of yesteryear, then Sir Nicholas Fairbairn emphasised the Thatcherite Scottish Conservatives. Elected an MP in Perthshire in 1974 with the tiniest majority against the SNP, Fairbairn was noted for his flamboyant dress and eccentric personality. Yet he was also noted for his right-wing views – and his opposition to devolution. As the *Herald* would note in 1987:

> [Fairbairn] warned of vastly increased taxation for everyone in Scotland if devolution went ahead, highlighted the higher government spending per head in Scotland compared with the rest of the United Kingdom under the present system, and claimed Scotland had a standard of living which those south of the border would not enjoy.

Notably, after his death in 1995, the SNP would win Fairbairn's seat, which was once one of the Tories' safest in Scotland.

Thatcher's *coup de grâce*, however, came with the poll tax debacle, which saw the Tory Prime Minister introduce the community charge a year earlier in Scotland than in the rest of the UK. The decision has led to significant debate to this day over whether Scotland was used as a 'guinea pig' to test the tax before it was promoted in England and Wales. Then Chancellor Nigel Lawson has vehemently denied such accusations. 'I can understand why the fact that the poll tax was introduced first in Scotland may have led some to suppose the Cabinet in London was deliberately using Scotland as a test-bed for the tax,' he once said, directly addressing the criticism. 'But nothing could be further from the truth.'

Despite his denials, however, Cabinet Office documents released in 2014 tell a different story. In November 1985, Thatcher adviser Oliver Letwin stated: 'You could make all the changes to grants, non-domestic rates, capital controls and housing benefit in England and Wales, but try out the residential charge in a pure form only in Scotland, and leave domestic rates intact for the time being in the rest of the country.' He added: 'If you [Thatcher] are not willing to move to a pure residence charge in England and Wales immediately, you should introduce a mixture of taxes but should rather use the Scots as a trailblazer for the real thing.'

In fairness to Lawson, while Letwin did advocate testing the poll tax on Scotland, documents from the same period show he was vociferously opposed. Lawson stated in one memo: 'A flat-rate poll tax would be politically unsustainable; even with a rebate scheme the package would have "an unacceptable impact" on certain types of household.'

The Letwins of the government won the day, however – and the poll tax would be introduced in Scotland in 1989, a year earlier than in the rest of the UK. Thatcher was characteristically unrepentant, of course, taking to the stage at her 1990 party conference in Aberdeen to chastise the Labour Party for stoking up opposition to paying the community charge in Scotland.

The then Scottish Secretary, Malcolm Rifkind, would complain about Thatcher's treatment of Scotland, although he himself supported the poll tax. 'She just assumed it was my job to represent the Cabinet in Scotland,' he said. 'I saw it as the other way round. The problem Margaret had was that she was an English woman and a bossy English woman.'

Indeed, it was the Iron Lady's refusal to back down in the face of such opposition in Scotland that irrevocably damaged the Tories' position north of the border. David Cameron would admit this himself shortly after he became Tory leader in 2006. 'A series of blunders were committed in the 1980s and 1990s of which the imposition of the poll tax was the most egregious,' he said. 'The decision to treat Scotland as a laboratory for experimentation in new methods of local government finance was clumsy and unjust.'

Of course, Scots did benefit from a number of Thatcher's policies, particularly right-to-buy – a position she obliquely sought to justify in her famous 'Sermon on the Mound' speech to the General Assembly of the Church of Scotland. However, that famous speech also angered many Scots, who saw it as an attempt to justify her more controversial policies. 'We are all responsible for our own actions,' she famously declared. 'We can't blame society if we disobey the law. We simply can't delegate the exercise of mercy and generosity to others.'

The damage had been done.

As an opinion piece in *The Herald* would later note:

In between [her] 1975 debut in Edinburgh and her tearful departure from Downing Street, Mrs Thatcher became a hate figure for many in Scotland.

She bore the brunt of the blame for the poll tax, introduced in Scotland a year earlier than in England, and was vilified for presiding over an industrial shakeout that shed workers in their thousands from mines, steel plants and other traditional industries.

But her supporters argued she was giving the economy the unpalatable medicine it needed, and also point to victory despite the odds in the Falklands.

Through it all, Mrs Thatcher gave the impression of being baffled at Scottish opposition to her policies.

Indeed, as a marker of how divisive Thatcher's legacy is in Scotland, one of Alex Salmond's final acts as First Minister in 2014 was to write off unpaid debts from the poll tax.

'The poll tax was a hated levy which poured untold misery on communities across Scotland,' he said in October 2014. 'It was a hugely discredited tax, even before it was brought in – and it was rightly consigned to history just four years after its introduction in Scotland. It is therefore not appropriate for councils to use current electoral records to chase arrears from decades ago.'

By 1992, even with Thatcher gone, the Tories would poll just over 25 per cent of the vote north of the border. Five years later, they would receive just 18 per cent of the vote in Scotland and return no Scottish MPs amid Tony Blair's landslide victory. As Margaret Arnott and Catriona Macdonald note in *Whatever Happened to Tory Scotland?*, Thatcher had seriously damaged the Scottish Conservative brand of Unionism by turning it from a patriotic idea into a political one.

'[Under Thatcher], the Union would be defended on ideological grounds to maintain central control throughout the UK,' they write. 'Here it was parliamentary sovereignty rather than popular sovereignty that was the defining practice. A different kind of Unionism was advocated by Thatcherites. Thatcherites were comfortable framing the Union to achieve ideological ends. Ideological ends which drew upon the ideas of the New Right.'

In the same book, Colin Kidd explains it more plainly, stating: 'Above all, there was the Thatcher factor, which took two forms, both a visceral dislike of Margaret Thatcher as a shrill, bossy Englishwoman, and a more substantive hostility to Thatcherism as an ideology markedly out of step with the traditional ethos of Scottish life.'

On the announcement of her death, parties were held in Glasgow and other parts of Scotland – though such celebrations were widely condemned both north and south of the border.

Thatcher's failure to deliver devolution – and her perceived Englishness – dealt damaging body blows to Toryism in Scotland.

The best evidence for this comes from Ruth Davidson herself, who has sought to distance her party from the Thatcher years. The Scottish Conservative leader has done her utmost to erase the legacy of the 1980s from the current political narrative.

Of course, she has also praised the Iron Lady for many of her policies. Speaking after Mrs Thatcher passed away in 2013, Ruth described her as 'one of the truly great Prime Ministers', adding, 'She defended Britain's sovereignty, helped win the Cold War, empowered thousands to own their own home by democratising property ownership and smashed the glass ceiling.'

Indeed, Ruth has also regularly praised Thatcher from a feminist perspective.

Coming home from school on the day the Iron Lady resigned in 1990, Ruth asked a friend's mother, 'Can a man even be Prime Minister?'

Later, after the former Prime Minister's death, she would suggest that Thatcher 'changed perceptions' for women in politics, while in the 2015 election campaign she chose to echo the famous image of Thatcher astride a tank in West Germany.

Eulogies aside, however, Ruth has been circumspect in her attitudes to Thatcher.

Her ally David Cameron also realised during the independence referendum that the Iron Lady's legacy was not to be praised in Scotland, urging people to not treat the vote as a 'chance to kick the effing Tories'.

In the run-up to her Holyrood triumph, however, Ruth attempted to remove Thatcher from the political narrative in Scotland completely. 'To be honest, that's not been the topic of conversation in Scotland for quite some time – we've had other things on our plate,' she said.

> I was six months old when Margaret Thatcher came to power. I was in primary school when she left office – so it's not really something for my generation or the generations that come after me. I'm thirty-seven. You can vote now in Scotland at the age of sixteen – so talk about Margaret Thatcher is the same as talking about Gladstone or Disraeli in terms of the distance that's there.

This attempt to distance herself from Thatcher was not a one-off, but rather a continuing feature of Ruth's leadership. Running for the role in 2011, she said she had 'no knowledge or memory' of the Iron Lady – a comment that proved controversial given her upbringing near Fife mining villages decimated under Thatcher's government. Such tactics are clearly prudent politics in Scotland, given Thatcher's legacy.

Yet, distancing herself from Thatcher is not the key to Ruth's success. Rather, drawing on her upbringing and early career, she has reinvented the Scottish Conservatives as the Unionist Party of the early twentieth century. Under Ruth, the Tories have once again become a party that at least appears to stand up for Scotland.

More travails would await the party before that point, however. As Ruth went to university and the world of work, the Tories in Scotland were still grappling with the upcoming referendum on devolution. That vote, unlike its predecessor in 1979, would lead to the creation of the Scottish Parliament.

It was a vote that would change the course of political history and Ruth's life.

CHAPTER 2

THE FIFE TORY

Ruth almost never survived childhood.

It was a winter's day, outside her parents' home in Fife, when the lorry hit her.

She was five years old. Her femoral artery was crushed, her pelvis shattered, her right leg broken.

Her terrified mother, Liz, rushed to her side. Her father, Douglas, who worked in the whisky industry and had previously played football for Partick Thistle, was at work.

'I remember feeling someone put a blanket over me on the tarmac,' Ruth said, recollecting the accident in 2016. 'Then I remember opening my eyes in the ambulance and my mum being there and looking dreadful. She looked 100 years old. Then I blacked out again.'

The doctors were not sure Ruth would survive. Her terrified parents were told her chances were 50/50. She would stay in hospital for months, trapped in a full body cast with pins in her leg.

Eventually, she would have to undergo reconstructive surgery and learn to walk all over again. Such were the extent of her injuries that she became an object for medical lessons at the local teaching hospital. 'They'd wheel me out in front of 200 medical students almost naked and broken. I was terrified,' Ruth told the *Daily Mail*. 'I remember getting my cast taken off and screaming the place down because they took it off with a circular saw and I thought they were going to cut through my leg.'

Back at her comprehensive school in Buckhaven, a working-class town in the east of Fife, Ruth suffered jibes and taunts from fellow pupils. 'It's tough when you're the only child in your primary school using a Zimmer frame. I was covered in scars and I got teased,' she said. 'But it just made me want to do better than everybody else. If people tell me I can't do something, then it makes me want to try twice as hard.' Yet she would also, rather sweetly, admit to being frustrated at not being able to play football or climb trees in the months following the accident. Indeed, her preference for trouser suits is because the scarring on her legs remains so bad to this day.

The memories of the incident were not just physical, however. The accident and the resulting experiences would prove a catalyst for Ruth's early political development and an example of her unique brand of Toryism. 'I was a young child but I will always remember the kindness of strangers,' she told the *Mail on Sunday* in 2015. 'I still had a full body cast when I was discharged from hospital – but a man read about my accident in the local paper and sent us an old World War One spinal carriage so my mum could take me outside for fresh air.'

The 1980s, of course, was the decade that Thatcher declared war on the idea of community. People could not – and should not – rely on others to help them, but rather take responsibility for their own destiny. Yet, even at an early age, Ruth was given a personal reason to refute this argument. As she herself recollects decades later, the 'kindness of strangers' was a notable advent in her recovery. While she received jibes at school – which can easily be dismissed as immaturity – the community rallied round her. The experience was something that stayed with her throughout her life and imbued her with a sense of duty to help others as she herself had been helped.

Indeed, it was not just a community spirit that Ruth discovered through her accident.

As she proudly recollected to a packed Tory conference in 2016:

> Three weeks ago, I was standing on a street stall on the Mound [in Edinburgh] when a man introduced himself. Retired now, he used to be a surgeon in the Sick Kids hospital in Edinburgh. He's the man who put me back together again when – aged five – I was run over by a truck. His skill saved my life, saved my legs, and his application is the only reason I'm standing before you today. The only reason I'm able to stand up at all. And I couldn't stop myself. Thirty-two years on and I bundled him into an enormous hug. I'm not sure it's really the Edinburgh way. But I couldn't help it.

Such a life-saving experience of public service clearly had a profound effect on Ruth and would lead her not just into politics but also into the army and journalism. It instilled in her a sense of duty, a desire to help people – and not just for personal gain and advancement.

These views would have been somewhat at odds with the Thatcherite Tory Party that surrounded Ruth as she grew up. The period was marked by privatisation, by cuts to public services and the welfare state.

But as her political career developed, Ruth would make much of this commitment – fostered at an early age – to both public services and local communities.

There is, of course, still the role of the individual in Ruth's recovery. It was she and she alone who had to face the jibes, the painstaking recovery and the surgeries. She had to fight both mentally and physically to recover. The experience taught her that individual determination can, with support, overcome almost any obstacle. Again, this characteristic, developed as a result of her accident and recovery, would remain with her into adulthood and prove crucial in her later political career.

It too goes some way to help explain why Ruth is a Tory rather than – as many might have expected – a Labour supporter. While she learnt that community and public service were important, she also realised that they alone could not deliver for her. She was required to make – often considerable – effort herself. The state and the community could therefore only be responsible for so much.

* * *

Ruth was not born with a silver spoon. She describes her background as blue-collar – and it is not far from it. Her parents, Douglas – who left school at sixteen – and Liz – who left school at fifteen – both grew up on council estates in Glasgow, in Castlemilk and Merrylee respectively. Located side-by-side in the Southside of Scotland's biggest city, the two areas were the epitome of post-war development. Council officials had travelled to the south of France to learn the lessons of urban development in Marseille, and their experiences are reflected in the project. The majority of the homes were three- or four-storey tenement blocks, entered via a common close. Unlike older, Victorian tenements, these properties came with interior bathrooms and hot water. Many were built with verandas in homage to their Continental origins.

But they soon fell short of their aspiration to act as a sanctuary for the working class. The areas became infamous for poverty and overcrowding. The city council's own planning body even referred to them as 'townships'. While they were designed as areas for people to both live and work, there was notoriously little employment and few amenities. Castlemilk, for instance, had only one pub and no cinema. A health centre would be built only in the 1980s – long after Ruth's father Douglas had left. The area also suffered from poor transport links and, with few jobs in the local area, many workers were forced to take several buses to get the Govan shipyards.

A bid to improve on the 1950s design saw the introduction of multi-storey blocks in Castlemilk in the 1960s, but these only served to worsen the pre-existing difficulties in the area and would be demolished in 2005.

Both Ruth's parents would therefore have encountered serious and real poverty growing up. For Ruth's father, he also would have been something of an outsider, having been raised a Protestant in a relatively Catholic area. Growing up in Glasgow during the 1950s and 1960s, the scourge of sectarianism would have still been rampant – and Douglas may well have experienced prejudice because of his background.

Like many men from his area and of his generation, Douglas

– the son of a factory worker and an auxiliary nurse, and generally known as Dougie – found solace through sport, specifically football. Growing up in Castlemilk it would have been a key activity for any young man, but he was clearly a natural talent. By 1966, he was signed by Partick Thistle, a Glasgow club based six miles north of his home.

Joining such a big side – Partick played in Scotland's top division – would have a major impact on Ruth's father's life. A team portrait from the time shows him looking wide-eyed, fresh-faced and enthusiastic. The choice of club is also interesting. The city's two biggest clubs – Rangers and Celtic – were closely identified with Protestantism and Catholicism respectively. The so-called Old Firm derby when both teams played was – and remains – a highly charged affair that goes far beyond football and into the realms of politics and religion. Partick Thistle was, however, a neutrals' club. The classic retort to any Partick fan is: 'Are you a Celtic Partick Thistle supporter or a Rangers Partick Thistle supporter?' Despite being a Protestant himself, the majority of his young friends would have been Catholic and this may have played a factor in his decision to choose a neutral club. (Though, as a young man just starting his footballing career, it is unlikely Douglas would have had his pick of clubs, so we should be wary of drawing too much inference from the choice.)

Like many footballers who show early promise, Douglas's career did not go from strength to strength and Partick Thistle would be the most senior club he played for. His next move would be to Selkirk FC – a Borders team that lacked the prestige of Partick. Here, Dougie would play as a midfielder for much of the 1970s and early 1980s. With wife Liz at his side, it would also be where they decided to start a family.

*   *   *

Ruth was born on 10 November 1978, in the Simpson Memorial Hospital in Edinburgh because the local hospital in Selkirk had no maternity facilities.

Alongside her older sister, she spent her earliest years in the Borders town, while her father – now retired from football – managed a mill for Laidlaw & Fairgrieve in nearby Galashiels. Such surroundings were a far cry from the suburban slums of Douglas's and Liz's youth. Selkirk – with a population in the low thousands – is a picturesque early Victorian town. Woollen mills – where Douglas now worked – had arrived with the industrial revolution. While the industry had declined somewhat since the Second World War, efforts to rebalance the local economy – with the advent of both electronics factories and tourism – had been largely successful and the area remained fairly prosperous.

It is also – again, unlike Glasgow – deeply Conservative territory. In the 1979 referendum, the Borders would be the mainland Scottish area most vehemently voting No to devolution. This would have suited Ruth's parents, who, despite their working-class upbringing, became committed Tory voters from a young age.

Selkirk itself also makes much of its local traditions. For instance, Selkirk Common Riding is an event that takes place every June to commemorate the Battle of Flodden, a sixteenth-century English victory over Scotland. Such festivities would have well suited the young Davidson family, who were thoroughly small 'c' conservatives and, with Douglas's new management job, well on the way to becoming definitively middle-class.

Ruth was three years old when her father, now a career-driven industrialist, took up a job in the whisky industry and the family upped sticks to Lundin Links in Fife. The transition would not have been difficult for the family of four. Based on the east coast of Scotland, north of Edinburgh and about eighty miles from Selkirk, Lundin Links would have had much the same small-town feel as their former home in the Borders. It is famous for its two golf courses, despite them being somewhat overshadowed by nearby St Andrews. The major difference for Ruth's parents, however, would be political. In contrast to the decidedly conservative Selkirk, Lundin Links and Fife was a much more Labour area. Clearly, this had little impact on Ruth's views in later life, but it is worth noting she would grow up around many working-class people who would not share her later passion for the Conservative Party.

Indeed – as well as the accident that almost killed her – it is from this age that Ruth begins to remark on the Davidson family dynamic. It was from Douglas, Ruth would later suggest, that she got her moral compass, while mother Liz 'dealt with the day-to-day stuff in the house'. This is not wholly surprising. Douglas was clearly an ambitious and capable businessman. Despite having left school at sixteen and enduring a far from disastrous – but hardly wildly successful – career in football, he was anxious to get on in life. He had, in short, exactly the kind of 'striver versus skiver' personality that embodied Tory political views. He was upwardly mobile, but through his own hard work. It was an attitude that clearly influenced Ruth and is reflected in her ruthless determination to succeed.

Yet Ruth gives us a further insight, not just into the character of her parents, but also into their views. Clearly, Douglas was now successful enough that Liz did not need to work to support the family. This is not to suggest the Davidsons were wealthy – they weren't – but they were certainly comfortable. But it is the traditional relationship of the marriage that is most striking, and again reflects that 'small c' conservative background that was so dominant in Ruth's upbringing.

For her education, Ruth would attend the local primary and comprehensive secondary, Buckhaven High School, the motto of which is, appropriately for Ruth, *Perseverando* – perseverance.

While her traditional parents might have preferred to educate her privately, there is no evidence that this was considered. In any event, sending both Ruth and her sister to a fee-paying school would have been an expensive prospect and beyond the means of a single-earner household.

Buckhaven High School showed Ruth a cross-section of Scottish society, allowing her to mix with local working-class children from across the coastal villages of east Fife. Clearly this experience helped provide Ruth with much of her bonhomie and 'natural' touch that would serve her well in later life – and there is no evidence to suggest she was anything but happy when mixing with her classmates.

'Buckhaven High is quite a long way from being a private school,' she told *The Scotsman* in 2012. 'It takes its pupil base from what I believe is euphemistically called a socially depressed area, and it had all the attendant problems that go with that of drugs and violence and all the rest of it, but my teachers were amazing.'

Of course, as Ruth herself suggests, comprehensive education brought with it certain aspects that probably delighted her at the time – if not her parents. The future Tory leader, for instance, admitted to smoking marijuana while attending the school. In 2015, she told a general election debate audience at Glasgow

University that she had tried the drug 'once or twice'. 'I went to Buckhaven High School, what do you think?' she joked, when asked about it by a member of the audience. Like other party leaders, she suggested it made her feel 'really sick'.

But generally she is more circumspect on her time at BHS, as locals know it. 'Buckhaven High School in the early '90s was a community where you saw all sides of life,' she told the *Daily Mail*.

> It had an ethos where, despite people's backgrounds, strengths, weaknesses, or because of them, people respected each other and helped each other. What people did or were back then is less important than how the experiences shaped them into the positive forces we all can be now. We learn from our mistakes, and if we've made mistakes, there is pride in learning from them and moving forward and helping others either avoid them, or deal with them. I'm proud of Buckhaven High School – I've been back many times since – and privileged to have shared classes with the people who showed me a much bigger picture.

Indeed, despite her injuries from her earlier accident, Ruth was an active participant in school life. She played the clarinet and was a member of the ski club. From an early age, too, she showed her love of taking centre stage, setting up a theatre group with friends. One of the productions she put on was *The Sisterhood*, an adaptation of a Molière farce, where she played a matriarch-type figure, a bit like Maggie Smith in *Downton Abbey*. She would later boast she was the first girl to be selected for the under-fourteen football team, while she also took up a part-time job as a kitchen porter during her teens.

It did not take long, however, before politics became a part of Ruth's life. 'I've always been a Tory,' she told the *Edinburgh Evening News* in 2014.

> I was outed when I was sixteen when a newspaper ran a feature on 'Saffy Syndrome' focusing on girls who were like the daughter in *Absolutely Fabulous*. My school put me forward for it as I was so sensible, and so I was outed as a supporter of the Conservatives. The other kids didn't care, but some of the teachers got a bit sniffy.

As well as politics, however, Ruth was, and remains, deeply committed to God.

A member of the Church of Scotland, she believes Christianity can provide a 'moral compass' for youngsters.

Of course, it is relatively unusual for a woman of her generation to be so committed to Christianity. The Church of Scotland – like many other denominations – has experienced a sharp decline in membership over the last several decades. Indeed, since the 1980s, surveys have repeatedly found congregations getting smaller and smaller, with the Church of Scotland – often known as 'the Kirk' – being particularly badly hit.

But while her faith was born in childhood, it has stuck with her throughout her life. Indeed, if Ruth's determination and belief in the individual came from her father, then her faith came from her mother. Douglas was religious but not hugely committed, attending church only for major festivals like Christmas and Easter. Liz, on the other hand, was a firm believer and committed Church of Scotland activist. She was the superintendent in her local congregation and imbued Ruth with a love of God.

Ruth's faith is therefore not 'casual' or a mere question of identity. On the contrary, she has been regularly and actively involved in church life. She would, for many years, follow in her mother's footsteps and become a Sunday School teacher.

There is, however, more than just parental influence here. Clearly, if Ruth wished, she could have followed her father's more laissez-faire approach to faith. But the church provided Ruth with a sense of grounding – and there is no doubt her earlier accident and remarkable recovery will have played a part in developing her religious beliefs. 'I am a member of the Church of Scotland, I attend services, I believe in God, I appreciate my own faith,' she told the BBC in 2011. 'I think the grounding that I've had through my own church has helped me shape my views on the world – my views on tolerance, on love, on appreciating other people, on service or on duty – and I don't think any of these things are bad things.'

Yet, despite her strong grounding, Ruth has often struggled with her religion. Much of this can be put down to the strains of modern life. Her career would force her to live in a number of different cities across Scotland, so she regularly moved churches. Before politics, her work both as a journalist and as a soldier meant she was often busy at weekends, so her attendance slipped. The decline of her mother's influence may also have been a partial factor, but Ruth's faith is personal, not a feint to placate parental desires.

Her key issue was trying to grapple with – or perhaps marry – her devout religious faith and sexuality. As a child, Ruth had dreamed of a traditional marriage in a church. Much of this, of course, will be down to popular culture and the dominant social norms, which were – it goes without saying – less tolerant than they would be today. The prevailing wisdom in working-class Fife in the 1980s as Ruth grew up would have been deeply sceptical of homosexuality – as she herself notes. 'I don't think anyone was openly gay at my school,' she said. 'I think everybody who is gay thinks a lot about how it will affect their family and friends.'

Yet being a church-going, Sunday School-attending believer, undoubtedly put extra strain on Ruth's understanding of her sexuality. Conventional marriage designs would have been instilled in Ruth from an early age. As a member of the congregation, she would have been surrounded by people who believed – in a religious sense – that marriage could only take place between a man and a woman. Her traditional upbringing will have only reinforced the sense that there was a 'right' way to do these things. 'I thought I was destined for the big white wedding and the chap on my arm and all the rest of it, and then it wasn't to be,' Ruth told the BBC in 2015, with perhaps a hint of disappointment.

It was not until her mid-twenties that she came out as gay, but her comments on the subject reflect the deep-seated struggle she endured with her sexuality. She told the BBC in the same interview that she had 'known for a few years' that she was gay before she made it public, suggesting that in her teenage years she struggled to come to terms with her sexuality. A friend said that, not unusually, she engaged in heterosexual relationships before coming out as gay.

All of this is not at all unique or surprising, but there is little doubt that Ruth's conservative background – not to mention her own views – would have made the process more difficult. It is worth noting that her decision to come out came after she left university and was away, geographically at least, from the orbit of her parents and her childhood church.

'It took time for me to come to some sort of peace with myself about it. It's something I struggled with, I didn't want to be gay,' she said in the 2015 interview.

> I'm not sure how many people do, and it's been amazing the difference even in my lifetime how things have changed, but I did struggle with it for a number of years before I would admit it to myself, never mind to anybody else. But there comes a point at which you make a decision and that decision is either that you're going to live a lie for the rest of your life, or you're going to trust yourself. That's what I had to do.

Like many denominations, the Church of Scotland has a difficult – some might say chequered – history in relation to equal rights. Their General Assembly had made moves towards recognising homosexuality. In 1994, when Ruth was still a teenager, they considered a report that concluded 'among other things, that cohabiting couples, whether heterosexual or homosexual, may well display all the marks of loving, faithful and committed partnership, and should not be thought sinful'. Yet, in the face of opposition, the issue was kicked into the long grass, meaning official church policy remained that homosexuality was a sin. It would not be until 2005 and the legalisation of civil partnerships in Scotland, that the Church of Scotland fully permitted same-sex relationships.

Interestingly, Ruth herself does not identify the Church of Scotland as being specifically problematic, but rather Christian teaching more widely. 'I was in the BBC, so it wasn't a workplace issue, I think it's fair to say – that's where I was working at the time – so that was fine,' she said.

I think the biggest issue for me actually was the issues with my faith. To read Paul's letter to various churches around the globe talking about 'homosexual offenders' – the phrase in the international version – and talking about idolaters and adulterers and thieves being ranked together was very, very difficult.

The prevailing social attitudes of the church have, naturally, changed over the course of Ruth's life. It is now much easier to be gay and a committed member of the Church of Scotland. Ruth said she received thousands of congratulatory messages from churchgoers after she announced her engagement to her partner in 2016. But not every member of the church was accepting – and their criticism clearly stung Ruth. She told former Church of Scotland moderator the Very Rev. Dr Lorna Hood in 2016: 'The accusatory nature that people take, the hurtfulness, the kind of venom that is behind it, and sometimes it does feel venomous, is much more against the teachings of the church that I'm a member of, and of the faith that I profess.'

Clearly, while Ruth is angered by such abuse from fellow Christians, she believes they are the outliers rather than the norm.

Whether Ruth would continue to hold her religious faith so strongly had attitudes not changed – or at least started to change – is open for debate. What is clear is that her beliefs added to the strain on what was already a difficult moment in her life.

And what do her family make of it? Ruth has, rather cagily, only gone so far as to say they are 'accepting'.

Away from her home and religious life, Ruth has been open about her sexuality, without flouting it unnecessarily. As her public profile has increased, she has benefited from Scotland – or perhaps Scottish politics – taking a more progressive attitude towards being gay.

Until late 2017, Scotland's three main political parties were led by women, and Ruth's former Labour counterpart, Kezia Dugdale, is also gay, as is UKIP's David Coburn, while the Green Party's Patrick Harvie is bisexual. Such a scenario means that Ruth, rather than being an exception, is actually in the majority. This means that while her sexuality is something that people know and might note, it is not unusual in the way it would be if, for instance, she were a party leader in Westminster.

Indeed, Ruth has also been actively supportive of other political colleagues who have come out as gay, most notably the Secretary of State for Scotland, David Mundell. Having struggled with her sexuality herself, Ruth clearly has a personal reason to support others in the same position. After Mundell came out, she said: 'Really proud of my friend David today. I know that David didn't make [this] statement lightly, but approached it in his typically thoughtful and positive manner. He has my wholehearted support, as well as the support of the wider Scottish Conservative family.'

That is not to suggest, however, that Scottish politics – or Scotland itself – is some rose-tinted utopia of tolerance and progression. Ruth has regularly suffered slurs at the hands of internet trolls, with the proliferation of social media making direct abuse easier and more prevalent. In one such instance, she was told by an SNP member that she needed 'a good c*ck, not a lesbian battery one'. The party suspended the member in question, but such behaviour was not a one-off. Away from social media, a comedy sketch at a pro-independence rally in 2016, for example, referred to her as 'Ruth Dykey D'. The comment was widely condemned, though an SNP MP described it as 'hilariously irreverent satire' before later apologising.

But, being robust as ever, Ruth has had no qualms about calling people out for abuse. 'As an openly gay politician, I also get a significant amount of homophobic abuse, and I feel a responsibility to challenge that,' she wrote in the *Daily Record*.

> I don't want young LGBT people reading my timeline and thinking that that sort of language is OK. I don't want them believing that the only response is to just sit passively and take it. It is important to me that I retweet, highlight or challenge a cross-section of homophobic abuse I receive so young people feel able to do the same. We are allowed to say, 'No, this is not acceptable.'

Ruth has taken an admirable stand in this case, but it is interesting to contrast her language here with her earlier comments on the hurtful abuse she has received from fellow members of the church. Homophobic abuse online – often from supporters of opposing parties – is clearly viewed as being a political issue. It is seen as a question of education and reminding people that such comments are not acceptable. Abuse – or 'venom', as she put it – from fellow Christians, however, is clearly more stinging, which again reflects the importance of religion in Ruth's life.

*   *   *

After finishing at Buckhaven High School, Ruth went to Edinburgh University. It was not her first choice. Ever the tomboy, she would rather have joined the army, but the injuries sustained as a child ruled her out of officer training at Sandhurst.

Nevertheless, Scotland's capital has always held an affinity for her. Apart from being the place of her birth, it is also the closest city to Fife. Around forty miles from her home town of Lundin Links, Edinburgh was close enough for her to retain close ties with her parents, but also far enough away that she could enjoy herself uninhibited. Ruth would throw her eighteenth birthday party there – enjoying her first drink in a city pub.

But, for a woman who had grown up in the sleepy towns and villages of the Borders and Fife, it was also something of a cultural metropolis. With the university based in Edinburgh's south, Ruth was just a short distance from the Royal Mile and institutions like the National Museum of Scotland and the Scottish National Portrait Gallery.

The capital, of course, can have a reputation as a somewhat snobbish and cold city – a description that is often contrasted with Glasgow as a warm and friendly place. Ruth herself would experience feelings of caution about the city – particularly about some of her fellow students. 'There are these people who are twenty or twenty-one, have had a gap year in Tanzania, who have this sheen, this brio, this impenetrable confidence that their entire life is mapped out for them,' she said of her fellow classmates, many of whom would have been upper middle class and English – a far cry from Ruth's background. 'They are going to end up married, in the Home Counties, with a lovely wife called Tilly – he's got a Mercedes, she's got a Land Rover and they have a pony called Trumper for their daughters. It was intimidating, that level of self-confidence,' she said.

Ruth would later suggest she 'found it really tough' ingratiating herself in the society of Edinburgh University, which was a far cry from Buckhaven High School. But studying English – as well as American political history – at Edinburgh would further instil her affection for the city she would later represent. One poem in particular, Norman MacCaig's 'November Night, Edinburgh', sums up her love for the city. 'I love those nights in Edinburgh that the MacCaig poem describes – you don't get that in the west because it's damper,' she told the *Edinburgh Evening News* in 2014. 'Edinburgh does this time of year very well – the change from autumn to winter, why would you be anywhere else?'

While she was attentive in her studies – she would graduate with a 2:1 degree after her four-year course – she also continued to be active in the extracurricular scene. Debating became a particular passion, with a fiery and determined Ruth even then eager to trounce her opponents.

Having graduated, and with a military career seemingly now ruled out because of her childhood injuries, Ruth instead returned to her native Fife to take up a career as a journalist. The *Glenrothes Gazette* was as good a place as any to train as a journalist.

The *Gazette* was, by Scottish standards, a relatively new newspaper when Ruth joined, having been founded in 1962. The weekly, based in the Fife town of the same name, had a circulation of around 6,500 – a significant readership.

It was, of course, an area Ruth knew well, having grown up just eight miles away in Lundin Links. Glenrothes, like many post-industrial Fife towns, has high levels of unemployment and social deprivation. Almost a fifth of the town ranks among the most deprived areas in Scotland and, like many trainee reporters, Ruth would start with the hard graft of drugs deaths, court and crime. Yet she would also cover the council beat – a mainstay of local journalism. Much of this revolved around planning applications and drumming up local anger about unpopular decisions – but it was nevertheless a fundamentally political beat. Ruth would come to know many local politicians and witness first-hand the often dry machinations of local government. Starting the role at twenty-one, she remembered her time at the *Gazette* – and specifically covering the council – fondly. 'The thing that was most interesting in my time at the *Gazette*, given what I do now, was learning all the local government stuff, which is something I knew nothing about before I started work in Glenrothes,' she said.

With a personable character, Ruth clearly enjoyed the regular interaction with people that being a local journalist entails. 'I particularly remember doing a piece about the Leonard Cheshire Home in the town and being really impressed with that ... I still have all my cuttings from every single paper that I wrote for.'

That Ruth would, years later, single out her story on the Leonard Cheshire Home – a charity facility that supports people with disabilities – is perhaps rooted in her own experiences following her accident as a five-year-old. As a young reporter, Ruth was clearly so touched by the compassion shown by volunteers – and as others had shown her – that the memory stayed with her.

Like most cub reporters, Ruth did more than her fair share of grunt work. Copies of the weekly paper from her time there reveal a plethora of reports on church meetings and coffee mornings. She was also landed – perhaps not to her chagrin – with writing the regular 'Couch Potato' TV column. A beaming byline picture of a youthful Ruth would be accompanied by a review of the latest offerings on the box, with the future Tory leader giving a pertinent insight into the latest soap opera plots and cooking shows.

In more serious areas, a news story on the candidates for the Central Fife constituency provides a clear example of how quickly Ruth's career would take off. For the piece in the early 2000s, almost a decade before she entered politics, she interviewed one Jeremy Balfour – the Conservative hopeful – who would not win a seat until the 2016 Holyrood election, where he serves under Ruth's leadership.

Two pieces from her time at the *Gazette*, however, are worth exploring in more depth. The first is an opinion piece she wrote shortly after starting at the paper in February 2000. This regular 'First Person' column gives a valuable insight into Ruth's early views on politics – and the Union – and is worth quoting at length. The column begins by recounting a speech Ruth was invited to give at the Edinburgh University Debating Society to celebrate Burns Night. 'As I knew that about half of my audience would be from places other than Scotland I decided that the main theme of the speech was to be Burns' politics, patriotism and quintessential Scottishness,' she began, before going on to describe what she believes it means to be Scottish – and British. 'In Burns' day it was not hard to find a republican image of what it was to be a Scot,' she wrote.

> Only thirty-five years after the last Jacobite uprising, and with the Union of the Parliaments a fading, but still painful memory, it was easy to identify Scottishness with rebellion and anti-establishment feelings.
>
> But what about today?
>
> For a country that is so fiercely proud of its distinction from the other home nations, there is still very little consensus of what our identity should be.

For Ruth, however, the answer was not a nationalist's view of Scotland, but rather a patriot's.

Scotland's image has changed a lot down the years.

At the start of the twentieth century, the focus shifted away from the highland, tartan-clad crofter and moved to the Glasgow shipbuilder.

So proud were we of our heavy industry – and with good reason – the hard-drinking, bonnet-wearing, Scottish hardman acted as the flawed template for the nation as a whole.

Fast forward to today and we're now bombarded with headlines declaring 'tartan-chic' and so fashionable has it become that those in the know are warning us that being Scottish is the new black.

The 1995 film *Braveheart* – a historically inaccurate if enjoyable biopic of the Scots rebel William Wallace – had 'ignited the passions of young people who had never stopped to think about their culture', Ruth said. The Mel Gibson film had left them feeling 'hard done by'. But she added:

We've spent so long defining ourselves as 'not English' and 'not European' that we seem very confused about what we have become.

Kids who thought the Highland clearances were breaks in between the trees [have] suddenly complained of their long oppression at the hands of the English and the tide of anti-English feeling rose to a disturbing level.

Ruth argued – perhaps incorrectly – that this would not be enough to push Scotland towards independence.

Five years on [from the release of *Braveheart*] and the predicted surge in nationalism didn't really materialise.

The SNP's prediction of a completely independent Scotland in fifteen years' time looks increasingly unlikely.

The parliament at Holyrood, for all its significant flaws – and there are many – is trying to address social issues.

This is a much better situation than just shouting from the sidelines in Westminster, moaning that no one is paying us enough attention.

Such views show that – even before she became professionally political – Ruth held a disparaging view of the SNP. The future Tory leader valued the Union and – to an extent – devolution, but did not believe Scotland should – or would – get special treatment. At the time of writing, Scotland had just held its first devolved election – and, amid the exuberance of that occasion, Ruth's opinion would have been somewhat controversial. However, it also reflects the typical Tory view at the time – that devolution was fundamentally wrong.

Indeed – while Ruth would go on to support modest further devolution, at least in public – it is particularly striking how closely the views she held when she was just out of university match those that would dominate her political career in later life. Her column concludes: 'Scots are no longer wearing their nationhood as a defiant apology, embarrassed by their perceived parochialism.' Scotland was, Ruth wrote, 'aware of our history but not still wallowing in it'. Just eleven years later, Ruth would be making the same arguments on the floor of Holyrood.

While such opinion pieces provide valuable insight into Ruth's thinking at the time, the majority of her work at the *Gazette* was dominated by writing news. One story in particular is worth noting.

Section 28 of the Local Government Act of 1988 stated that local authorities shall not 'intentionally promote homosexuality or publish material with the intention of promoting homosexuality'. Introduced by Thatcher's government, it was controversial at the time and would remain so. No charges were ever brought under the act, but critics argued it caused bodies to self-censor in a bid to avoid a possible prosecution. This was particularly concerning for local authorities, who run public education. While teachers could not be prosecuted under the act, councils – who managed them – could, leading to confusion about what could and could not be discussed in classes. Members of staff became reluctant to discuss homosexuality during sex education classes, for fear of falling foul of Section 28. Given it was introduced in 1988, at the height of the HIV/AIDS outbreak that was associated with the gay community, this was particularly concerning for LGBT rights activists, who feared children would not be properly briefed on safe sex, among other things.

The New Labour government attempted to repeal it in 2000, but was defeated in the House of Lords. Tony Blair's government argued that Section 28 was 'a barrier to building a supportive and tolerant society'. With a firm majority in the House of Commons, Labour were able to vote through the repeal, but it was defeated by a campaign led by the Tory Baroness Young in the second chamber. Summarising her arguments, she said: 'The centre of this debate is children, children in schools, children who in my opinion ought not to be treated as if they were adults and in a position to make an informed choice about alternative lifestyles, about which they cannot possibly have the experience to judge.'

Despite the defeat in 2000, Holyrood would lead a separate campaign to remove the clause from the statute book. The move was fraught with difficulty, with Stagecoach's Brian Souter – who is also a prominent SNP donor – launching a campaign against the plans.

Ruth covered the various elements of the campaign herself in the pages of the *Gazette*. Her coverage was truly professional – balanced, objective and impartial. She freely described the Holyrood bid to repeal Section 28 as 'controversial', quoting from her interviews with local church figures – including from the Church of Scotland – who opposed the repeal. What internal conflicts such reporting caused – if any – are unknown. But it cannot be easy to be a gay trainee reporter and have to take quotes from people describing homosexuality as a 'perversion'.

By the end of 2000, Section 28 would be repealed in Scotland – and in the rest of the country by 2003. While Labour had retained its support for the repeal, the Conservatives eventually changed their position, allowing their members a free vote on the proposal. Baroness Young – the chief opponent of the change in the House of Lords – had passed away in 2002 and the bill passed. Ruth would later describe the introduction of the clause by Thatcher as 'wrong ... pure and simple'.

Like many trainee journalists at local newspapers, however, Ruth – always ambitious, always sure of herself – had her eye on bigger things.

Leaving the *Gazette*, she moved first to Kingdom FM, a commercial radio station, also based in her parental home of Fife. Good training, perhaps, but she would be quickly transferred again, first to Real Radio and then – more permanently – to work for BBC Scotland, both in radio and as a documentary maker. A later *New Statesman* profile describes her broadcast performance as 'fluent, well prepared, interested in whomever she was talking to'. In the same piece, her former producer Pat Stevenson recalls her as a 'fantastic interviewer', describing her as 'incisive and forensic'.

It was during her time at the national broadcaster that she was sent to cover the aftermath of the war in Kosovo.

The brutal conflict, which began in 1998, was fought between ethnic Kosovars and Slobodan Milošević's Serbia. The war ended in 1999 after a bombing campaign by a NATO coalition, including the UK, brought Milošević to his knees. The situation, however, remained unstable and NATO provided a peacekeeping force for the region. It was this operation that Ruth went to cover – and it once again rekindled her love of all things military. On her return, she signed up to the Territorial Army as a signaller, inspired by the troops she met in the Balkans. 'I was sent to the Balkans at the end of the Kosovo war as a reporter and I have never been more proud of being British in my life than watching British troops with a Union Jack on their arms, believing in something, pulling their weight,' she told a Wembley audience in 2016. 'That's what caused me to join up and serve,' she added.

The Territorial Army was, in Ruth's own words, the making of her. Her role taught her the value of leadership and teamwork. Her motivation to sign up was clearly down to the sense of duty and community that had been fostered in her from such a young age.

Her chosen unit was 32 Signal Regiment, based in the west of Edinburgh. Founded in 1967, the regiment prides itself on its communications ability, and its members would serve on operations in both Iraq and Afghanistan in the late 2000s, albeit after Ruth's time.

One of her commanding officers, Colonel Steve Bargeton, remembered Ruth as a plucky and determined soldier. He said she was marked out at the start as a potential officer – a potential leader – which is how they came to meet. Bargeton was tasked with organising a fast-track officer recruitment course for the Territorial Army, which was run out of the Barry Buddon base in Angus. Over the course of a year, almost every weekend the recruits would be put through mentally and physically challenging training, with the aim of being sent to Sandhurst afterwards. 'Ruth was one of the stand-out candidates we had,' Bargeton remembers.

> There were probably around fifty or so people on the course and one of my jobs was to think about them in terms of who would definitely succeed, who was a maybe and who we thought would struggle. I suppose it was a bit like *The X Factor* really. There were the definite ins, the definite outs and then the maybes. Ruth always looked like a good prospect.

While she was not the fittest of the candidates, Bargeton says, she showed great mental resilience.

> It was often very gruelling. You'd spend hours carrying heavy kit, planning attacks, marching – it takes it out of you. Some other people were perhaps physically fitter and Ruth had to work harder. But she had the mental strength to deal with it. Anyone can train more, but Ruth had something that can't be taught.

Ruth's great strength, according to Bargeton, was in the field.

> She did extremely well at battle camp, which is a ten-day intensive course. It's not SAS training, but nevertheless it is

ten days in the field. You've got to have your personal admin sorted out, you have to be switched on about how you look after yourself, you have got to be sharp giving orders, receiving orders, executing orders. There's a lot of physical stuff, a lot of patrolling. And of course, there's a lot of commanding. There's this way of commanding men – ultimately, you have to get people to buy into what you want to do – and Ruth had that.

Amid the gruelling training, Ruth gained a reputation for looking out for soldiers who were struggling, Bargeton says. 'She was a banker,' he added, meaning that Ruth was dependable.

As the weekends of training wore on, Ruth became a great figure in the mess, Bargeton says, joining in the camaraderie with fellow soldiers. 'She was always up for having a few beers and having a laugh. But she'd always be up for training on time,' he recalls.

Bargeton does not remember Ruth being particularly engaged with politics at the time, although he suggests – along with sex and religion – it was something no one talked about.

But her time as a signaller was to be brutally cut short. During her training to become an officer at Sandhurst, her frailty from her old injuries came back to haunt her.

'I never saw active duty overseas, but I did the officer training in Scotland and then the real exams at Sandhurst – which is where I badly injured myself,' she told the *Daily Mail*.

For the physical courage test we had to jump through a glass window and I volunteered to go first, as I do, but the sandpit behind the window had frozen solid. I landed awkwardly on my neck and cracked vertebrae. I spent almost two weeks in hospital and had to wear a back brace.

Despite being keen to continue in the forces, Ruth was told she was now an insurance risk. Once again, Ruth suffered not just a physical scar but a mental one too. Her sense of disappointment at not being able to do something she was so passionate about would have been palpable. In others, the rather absurd bureaucratic parlance of being an insurance risk might have fostered resentment. But there is no evidence to suggest that Ruth – who had valued public service since her early treatment in the NHS – felt anything other than frustration at a potential career path being closed.

Indeed, Bargeton believes she would have made an excellent officer – and questions whether she would have gone into politics had she not been injured. 'There's no doubt she was very well suited to army life,' he said. 'She was keen, passionate and a very good leader. I think it's what she really wanted to do.'

If joining the army was the making of Ruth, then having to leave was the making of her political life. Casting about with her military career in tatters, Ruth returned to the one constant in her varied life: politics.

CHAPTER 3

DEVOLUTION DANGER

While Scottish politics might have always been Ruth's calling, the same could not be said for her Conservative Party.

In 1997, Tony Blair won his now famed landslide, wiping out almost two decades of uninterrupted Tory government. The New Labour project, which began in earnest after Blair's election as leader in 1994, had totally reinvented the party, widening its appeal so far as to put even traditionally safe Conservative seats under threat.

Of course, the public – who had by then been governed by the Tories for eighteen years – were anxious for a fresh political movement. Blair himself was a likeable, competent and charismatic leader and, under the New Labour banner, supported policies that were palatable to a broad cross-section of voters. Labour's vote share south of the border would jump to almost 44 per cent, with dozens of seats switching hands.

It could be argued that the modernisation of Labour was an English, rather than Scottish, phenomenon. Certainly, the

Labour Party had struggled to pick up votes in England beyond its traditional heartlands during the 1980s. In contrast, support in Scotland had remained steady and even increased over the same period. The New Labour project was in part designed to address the imbalance.

Blair himself – despite going to school in Scotland – represented a seat south of the border and had a fundamental air of cosmopolitan London in both his attitudes and his outlook. This was particularly noticeable when contrasted with Blair's predecessor, John Smith – the Scot who, until his untimely death, was destined to lead the modernisation project that eventually fell to Blair. Blair's usurpation of Gordon Brown during the leadership contest that followed Smith's death adds further weight to this view.

But the nuances of such an argument ignore the bigger picture. New Labour – like Thatcherism – was designed to provide political renewal for Britain as a whole. The 'cool Britannia' mantra was a gimmick embraced by the youthful, guitar-playing Blair. Yet it had a deeper resonance too – one of Britain reasserting itself in the world on the basis not of jingoistic patriotism, but rather a love of modernity. New Labour was, crucially, an update of social democracy for the twenty-first century – and it was therefore able to appeal across the country.

This allure is reflected in the 1997 general election result in Scotland too, which was a disaster for the Tories. Despite the swing against them being lower north of the border than south of it, the Tories won no seats in Scotland. Foreign Secretary Malcolm Rifkind and Scottish Secretary Michael Forsyth were two high-profile casualties of the apocalyptic performance. With 17.5 per cent of the vote – their lowest showing in Scotland to date – the Tories were decimated.

It was the culmination of decades of policy failure that increasingly led the party to become disassociated from Scots voters. While Thatcher's neoliberalism reinvented the Tories in England after the collapse of empire and the decline of nationalism, it had little or no cachet in Scotland. The Tories had become an English party.

As with any defeat, the recriminations within the Conservative Party were frenetic and bitter. Moderates and hard-liners – at least those who had not lost their seats – blamed each other for the rout. In England, it was clear the Tories had no credible response to Blairism and that they would not for some time.

In Scotland, however, there was an opportunity for more serious and reflective soul-searching. While they had been wiped out north of the border, the result was not the shock experienced by those in England. The Tory vote share had been declining for some time, leading to a sense of the inevitable about their final collapse.

Some Scottish Conservatives recognised that the Tories' apparent 'Englishness' was to blame. 'We have been perceived, wrongly in many cases, as an English party with a branch office in Scotland,' said Arthur Bell, chairman of the Scottish Tory Reform Group. 'I think that has got to go. There are fundamental changes coming in Scotland which will not allow us to survive at all if that perception is maintained.' Future party leader Annabel Goldie would warn that the party faced 'extinction' in Scotland if it did not change.

Then Scottish Secretary Michael Forsyth had already bid to put the Tories on a distinct footing in Scotland, publishing a separate manifesto for the 1997 election and using the lion rampant as the party's logo – but, as David Torrance points out, this 'amounted to too little, too late'. One of Blair's key manifesto proposals, meanwhile – again reflective of New Labour's relevance to Scotland – was to hold a referendum on the creation of a Scottish Parliament. Such a move should have offered the Scottish Conservatives the chance to redress the balance of their perceived 'Englishness'. By backing devolution, the Tories could have begun to cast off perceptions that they were anti-Scottish and a 'branch office'. But many in the party remained fundamentally opposed to countenancing even a transfer of powers.

Matters came to a head during the 1997 Conservative conference in Perth. Delegates had gathered to discuss their response both to the creation of a Scottish Parliament and to the wider issues of identity afflicting the party north of the border. The scenes would be tense, with many senior members of the party opposing not just devolution but even the notion of a semi-autonomous party north of the border. The Scottish Conservative and Unionist Association president – and future Tory leader in Scotland – David McLetchie said: 'We can have a substantial degree of autonomy, but the idea of an independent breakaway party is a complete nonsense.'

Forsyth, addressing delegates at the Perth conference, was even more forthright. 'We Conservatives and Unionists have always stood for what we believed in,' he said. 'If, in the wake of election defeat, we were now to stand supinely aside and nod through the most disastrous reversal of our constitutional stability since 1707, we would deserve to be relegated to a footnote in history.' While the conference overwhelmingly backed his view – echoed by new leader William Hague, who branded the devolution vote 'flawed' – there was dissent.

Factional infighting was further fuelled by reports that

'devo-realists', as pro-devolution Tories were known, were being 'bankrolled' by like-minded German Christian Democrats. The situation became so frantic that right-winger Lloyd Beat, the chairman of the Conservative Political Centre of Scotland, claimed the 'devo-realists' represented the same threat to the Tories as Militant had done to Labour a decade earlier.

In the end, a motion calling for the party to continue campaigning against a Scottish Parliament was passed with widespread support.

Matters were hardly helped by Margaret Thatcher's decision to intervene in the debate, despite having been out of office for almost a decade.

She wrote in *The Scotsman*:

What is at stake – in the case of both the propositions on the ballot paper – is nothing short of the Union of the United Kingdom itself. And the constitution of our country is a matter of the gravest moment for all of us, north and south of the border, although you would never think it from the shallow and cynical manner in which the government is proceeding.

The decision to oppose devolution was widely out of step with Scottish political thought and would cost the party dearly in coming elections. When the referendum was held on 11 September 1997, almost 75 per cent of Scots voters backed the creation of the Scottish Parliament. A further 63 per cent of voters also backed tax-raising powers for the new Parliament, which was offered in a second question on the ballot. Given its opposition to devolution, however, the Tories were doomed to fish among the 25 per cent who voted No.

The aftermath of the 1997 election can therefore be seen as a watershed moment for the Scottish Conservatives. Their failure – despite the efforts of some – to support even a token transfer of powers not only failed to address their identity crisis, it reinforced it. The perception that the Conservative Party was 'English' was compounded into being 'anti-Scottish'. It is extraordinary that, despite their steady decline since the 1960s, so few in the party recognised this danger. Of course, much of the opposition to devolution was principled, drawing from an ideological belief in the Union, which they believed had served Scotland – or perhaps Britain – well for three centuries. But whether the opposition was born out of principle, stubbornness or stupidity – or perhaps all three – it would cost the Conservatives dearly and significantly stall their recovery.

Indeed, for wider Scotland, the 1997 vote to deliver a Scottish Parliament was undoubtedly seismic. Alex Salmond said it would be the catalyst that would see Scotland gain independence in his lifetime. 'We will shortly begin work on our manifesto but I can say right now that its centrepiece will be the pursuit of an independent Scotland. I have no doubt we will achieve that aim within my own lifetime,' he said after the result.

Certainly, Blair himself recognised it was a significant moment, even if he was less confident in predicting the future than his SNP counterpart. 'This is a good day for Scotland and a good day for the United Kingdom too,' he said. 'The era of big, centralised government is over. This is a time for change, renewal and modernity. This is the way forward. I believe that we now have the chance to build a modern constitution for the whole of the United Kingdom.' Privately, however, Blair had serious reservations about devolution – as did others within the Labour

Party. 'I was never a passionate devolutionist,' he wrote in his autobiography.

> It is a dangerous game to play. You can never be sure where nationalist sentiment ends and separatist sentiment begins. I supported the UK, distrusted nationalism as a concept, and looked at the history books and worried whether we could get it through. However, though not passionate about it, I thought it inevitable.

Donald Dewar – who would go on to be the inaugural First Minister of Scotland – suggested the result had exceeded all his expectations.

It is understandable that Labour – now the party of government – would have reservations about devolution. No government is apt to give up power lightly – and for Blair's party the stakes were even higher, with Scottish constituencies representing a significant portion of their majority in the House of Commons. Two key differences separate the Labour and Tory positions, however. Firstly, Labour figures kept any reservations about devolution private. Blair's comments quoted above, for instance, were only made in his autobiography, published more than ten years after the devolution referendum. Secondly, whatever private reservations there were, Labour had publicly backed – and delivered – devolution. If we contrast that with the Tory position of publicly opposing the transfer of powers, it is easy to see why Labour would enjoy early successes in Scottish elections.

With the benefit of hindsight, Forsyth and the anti-devolutionists could claim that they were on the right side of history. Devolution has arguably allowed the Scottish National Party to surge electorally – ultimately resulting in the referendum of 2014 and perhaps another in the near future. Without devolution – and trapped in a UK-wide, first-past-the-post Westminster system – it is unlikely they would have ever achieved the power necessary to threaten the Union itself. The late Labour MP and anti-devolutionist Tam Dalyell would describe the creation of the Scottish Parliament as 'a motorway without exit to a Scottish state'. Later he would be more frank, suggesting that 'feeding the SNP monster is misguided' because 'any form of devolution would never, ever be acceptable to them … Statehood was what their lives were about'. As in many areas, however, the West Lothian MP was an eccentric outlier. Such views were limited at the time – and the danger of devolution for the Union would not become apparent for many, many years.

The first election to the devolved Parliament would be held on 6 May 1999 – and the Tories began urgently hunting around for a coherent position on devolution. The initial overtures, as had often been the case, were good. Even William Hague had conceded that the Scottish Parliament would exist for 'quite a long time to come'. The former Scottish Conservative and Unionist Association president David McLetchie secured the role of head of the party in Scotland. While initially opposed to devolution, the solicitor and avid Hearts FC fan warmed to the idea, claiming it was 'an opportunity to get back on the pitch' and 'off the side lines'. Indeed, other party grandees had already moved to make the Scottish party more Scottish, with Sir Malcolm Rifkind claiming it should 'dare to differ' from Westminster. Party leader Hague himself declared at a rally at football ground Hampden Park, 'you are truly a Scottish party'.

Yet, while the rhetoric was there, the Tories had not truly

reformed. Many of the rank and file were still opposed to devolution, and Conservative opposition to the Parliament still loomed large in voters' minds.

The 1999 election campaign itself was rather nondescript. Labour were still buoyant after their 1997 triumph, and opinion polls consistently had them well ahead of their rivals. The SNP were predicted to do well throughout much of the campaign, but ultimately fell short of a shock result. Pollsters had the Tories and Liberal Democrats locked in a battle for third place.

Labour would fall nine seats short of a majority – winning fifty-six seats – while the SNP would return thirty-five. McLetchie's Scottish Tories would get just 15.5 per cent of the votes, notably down on their already disastrous showing in 1997. They returned eighteen MSPs through the PR list system – considerably more than some predictions of a lowly twelve, but hardly a resounding success. Nevertheless, they managed to just edge ahead of the Liberal Democrats, who secured seventeen seats, which can be viewed as a success of sorts. However, the centrist Lib Dems under Jim Wallace soon fell into coalition with Labour to form a government, allowing them to wield significantly more influence than their Tory counterparts. Only the election of notorious Scottish Socialist Tommy Sheridan and one Green MSP saved the Tories from the humiliation of being the smallest opposition party.

The result was deemed no fault of McLetchie, who retained a reputation as a competent leader. Bald-headed and cheery, his background in law and his rapier mind made him a notable contributor in Holyrood debates, regularly challenging the then Labour–Liberal Democrat coalition government.

Yet the crucial failing for the Tories in Scotland remained their inability to fully come to terms with the Scottish Parliament. As David Torrance writes: 'Although McLetchie's attacks on the Scottish Executive were often effective, it masked the absence of a clear, positive Conservative approach to a post-devolved Scotland.'

McLetchie's stated mantra was to be 'the Unionist opposition at Holyrood' – a position much of his party agreed with. He set out his beliefs most clearly in one of his first speeches to the Scottish Parliament, where he launched – as Ruth would more than a decade later – a no-hope bid to be chosen as First Minister. 'My candidacy will symbolise our determination to be a constructive opposition in the Parliament, working to make it a success for Scotland in the context of the United Kingdom,' he said. 'The Scottish Conservatives are the Unionist alternative to the Lib–Lab government that has been stitched up behind the backs of the voters, just as, time and again during the election campaign, we predicted.'

This policy of promoting the Union within the devolution settlement was not without its successes – the Tories would win the 2000 Ayr by-election against Labour, gaining their first constituency in the process. Of course, Labour was defending a wafer-thin majority of just twenty-five in the west of Scotland seat. Matters were hardly helped by the bizarre resignation of the sitting Labour member – Ian Welsh – who inexplicably threw in the towel after just 230 days in office. In a resignation statement, he attacked his colleagues as people who 'promise everything and deliver nothing'– hardly a ringing endorsement of his party.

Despite Labour's self-immolation, the Tories deserved to take heart from their victory. The Scottish Parliament constituency of Ayr shared its borders with the Westminster seat of the same name, which had been held by the Tories for almost a century until 1997. Despite being a curious mix of affluence and deprivation, the constituency had many markers for Tory success. It had a high rate of homeownership; a large proportion of the population were Church of Scotland members; and almost two-thirds of voters were over sixty. That the Tories were able to win back those voters reflected that McLetchie's 'Unionist opposition' strategy was not without support.

Yet the factionalism and infighting that had dogged the Tories since 1997 – perhaps longer – continued. A shift, for instance, to support free personal care for the elderly might have been electorally prudent but it caused deep ruptures in a party traditionally sceptical of state intervention. Another adopted policy position – to ban flavoured cigarettes – was ridiculed by party activists. As David Torrance points out: 'Attempts to reposition – or indeed "detoxify" – the party were confused and sporadic: there was no coordinated or ideologically consistent strategy.'

Such issues reflect that, while the constitution remained the most divisive issue within the Scottish Conservatives, ideological differences also existed. As is the case with the UK party, the moderates clashed with the hard-liners over what kind of policies MSPs should be pursuing. Indeed, many of those who were more positive about devolution were also on the free-market wing of the party, hoping that devolution could allow for less regulation and government intervention north of the border. While these ideological differences rarely boiled over into the public sphere, they did, as David Torrance suggests, make it more difficult for the party to present a coherent policy position.

William Hague, however, would insist his party was moving in the right direction. 'Since 1997, the Scottish Conservative and

Unionist Party has been turned around,' he would boldly – and incorrectly – tell Scots activists ahead of the 2001 general election. 'Our finances are improving, our membership is rising again and we have reconnected with the people of Scotland.'

He praised party head McLetchie, but perhaps most notably felt it necessary to insist the leader was independent. 'Above all, our party has found a distinctly Scottish voice. That voice can be heard in the calm, decent and persuasive tones of David McLetchie,' he continued. 'David and I understand what devolution means. It means fighting in Scotland as a Scottish party with Scottish policies. When David speaks, it's his voice you're hearing, not mine.'

Despite the strong rhetoric, however, Scots voters remained unconvinced. At the general election in June 2001 the party would fail to improve on its showing in the Holyrood elections two years earlier, polling just 15.6 per cent – although this time that was enough to get one MP elected. In the Tories' defence, Blair remained extremely popular at the time of the 2001 election, with the Iraq War still two years away. Hague, despite his abilities, had failed to make any inroads against New Labour in England, meaning success remained unlikely in Scotland, where they were starting from an even lower point.

Recriminations continued, however, with McLetchie's leadership questioned and the party's direction faltering.

The Scottish Parliament should have given the Tories a platform to assert themselves on Scottish issues. Indeed, McLetchie's noted success in the period – somewhat ironically given how the Tory leader himself would be forced to resign four years later – was forcing the First Minister, Henry McLeish, to resign. The roots of the so-called Officegate affair – involving undeclared rental income from rent in Glenrothes – dated back to 1987, but the issue came to light only in April 2001, six months into McLeish's brief tenure as head of the Scottish Executive. Persistent pressure from McLetchie was pivotal in forcing McLeish from office – and played well with traditional Tory values of propriety. But confusion over the party's constitutional stance continued to dog McLetchie and hamper any real electoral progress – and the benefits of any parliamentary successes.

MSPs persistently standing for House of Commons seats also added weight to the suggestion that the Scottish Tories did not take Holyrood seriously – although in fairness the talent in Scottish Labour too saw its future south of the border.

Some, such as future leadership contender Murdo Fraser MSP, were vocal in arguing for so-called fiscal autonomy – that the Scottish government would have to raise, as well as spend, money. Arguments such as this, however, remained *sotto voce* in the Scottish Tories.

Nevertheless, the 2003 Scottish election showed some improvement for the Tories north of the border. It was not – in purely statistical terms – anything like a resurgence or a triumph. The Conservatives constituency vote would rise 1 per cent across the country – totalling 16.6 per cent – while the regional list vote would rise a meagre 0.2 per cent. The result was enough for the Tories to maintain their eighteen members, in contrast to Scottish Labour and the SNP, who both lost seats. The Tories still remained, however, very much the third party of Scottish politics.

The headline figures did conceal a number of individual triumphs for the party. McLetchie – previously a list MSP – won the Edinburgh Pentlands constituency. The affluent seat enjoyed lower unemployment than the rest of Scotland and was in many ways ripe Tory territory. Yet demographics should not detract from the scale of McLetchie's victory, which saw him unseat a then Labour minister and future party leader Iain Gray. To win against such a big name was undoubtedly a coup for the Tory leader, and reflected his growing successes in the Holyrood chamber. His victory was coupled with that of Alex Fergusson, who won the (now abolished) seat of Galloway and Upper Nithsdale, defeating the SNP incumbent. Elsewhere, John Scott held on to his by-election victory in Ayr, increasing his share of the vote.

Such victories mattered little in the national picture, but they did reflect small shoots of recovery. Gaining and retaining constituencies showed that the Tories could win seats in Scotland in a first-past-the-post election, representing significant progress from their wipe-out in the general election of 1997 and their meagre gain in the same contest in 2001. McLetchie's victory in Edinburgh Pentlands against Labour – and Scott's ability to fend off the same party – also reflected something of a detoxification of the Tory brand. It was becoming acceptable again – at least in Holyrood elections – for affluent voters to back the Tories. While they had perhaps been attracted by New Labour centrism in earlier elections, they were now returning to their natural Conservative home. Fergusson's victory over the SNP was also cause for optimism, suggesting the Scottish Conservatives could perhaps convince the Tartan Tories who had deserted them over previous years to return to the party.

The importance of these individual victories, however, should not be overstated. Certainly – as would prove the case for the Tories themselves – the 2003 vote was something of an aberration for all parties. Sheridan's Scottish Socialists, for instance, would return an impressive – if equally short-lived – six seats. The Greens would also win an extra six seats, taking their tally to seven. The gains of these fringe parties, largely at the expense of the SNP and Labour, could be seen as general voter dissatisfaction with the work of Holyrood to date.

The benefits of such results, however, would be short-lived for McLetchie. By 2005, his six-year stint as leader was over: he was forced to resign after freedom of information requests revealed he had claimed thousands of pounds for taxis to conduct Tory Party business. Tellingly, he resigned from the party because he feared the expense claims were becoming a 'distraction' from rebuilding support for the Tories north of the border. In truth, given the party's continued division over the constitution, it was probably a welcome distraction.

Resigning, McLetchie said:

I have been committed to the Conservative Party in Scotland for the whole of my adult life and what it stands for is far more important than me personally. I recognise that the recent coverage surrounding my expense claims has been damaging and is a major distraction from our efforts to rebuild support for the party in the country.

It was a sombre resignation from a man who had kept the Tories alive in Scotland, if not revitalised them.

The party had still fundamentally failed to marry devolution and Unionism – and it needed an answer fast.

*   *   *

Murdo Fraser was perhaps the greatest leader the Scottish Conservatives never had. Of course, he is now known for his

2011 battle for the leadership with Ruth. But, with the benefit of hindsight, it was in 2005 – following McLetchie's resignation – that he should have run. Fraser had a clearly defined position on devolution, believing it could be used as a vehicle for Conservative values north of the border. With the membership still deeply sceptical, it is unclear whether he would have won in 2005, but, as a relatively experienced and certainly competent parliamentarian, he would have had a good chance.

As it happened, the democratic process was swiftly overruled by the party executive, who rushed to appoint McLetchie's former deputy, Annabel Goldie. As is often the case, a quick and smooth transfer of power was preferred to a potentially divisive – and public – leadership battle. Yet that is exactly what the Scottish Conservatives needed: the opportunity to clear the air and elect a leader with a definitive position on devolution that the party could get behind. McLetchie's resignation and the appointment of Goldie can therefore be seen as another watershed moment. As in 1997, the Scottish Conservatives had a chance to overcome their perceived 'Englishness' with a clear and frank debate – but the opportunity was shut down in a knee-jerk reaction.

Like McLetchie, Goldie was a former solicitor and a confident performer in the Holyrood chamber. Yet, also like her predecessor, she lacked the will to truly tackle the question of devolution in the Scottish Conservatives. Her manifesto team's recommendation of adopting full fiscal autonomy as a party platform, for instance, was swiftly shut down. While she espoused the rhetoric of post-devolution politics, she failed to deliver on the policy. And again, familiar voices argued for change.

Brian Monteith, first a Conservative, then an independent, MSP, wrote in 2006: 'Once people are able to see that the

[Scottish Tory] party is willing to put Scottish interests before party interests, then they should be willing to listen to what it has to say.'

However, these lone voices continued to go unheeded and the party would continue to struggle electorally. The constitution would remain a major dividing issue and a crucial stumbling block to voters, who found the Tories' incoherence on – if not incomprehension of – devolution deeply unappetising.

The party would continue to enjoy mixed fortunes during the 2007 Scottish elections – Goldie's first in charge. Again, there were some positives, particularly looking at individual results. The Tories not only held on to their three constituencies from 2003 (with McLetchie's taxi debacle not appearing to concern the voters of Edinburgh Pentlands), they also gained another constituency, with John Lamont – who would go on to be a key player in Ruth's rise to power – winning the Borders seat of Roxburgh and Berwickshire. The future Chief Whip gained an impressive 10 per cent swing against the incumbent Liberal Democrats, meaning the Tories returned four constituency seats for the first time. As with other areas where the Conservatives had enjoyed individual successes, the Borders was traditional Tory territory – rural, relatively affluent and staunchly Unionist.

But steady – if painstakingly slow – progress in winning constituencies could not detract from the Tories' overall performance. Across the country, Goldie's first election in charge saw a 1 per cent drop in the regional vote, while there was no growth in the overall constituency vote. The decline in the list vote meant that they lost two seats, leaving them with a net loss of one seat overall and just seventeen members in the Scottish Parliament.

Clearly, voters remained reluctant to endorse the Tory Party across the country. This aversion remained largely down to their incoherence on devolution, but their right-wing agenda on domestic matters can hardly have helped. The Tories' rather dour 2007 election manifesto introduction is a useful example. It describes devolution as being a 'disappointment'. In an attack on the Lab–Lib coalition, but also implicitly on devolution itself, it adds:

> It has failed to deliver on the issues that matter most to [the people in Scotland], like housing and public services. It has allowed itself to become embroiled in issues which attract a great deal of attention, but deliver little benefit to the nation. And too many MSPs have used their office as a platform to grandstand on issues that have nothing to do with them, and are not within the competence of the Scottish Parliament. There must be change.

The unduly negative message reflects the continued Tory division – and incoherence – on devolution. The party believed the Scottish Parliament was an inconvenience – and a potentially dangerous one. This stood in contrast to Labour and the SNP, who had a more positive message on devolution, believing it could, in short, be used to make Scotland a better place. Of course, the rhetoric often failed to match the reality, but this mattered little to voters at the polls, who have consistently shown a desire to make a success of devolution.

It is possible that the Tory vote may also have suffered in 2007 because of a confusion among the electorate about how to vote. There were a high number – almost 142,000, or 7 per cent of total votes cast – that were rejected as invalid. This was blamed on a poorly worded single ballot paper used for both the constituency and list vote. It told voters they had two votes – meaning one constituency and one list vote – but it is thought many instead voted twice on the list instead, rendering their votes invalid. The confusion was described as a 'disgrace' by the BBC's political editor Brian Taylor and led to legal challenges. It is unclear, of course, how many Tory voters may have had their ballots rejected, but it is certain some would have. Nevertheless, this cannot excuse the party's poor electoral performance.

Despite the poor result for the Tories, the 2007 election did offer them opportunities that had hitherto not been forthcoming.

Alex Salmond's SNP had gained twenty seats and were now the largest party, with one more MSP than Labour. The result led to the advent of an SNP minority government for the first time. Unlike the Labour and Liberal Democrat coalition, Salmond's lack of a majority presented an opportunity for Goldie and the Tories. Short of votes and unable to form a coalition, the Tories were able to offer support – and gain concessions – from the nationalists, notably in relation to budgets. The SNP, for example, conceded ground on tax relief for small businesses in return for Tory support.

'What we got out of that budget was credibility,' explained Tory MSP Derek Brownlee, who was authorised to conduct the negotiations with SNP Finance Secretary John Swinney. 'It was the first time we'd led the news in ages and it was seen as quite the coup.'

Indeed, not only had the party gained concessions from the SNP, they had also – as Monteith suggested in 2006 – put aside political game-playing for the good of the country. The move provided a taste of what would become Ruth's guiding mantra almost a decade later: 'Strong Opposition'.

The Tories were helped in this cause by the indecisiveness of the Scottish Green Party. Even with the Scottish Conservatives, Salmond was still short of a majority for his budget, and looked to Robin Harper and Shiona Baird's party for support. In 2009, he was promised their agreement, only for the Greens to U-turn at the vote, causing the budget to fall. While it was a one-off moment – the same budget would eventually be resubmitted and passed – it strengthened the Tories' hand as a reliable partner for the SNP government. In the eyes of voters, it also showed that the Tories were pragmatic and mature, and willing to work in the national interest.

However, just as the party appeared to be rediscovering its Scottishness, the Calman Commission came. Again, as was so often the case for the Scottish Conservatives, the initial overtures were good. The Tories had supported setting up the commission, which took its name from its chair, Sir Kenneth Calman, in a cross-party parliamentary vote. The onus of the commission was to explore how devolution had worked and, more importantly, where it could be substantially improved.

Its conclusions were not to the Tories' liking, but nor were they unpredictable. The essential tenet of the final report was that the Scottish Parliament should raise – as well as spend – public money. As we have seen, this was an idea supported by some Conservative MSPs, who believed, firstly, that tax-and-spend powers would foster more responsibility in the Scottish Executive, and, secondly, that they could be used to turn Scotland into a more business-friendly region. Such views, however, were in a minority, and – despite having supported the founding of the Calman Commission – the leadership announced its MSPs would not give evidence to the review. This was presumably for fear that they would speak out of turn and expose the – already poorly hidden – Tory differences on the future of devolution.

The Scottish Tories' difficulties over the commission would lead Alan Cochrane to describe them in the *Daily Telegraph* as being the stupid party rather than the nasty party.

He added:

Having been instrumental in setting up the commission, the Scottish Tory leader is now telling her band of brothers and sisters to have nothing to do with it – for fear of embarrassing the wider party who haven't as yet come up with a considered view about what to do about more powers, especially those concerning the raising and spending of taxes.

Cochrane – an influential columnist close to many in the Scottish Tory Party – dismissed suggestions that the Conservatives' confusion over the commission had anything to do with the upcoming general election.

Instead, he argued:

There was never any chance of the party presenting a united front on taxation, which was always going to be the most contentious of the issues before Calman.

And there has never, ever been the slightest sign that Miss Goldie was prepared to do what leaders are supposed to do – namely 'lead' – on the matter. Her views on it are shrouded in mystery.

With a considered party view impossible and firm leadership not forthcoming, the Scottish Tories should never have backed setting up the commission.

Factionalism re-emerged with a vengeance, with Goldie eventually endorsing the commission's proposals. Somewhat reluctantly, she stated:

> Whatever we do to the devolved settlement must be built to last, a secure legacy from this generation of MSPs to a future generation of Scots.
>
> I am a committed Unionist. I will do nothing which puts at risk a partnership which for centuries has served our nation well. That is the agenda of another party.

As David Torrance notes, 'It appeared grudging.' Others MSPs in Goldie's party were even less enthusiastic about the proposals, and threatened rebellion, which could explain Goldie's dithering on the issue despite having initially backed setting up the commission. In his *Telegraph* column, Alan Cochrane reported that as many as sixteen backbenchers were preparing to rebel. 'Tory MSPs are pressing Miss Goldie to ensure that any such motion [on the Calman Commission] does not offer wholehearted support for [its recommendations],' he wrote.

'Otherwise, they will table their own amendment which merely "takes note" of the commission's recommendations. They believe that potential Tory voters are much less enamoured of extra powers for the parliament than is Miss Goldie and see it as a step too far towards independence.'

Such views were not confined to MSPs, with Lord Forsyth branding Calman's proposals as tantamount to 'appeasement' of the Nationalists.

Once again, the Tories' deep-seated divisions on devolution had been laid bare for the voters to see. It would be deeply damaging that – more than ten years after the Scottish Parliament was created – they still had no coherent or cohesive position on devolution.

Yet while the Tories continued to wrestle with devolution, they would also undergo a major overhaul of their own.

The 2010 Sanderson Commission was set up to review why the Tories were stagnating in Scotland. Written by Lord Sanderson, the report sought to explain why, despite coming first in the 2010 general election, the Conservatives returned only one seat in Scotland. Its findings would prove crucial both to the fortunes of the party and to Ruth herself.

Sanderson's chief recommendation was that there should be a party leader in Scotland with complete control of party policy north of the border. Such a suggestion might seem obvious, but both Goldie and McLetchie had only been the heads of the party in the Scottish Parliament, and were still beholden to Central Office in London.

And it was not just a lack of control that was hampering the party – but a convoluted and confusing structure.

As the Sanderson Report stated:

> The Scottish Conservatives currently have a UK leader, a Scottish parliamentary leader, a chairman (who is also the Party's chief executive officer), an elected deputy chairman (who is the leader of the Party's volunteers), as well as political leaders in the parliaments of Westminster and Brussels...
>
> The Scottish Conservatives' structure has to take account of the importance of the Scottish Parliament in Scottish politics and this must be reflected in the scope of the Party's leadership.

RUTH DAVIDSON

The recommendation of a new, more powerful leader grabbed the headlines, but the report was actually much wider-reaching. As well as tackling the question of leadership, Lord Sanderson would list the 'consistent themes' of the report as the need for 'a distinctive Scottish identity, a welcoming and broader Party, increased decentralisation of the Party structure and the empowerment of the members'.

One of the reforms that would prove key to Ruth's later success in 2016 was the reorganisation of the party's regional structures in Scotland. 'We ... examined the operations of constituency associations across Scotland,' Lord Sanderson stated in the report.

It is clear there is real cause for concern about the Party's organisational strength at a local level. Many associations are, in effect, moribund. This is undoubtedly a symptom of a lack of professional campaigning staff in constituencies and has led to an over reliance on centrally employed staff (who need to focus on national election campaigns) to provide local support.

He added: 'While targeting and a focus on winnable constituencies are vital for election campaigns, effective campaigning requires strong local associations throughout the whole of Scotland.' Reform of these local associations would prove key for the Tories, who were able to grow in areas across Scotland in 2016 where they had previously struggled.

One crucial idea the Sanderson Report rejected – which would play a key role in Ruth's leadership bid against Murdo Fraser – was the notion that the Tories should rebrand in Scotland. 'Because of the Party's lack of electoral progress and the negative perceptions that exist, many Party members are concerned the Scottish

Conservatives brand may be damaged', the report stated. 'Some members and external commentators have suggested the Party should change its logo to emphasise its Scottish focus and commitment, or even change its name if it is to win more trust and support.'

Such suggestions were, however, deemed unnecessary, as long as the party rediscovered its distinct message, the report argued. 'The Scottish Conservatives need to communicate a distinctive vision for Scotland and the values and beliefs for which the Party stands,' the report stated. 'The party must also communicate information about its work more widely and listen to and engage more with interest groups across the country,' it added, stating the obvious.

Yet Lord Sanderson was categoric that the Conservative brand remain intact north of the border. 'With regard to the Scottish Conservatives brand, the problem is not the Party's name or logo, but its failure to convey clearly and consistently what it believes in and stands for,' Lord Sanderson wrote, before adding even more bluntly: 'There is no requirement to change the party's name.'

The report as a whole was well received among aficionados of the party north of the border. Iain Anderson, writing for Conservative Home, said: 'The Scottish Conservatives 2010 Commission ... may yet turn out to be one of the most radical sets of proposals put on the table within the Conservative Party across the UK.' The Scottish Conservative-leaning website Think Scotland, meanwhile, branded it 'worthy'. But it added a note of caution: 'We are already one month on from the Commission's report and if you scratch below the surface it is easy to find a range of influences within the party seeking to stop implementation of one, another or all its recommendations in order to serve their own particular interests.'

Certainly, the report would not be enough to save the party from disaster in the 2011 election, given the recommendations were adopted only afterwards. But, as the party approached the Holyrood election, the Calman and Sanderson Reports offered opportunities for the Scottish Conservatives – both for dithering and for decisiveness.

It was time for Ruth to enter the stage of Tory politics – a decision that would change the future of her party and the political make-up of the country.

CHAPTER 4

EARLY MANOEUVRES

Malcolm Macaskill knew this was his chance.

The 51-year-old businessman had impeccable Tory credentials, or so he thought. Not only had he campaigned for the party for many years, he had also convinced wealthy friends to provide much-needed donations to the cause. He never expected to win Rutherglen and Hamilton West in the 2010 general election, but topping the Glasgow list for the Scottish election for the next year was his pay-off. Mr Macaskill was – barring some extraordinary happening – guaranteed to get elected.

Yet the extraordinary happened.

Just days before the 2011 Scottish election campaign was due to start, he was summoned to a meeting of Tory top brass. There, Andrew Fulton, Scottish Conservative chairman, told him he was being deselected. The grounds for his sudden removal were ostensibly that he had failed to disclose that he had twice been bankrupt. The 51-year-old was stripped of his position on the list – which was a guaranteed seat – as well as his constituency

candidacy. In his place came the 32-year-old gay ex-soldier who
had entered politics only two years earlier.

For Ruth, it was the crucial step on a ruthless political career
that would be pock-marked with Machiavellian intrigue.

And this was just the start.

* * *

Ruth's decision to enter political life came largely from having
little else to do after her army career ended prematurely. She
herself claims that she was inspired by David Cameron's call,
post-expenses scandal, for a wider selection of people to get
involved in politics. There may be some truth in this, although
Ruth has always been political. Since her accident aged five, she
has been inspired by public service, as was clearly reflected in her
early career choices in both journalism and the army.

In fact, she was so keen to start working for the Tories that
one party insider said she initially applied for a job archiving
newspaper cuttings in the party's Holyrood office. She was told –
quite rightly – that she had more to offer and was promptly given
a role in the then party head Annabel Goldie's office. Journalists
at the time – with whom she had some dealings – remember her
as a boisterous, if a little nervous, parliamentary aide. She tried
hard to fit in with 'the corridor', which then – only slightly more
so than now – was dominated by men.

One reporter said he was struck by her bluntness and banter,
which was uncommon among the more stuffy Conservatives who
dominated the party at the time. Yet he also felt it was somewhat
forced – the laughs were a little too loud, the jokes a little too
lewd. She wanted to fit in and tried hard to do so. Ruth, of course,

had always been something of an outsider, having had to deal with bullies at school after her accident, as well as coping with the masculine-focused world of the military.

Her work with Goldie gave her valuable political experience. She saw first-hand the characters and personalities of many of the MSPs she would soon lead. As well as getting to know journalists – some of whom she would have already been familiar with through her work at the BBC – she also befriended party staffers.

But Ruth had more to offer the party than being a behind-the-scenes figure. She was earmarked for elected office, although it is worth pointing out that, in the late noughties, there was not a plethora of talented candidates looking to run for – mostly unwinnable – seats for the Conservatives. So, as with most politicians – and more so for Scottish Tories – her first bid for a seat was doomed to failure.

Glasgow North East (which largely overlapped with the former Glasgow Springburn constituency) had always been a Labour stronghold, backing the party in every election since 1935. It is a deeply deprived area, home to housing estates and tower blocks that suffered particularly under Margaret Thatcher's premiership. Drug addiction and associated gang-related crime are a prominent feature of the constituency, which once boasted the tallest public housing scheme in Europe at Sighthill. It was – and remains – absolutely not Tory territory.

Ruth, of course, had some strengths that she could fall back on. Not only did she have a deeply determined personality – it would need to be – but she also had some familial links with the city. While her parents hailed from Castlemilk, which was outside the Glasgow North East constituency, the demographics of the two areas were similar. Her state school background, as well as the confidence she had gained as a reporter, would also help her on the campaign trail.

Indeed, the 2009 by-election that gave Ruth her first campaigning experience was not a foregone conclusion. It was triggered by the resignation of the House of Commons Speaker, Michael Martin, in the wake of the expenses scandal that had, in some ways, prompted Ruth's foray into politics. Her platform was to be one free from 'smears and fears', she claimed in a rather flowery and naïve statement. 'I am honoured to be the Scottish Conservative and Unionist candidate for Glasgow North East,' she said after her position was announced.

I will begin by pledging to fight an honest campaign. Since the controversy over MPs' expenses, people have lost trust in politics and as a result I think it is important to fight a campaign that engages people rather than turns them off politics.

I may disagree with the other candidates on many issues from justice policies to the economy, but that doesn't mean we shouldn't fight a clean and honest campaign.

We should be focusing on what matters to people in Glasgow North East, not on doing each other down by resorting to smears and fears.

This statement was followed up by a series of bullet-point pledges she promised to adhere to during the campaign, including 'not to mislead the public' and to make 'honest and reasonable promises'.

The fact that Tory MPs had been among the worst offenders in the expenses scandal was clearly a reality Ruth hoped voters would not realise – an early example of the political expediency that would come to play a key role in her leadership.

The then Tory leader David Cameron also issued a statement supporting Ruth's candidacy. While this is not wholly unusual – leaders from all parties often endorse candidates, particularly in by-elections – it does show that Ruth was already being taken seriously by the Conservative Party.

The by-election itself, however, remained a tough sell for Ruth. While no major parties had contested the Speaker's seat since 2001 – as is Westminster convention – there was a crowded playing field for Ruth to navigate. The SNP appointed David Kerr as their candidate – a member of hard-line Catholic sect Opus Dei – while Labour chose Willie Bain. The most dramatic intervention, however, came from John Smeaton. The airport baggage handler had shot to fame as one of those who helped foil an Islamist terrorist attack on Glasgow Airport – and contested the by-election on an anti-establishment ticket. 'The Labour Party have had thirty years to bring investment and jobs into Glasgow North East,' he said, announcing his candidacy.

I haven't noticed much difference and I know from strolling round the constituency that folk living there haven't noticed many changes either.

Well, I can. And, if I'm elected, you'd better believe it: I will. I'll bring a storm down on Westminster, knock down doors and badger them until they listen. No messing.

While to many his standing might have seemed like a joke, the bookies disagreed. The have-a-go hero – who was funded by a former director-general of the Conservative Party – was given the third-best odds to win the seat.

In the end, the contest proved something of a damp squib. Labour romped home on a turnout of just over 33 per cent. Ruth kept her deposit, receiving 5.2 per cent of the vote and coming third. It was a decent, if unremarkable, result for the future Tory leader, although she almost suffered the ignominy of being beaten by the BNP, who were just sixty-two votes behind her. The influential Conservative Home website described it as a 'creditable' result, while Ruth herself said she was 'delighted'. Clearly in an upbeat mood, she added:

> Glasgow North East was always going to be a difficult fight for us but we came third and held onto our deposit. This contrasts with similar by-elections before 1997, when Labour was the third place party it lost its deposit [both in Newbury and in Christchurch in 1993]. I personally have loved the campaign and have enjoyed meeting the great people of Glasgow North East, seeing what good is going on in local communities as well as seeing what needs to be done to improve people's lives.

Just a year later, Ruth would return to fight the same constituency – although not without controversy.

* * *

'I have lived and worked my entire life in Scotland. Never been anywhere else, never wished to be. I'm Scottish to my bones.'

Or so Ruth claimed in a 2011 *Newsnight* hustings.

The problem was, it was not strictly true.

After coming third in Glasgow North East, Ruth was short-listed to fight the Midlands constituency of Bromsgrove for the 2010 election. The former MP, Julie Kirkbride, had, like Michael Martin, decided to step down in the wake of the expenses scandal. Of course, there were five other candidates on the list, including Sajid Javid, who would go on to win the contest. However, Ruth's seeming willingness to desert the people of Glasgow North East in favour of a safe English Tory seat played badly.

Her spokesman would insist she went down to see the Bromsgrove Conservative Association out of 'courtesy', after being placed on the list by Tory Central Office in London. This explanation, however, seems flimsy at best, with the episode underlining Ruth's ruthless streak – and her ambition. Clearly, following her forced retirement from the army, Ruth was anxious to get on with her political career quickly. As we have seen from her early life, she is always determined to recover from defeat as quickly as possible. But the *Sunday Herald* reported that many Scottish Tories were 'irked' by the move.

In the event, she did not even make it down to the final two candidates – how different history could have been – and was forced to return to run again in the unwinnable Glasgow North East.

Again, she had little hope of winning, although, facing an unpopular Brown Labour government, she would have hoped to improve. The Conservatives were tipped to win the election nationally, with Tory leader David Cameron consistently out-polling his Labour rival.

'Vote Ruth Davidson for the change we need', screamed her election leaflet for the campaign. Fresh-faced and sporting a longer haircut than her later bob, the leaflet is adorned with pictures of her with David Cameron, as well as commitments to protect local services.

In the end, she gained an extra 500 votes on a much higher turnout – but she was pushed into fourth place by the Liberal Democrats. The 'I agree with Nick' mantra clearly had an impact in Glasgow, as elsewhere, with the Tories failing to win a majority and entering into a coalition with the Liberal Democrats.

Ruth's failure to dramatically improve the party's standing in Glasgow, however, does not seem to have undermined her standing in the Scottish Tories.

On the contrary, she would be ruthlessly promoted.

* * *

Glasgow had been Ruth's adopted home for ten years, so it was a logical place for her to stand for Holyrood in the 2011 campaign. That it was the old stomping ground of her parents also helped.

Yet the second city of the empire also had one of the most fraught Scottish Tory branches in the country. Even before the coup against Macaskill, concerns were raised about allegations of vote rigging for the regional list in the city, where Ruth would initially rank second. David Meikle, Glasgow's only Tory councillor, expressed his concerns along with another candidate amid fears that a sudden influx of new members could have skewed the result. He also claimed a number of ballot papers appeared to have been filled in by the same person. Meikle demanded an investigation, but was shown the cold shoulder by the party hierarchy, leading him to withdraw from the regional ballot. There were, he said, 'serious question marks over the rankings result' for the Tory regional list.

Just days earlier, Macaskill had been stripped of station and rank by the Tory Party chairman, paving the way for Ruth's election. Macaskill, who quit the party in the wake of the fiasco, later hinted that there may have been political intrigues behind his removal. He received a five-figure payout from the Scottish Conservatives over his deselection after he threatened to take them to court. 'The treatment that I have been subjected to, along with the evidence that I have gathered, has convinced me that the party machine in and around Edinburgh Central Office is rotten to the core,' he told the *Sunday Herald* in 2012. 'I no longer wish to remain a member of such an inept and morally corrupt organisation.'

He added:

Some have suggested that there was perhaps always a greater plan. In dismissing me, the next in line on the regional list was Ruth Davidson, who had earlier failed to be selected as a constituency candidate in other parts of Scotland. History shows that not only was Ruth elected in my stead, but she also went on to become the party leader in Scotland.

On 4 April 2011, with just over a month to go until polling day, Ruth was confirmed as the number one candidate on the Glasgow region list. The infighting and intrigue had seen the list for the city dwindle to just four candidates, but Ruth was nevertheless at the top and almost guaranteed victory. For her, the selection was the crowning achievement of a quick rise in Scottish politics. Ruth's determination to succeed had played a key part. But the influence of her connections in the party, stemming from her work for Goldie, should not be underestimated either. While there would be few people lining up to contest Glasgow North East, backroom machinations could well have played a role in her securing the top spot on the party's list.

Despite Ruth's success, however, the 2011 election would not be one the Tories would want to remember.

CHAPTER 5

GATHERING STORM

Elections are often defined – or at least remembered – by one bizarre incident. The 2005 general election is John Prescott throwing a punch after being egged; 1992 is a hyperactive Neil Kinnock exclaiming, 'We're all right.'

The 2011 Scottish election is remembered chiefly for the Subway debacle.

Labour leader Iain Gray – his party already slipping in the polls – had planned a pleasant walkabout in Glasgow to meet and greet voters. The TV cameras had been invited. It was a sunny day – the perfect chance to introduce the relatively unknown Labour leader to a wider audience.

But arriving at the city's Central Station he was confronted by the somewhat extravagantly named 'Scottish Resistance'. This clique of placard-waving wackos, led by serial agitator Sean Clerkin, proceeded to harangue an increasingly terrified Gray across the city. Refusing to engage with them, but also unable to engage with voters, Gray eventually fled into a Subway before he and his assistant were forced to make an escape in a cab. The entire embarrassing incident was captured by the TV news crews. To top off a bad day, Gray would then compare the 'sandwich shop stand-off', as it was dubbed in *The Scotsman*, with his experience of the Rwandan genocide and the killing fields of Cambodia.

He said:

> I spent two years working in the civil war in Mozambique, I've been to Rwanda two months after the genocide, I walked the killing fields in Cambodia and I was in Chile three days after Pinochet was demitted from office.
>
> I've been a lot of places, seen a lot of things – that certainly wasn't the worst of them.

It was the defining moment of the election and one that proved fatal for the previously relatively unknown Gray. Yet it is also notable because, a week earlier, the same group had confronted Annabel Goldie. The plucky Tory leader, however, stood her ground and fended off the ambush, without the need to retreat to a branch of an American fast-food franchise. Of course, the Tories had their share of mishaps – their only MP David Mundell was hit with a key lime pie on his way to a wine and cheese-themed Tory fundraiser in St Andrews. But Goldie's handling of 'the Resistance' was one of a series of strong performances by the Conservative leader during the campaign.

Her party faced a 'rocky start' in the race for Holyrood following Macaskill's resignation. But, according to *The Scotsman*, 'the row was dispensed with early on and the Tories' determination to tell it straight paid off.'

(This may have been the case for the election itself, but it would come back to haunt Ruth months later.)

The Tories' campaign – badged up as 'common sense for Scotland' – focused primarily on reforming public sector spending and boosting opportunity. Key – and controversial – pledges included reintroducing prescription charges and some university tuition fees, both of which were now free in Scotland. Indeed, Goldie focused on the relative success of gaining concessions out of the SNP minority government. 'To those who say to me "You can't deliver", I say to them "Oh really, well just look at what we have delivered for Scotland over the last four years",' she wrote in the 2011 manifesto.

More bluntly – and not included in the manifesto – she said there would be 'no bullshitting' during the campaign, adding, 'Give me more and we will deliver more for Scotland.' Goldie also supported Cameron's austerity agenda, insisting voters would 'back a party that told it like it is'. This strategy stood in contrast to UK coalition partner the Liberal Democrats, whose leader in Scotland, Tavish Scott, rather floundered as he attempted to distance himself from the Westminster government.

Goldie – who was a popular character in Scotland, according to polling – also proved an able antagonist in the election's televised debates. At one point, the Tory leader threatened to grab her opponents by the 'short and curlies' – a comment that drew widespread praise, if not tangible results.

Crucially, however, Goldie still struggled to clearly define the Tories north of the border as a Scottish entity. Cameron himself realised this and attempted to recapture some of the spirit that had served the party so well pre-1955. 'Alex Salmond and Iain Gray think this election is all about them,' he told around 150 people while on the campaign trail at Inverness Town House.

Here's a novel idea: shouldn't this election be about Scotland and the Scottish people? They don't want senseless mudslinging. They want straight talking and delivery on the issues that matter. It's only Conservatives who offer both. Let me tell you, there's no politician who tells it straight like Annabel Goldie.

The Prime Minister, who had to run a gauntlet of protesters during his visit, went further in trying to emphasise his party's Scottish credentials.

'The Scottish Conservative Party is Conservative, yes, but it's Scottish, run by Scots, for Scots,' he said.

It makes decisions for Scotland. It does not take orders from Westminster. The judgements it reaches about policy, about manifestos, about who to partner with after the election, all that will be decided by Scots. It is, if you like, more Unionist but also more Scottish.

For voters, however, yet again the rhetoric did not match the reality. Internal party polling released after the election would reveal that just 6 per cent of Scottish voters believed the Tories north of the border put their interests first. More damningly, 38 per cent of the 1,500 voters surveyed thought the party put British interests first – while 50 per cent believed they prioritised English issues.

In contrast, a majority (52 per cent) of voters believed Labour put British interests first – suggesting Gray had taken the mantel of Unionism from Goldie. Unsurprisingly, 92 per cent believed the SNP put Scottish issues first.

There is no doubt that this dark polling for the Tories was

the result of their continued failure to put forward a coherent position on devolution. The debacle of the Calman Commission clearly still resonated with voters, with the Tories sending out mixed messages on the future of the Scottish Parliament. Indeed, many of the tangible benefits of devolution in voters' eyes, such as free prescriptions, were on a hit-list of things the Scottish Tories wanted to abolish. Such policies – while arguably sensible – led to the appearance that the Tories wanted to use Holyrood simply as an administrative hub, rather than a vehicle for real change.

* * *

Ruth had, after the tumultuous selection process, a quiet campaign. Having secured the number one spot on the list, she was all but guaranteed to be elected. She was also selected to run in Glasgow Kelvin – a constituency in the west of the city – some way from her previous stomping ground of Glasgow North East. Clearly, she was being elevated to seats she might – even tentatively – have more chance of winning.

The affluent constituency of Glasgow Kelvin, which straddles the city's merchant quarter, was once strong Tory territory. It contains Glasgow's three universities, and the equivalent Westminster constituency, in its previous guise as Glasgow Hillhead, was once a bastion of the Conservatives' Tam Galbraith. In a 1982 by-election, the seat would be won by Roy Jenkins and the Social Democratic Party, before eventually falling to George Galloway. That shift continued after devolution, with the Tories persistently placing fourth or worse in Holyrood elections – once, in 2003, facing the humiliation of coming behind the Scottish

Socialists. As the Tory Reform Group would note, 'The days when Glasgow Kelvin could be relied upon to be rock-solid blue are long gone.'

Ruth certainly faced a tough challenge, not that that perturbed her. Her election team was made up largely of students, but she sparked controversy when she appeared with Baroness Warsi, who had faced accusations of homophobia over election leaflets in which she criticised Labour for abolishing Section 28 and lowering the age of consent for homosexuality, claiming that it allowed 'schoolchildren to be propositioned for homosexual relationships'. One opposition candidate suggested the incident showed the Tories in Scotland needed to 'drag themselves into the twenty-first century'. It seems a curious accusation, given Ruth herself is gay. Yet perhaps it serves as an early example of how the opposition feared Ruth as a moderniser. The effort to smear her by association with Warsi could be seen as an opposition attempt to brand Ruth a typical Tory – despite all appearances to the contrary.

In the end, Ruth described her campaign, in which she regularly put in eighteen-hour days, as a 'whirlwind'.

* * *

As voters headed to the polls on 5 May 2011, Alex Salmond's SNP had produced a double-digit opinion-poll lead over Iain Gray's Labour. But the Tory support had hardly shifted, hovering around the 15 per cent mark or lower for much of the campaign. In the end, the party would record its worst ever result in Scotland, securing just 13.9 per cent of the constituency vote and 12.4 per cent of the list vote.

It was a devastating result. Although Labour recorded their worst performance in Scotland since 1931, they managed to secure swings against the Tories in a number of key constituencies.

The silver lining for the Tories was that they managed to hold on to three constituencies, all of which were in the relatively conservative Borders. David McLetchie, his public profile now diminished, lost his seat of Edinburgh Pentlands, but was returned on the list. Indeed, amid the SNP surge, many parties – most notably Labour and the Liberal Democrats – suffered far more significant losses: once-staunch Labour heartlands in cities such as Glasgow suddenly returned Nationalist MSPs for the first time. A similar phenomenon occurred in the north of Scotland, with Liberal Highland seats turning from orange to yellow. The Tories, in contrast, could take some comfort from still resonating with their voters in the south of Scotland. Nevertheless, the vote was enough for them to elect just fifteen MSPs, down two from 2007.

But this time, Ruth was among them.

While the 2011 result irrevocably changed the political landscape of Scotland, it also offered the chance for a Tory resurgence.

Not only would the Scottish Conservatives need a new leader, but Salmond had his SNP majority.

The independence referendum was coming.

CHAPTER 6

A NEW PARTY OR A NEW LEADER? OR BOTH

The 2011 election result became the night of the long knives for the leaders of Scotland's political parties.

Every major leader would be crushed in the SNP tsunami, a situation the *Sunday Herald* branded 'unprecedented'. Labour's Iain Gray and the Liberal Democrats' Tavish Scott were the first to go after their disastrous showing. Goldie, however, despite presiding over the Tories' worst ever result in Scotland, tried to hang on.

It also perhaps reflects the Tories low sense of self-esteem that Goldie did not feel it necessary to immediately resign. The party had recorded its worst ever result in Scotland but the sense was that was almost to be expected. Goldie did not see her role as reviving the Tories in Scotland – rather, her job as leader was to help them cling on, something she had arguably achieved. Indeed, she struck a defiant tone in interviews on the Friday after the election – but by Monday she would be gone.

It has been suggested that the party high command – including

Cameron – may have exerted pressure on the Tory leader to resign. An article in *The Herald* a few days after her resignation expresses bafflement at the decision – '[Goldie] had the strongest argument for staying' – but also hints at darker forces at work. Commentator Euan McColm went further ten days after the poll, writing in the *News of the World* that 'the knives were out for Goldie' long before the election and that the Tory talk has been 'for a year or more' about who would succeed her. Former Tory MSP Ted Brocklebank, writing in the *Mail on Sunday* on the same day, suggests Cameron may have 'lost patience' with the party's failure to make an electoral breakthrough.

But while she had to be pushed rather than jump, she decided to take a long time falling. Goldie announced she would stay on until a new leader was appointed – not in itself a remarkable decision, although the leadership election would not take place till the autumn. She would 'soldier on' until a successor was appointed, Brocklebank said in the same article, because 'traditional values such as courtesy, duty and loyalty are important' to her.

Nevertheless, the stage was now set for a long – and ultimately brutal – leadership battle. Nominations would not close until 23 September – some five months after Goldie announced she would stand down. In contrast, new Liberal Democrat leader Willie Rennie would be in place by mid-May, less than two weeks after the election.

For the Tories, it would also be the first – and, so far, only – contested leadership election the Scottish party has ever had. As the *Sunday Herald* noted, there was a 'fascinating scrap ahead'.

Murdo Fraser was undoubtedly the front-runner in the contest. The Mid Scotland and Fife MSP had been waiting in the wings for a number of years for the top job and had already served an apprenticeship as deputy. A sharp and skilled debater, he was 'widely regarded as one of the best performers in all parties at Holyrood' – according to *The Scotsman*'s Andrew Whitaker.

He had also been one of the few voices advocating for the party to embrace devolution as well as Unionism. The former solicitor had for several years recognised the Tories' problem in Scotland: that its attitude towards devolution had led it to appear 'anti-Scottish'.

In 2009, he would write: 'Whatever the justification for our stance against the formation of the Scottish Parliament, it put us in opposition to mainstream Scottish public opinion on the constitution, and as a Party we are still paying the electoral price for that.' While, as we have seen, this analysis holds a great deal of merit, it remained controversial. The Scottish Conservatives continued to be deeply divided over devolution, and Fraser's perceived radicalism on the issue – in reality just accepting what had already happened – would hamper his campaign.

There were also concerns about whether he could appeal beyond the Tory base. 'Murdo is a pretty unreconstructed right-winger. That's not what centre-ground voters are looking for,' a Tory Party insider said at the time. Certainly, the MSP held free-market, low-taxation views that, some would argue, were some way from David Cameron's 'Big Society' mantra, which was infecting the UK party at the time.

If Fraser had difficulties in convincing people he could turn the party around, so too did another grandee, Jackson Carlaw. The ex-car dealer is a shrewd and witty public speaker, but also, in the words of Euan McColm, 'your standard 1980s Thatcherite'. Andrew Whitaker, writing in *The Scotsman*, agreed, saying, 'It's hard to see him shaking things up too much.'

MSP Margaret Mitchell would also run, but she was deemed

a no-hoper and given little consideration in political commentary at the time.

That was not the case, however, for the final main contender – and Ruth's initial preference – John Lamont. A popular constituency MSP, Lamont had experience of Holyrood, having been elected in 2007, while also having the advantage of being just thirty-five.

Lamont, who indicated on 13 May that he intended to stand, was viewed as a moderniser – and Ruth, newly elected, warmly backed him.

As well as being close in age, the pair had also developed a behind-the-scenes bond while Ruth was working as an assistant to Annabel Goldie. Lamont had a reputation for being the Tories' fixer in Holyrood – he would later be appointed as Chief Whip – and the two would therefore have worked closely together on party discipline even before Ruth joined him as an MSP.

'Do I think somebody like John, who is young, professional, articulate and a proven winner, has a claim to being one of the contenders and is a serious and credible contender? Yes, I do think he has a claim,' she told the *Sunday Times* on 22 May.

> If we're looking to a leadership in the future, I'd like to see somebody who could bring in new people, who could attract new blood to the Conservatives and who has fresh ideas. With the collapse of the Liberal Democrats there is a big opportunity for a centre-right party but we need to connect with the people who agree with us and we've found that troublesome in the past.

These were not off-the-cuff suggestions from Ruth, but rather ideas that she had been building for some time. She had been impressed by the strength of her student campaigners in Glasgow – where she had been president of the Conservative Association – and was keen to reinvigorate the party with young blood. Indeed, her language reflects the mood of the Conservative Party at the time, which, under Cameron, had begun to emphasise its youth and vitality. Gone were the stuffy, tired old men who would be at home in the gentlemen's clubs of Pall Mall; in were the sleek, almost Blairite youngsters.

Ruth's notion that the Scottish Conservatives should 'skip a generation' was, of course, self-interested too. Indeed, throughout much of the *Sunday Times* interview, she could have been talking about herself, rather than Lamont. While she was publicly backing him – Edinburgh was rife with talk of his and her joint ticket – she was also contemplating an audacious bid for the leadership herself. A week before she came out for Lamont in the *Sunday Times*, she had already dropped quiet hints she was after the top job for herself. Indeed, Euan McColm's column on 15 May – just ten days after the election – suggested she would be the best candidate. 'If I was a Scots Tory with the flicker of a survival instinct, I would be cajoling and persuading [Ruth to stand],' he wrote.

Making Davidson Scots Tory leader would certainly be a gamble – but it would also be a calculated one. The Scottish Conservative party is dying on its arse. A lacklustre MSP group is sustained by a weak and out-of-touch support base. What it needs is a jolt to the heart. Davidson might provide that electric shock.

Yet his view, at that stage at least, was the exception rather than the rule.

Certainly, Ruth was keeping her cards close to her chest. She told the *Sunday Times* in the same interview in which she endorsed Lamont, using first-class political language, that she had 'no plans' to run for the leadership.

She added: 'My mum would kill me if I went for the leadership. My missus would kill me.' Ruth, however, is never one to shy away from a fight.

It was almost exactly 10 a.m. on Thursday 23 June when John Lamont's leadership bid imploded.

The 35-year-old, then the party's newly appointed justice spokesman, could have been forgiven if he thought his comments would be lost among the dozens of other speakers packed into Holyrood's half-moon chamber. Certainly, the Offensive Behaviour at Football and Threatening Communications Act was – and remains – one of the more controversial pieces of legislation the Scottish Parliament has passed. Designed to tackle sectarianism, its genesis was a series of letter bombs sent to a number of prominent Celtic supporters – including the club's then boss, Neil Lennon – in 2011.

Lamont began his speech well, suggesting that the blight of sectarianism must be tackled and that MSPs were agreed on that. However, as he moved into the final part of his speech, he fatally stumbled, insinuating that Catholic schools were responsible for encouraging sectarianism. 'The education system in [west central] Scotland is effectively the state-sponsored conditioning of those sectarianism attitudes,' he told MSPs.

I say that as someone who believes that as a Christian country we should do more to promote Christian values in our young people and to support religious education in schools. In those small pockets of west central Scotland, those attitudes are being entrenched at home and in the wider community.

The reaction to his speech – which, taken as a whole, was reasonably balanced and well rounded – was instantaneous and scathing. SNP minister Roseanna Cunningham described it as 'an astonishing diatribe'. More damagingly, the church also branded the comments 'offensive' and 'malicious'. The Bishop of Motherwell, the Rt Rev. Joseph Devine, said: 'The claim that Catholic schools are the cause of sectarianism is offensive and untenable. There has never been any evidence produced by those hostile to Catholicism to support such a malicious misrepresentation.' Alex Salmond, now First Minister, called on him to either apologise or resign as the party's justice spokesman.

Lamont would defend his comments, claiming that they had been 'misrepresented' while simultaneously insisting that there were 'issues' in faith schools in the west of Scotland. He would also continue to entertain ambitions to run for the leadership, but the damage had been done. Ruth's preferred candidate was finished – and she would step up.

One Tory insider has suggested that Lamont deliberately set himself up to implode, arguing that his intention was only to help Ruth's chances. Certainly, Lamont had always had ambitions to be elected in Westminster – he continued to fight, and eventually, in June 2017, won, the House of Commons seat of Berwickshire, Roxburgh and Selkirk. He had previously stood in the constituency, which covers many of the areas he represents as an MSP, in 2005 and 2010, increasing his share of the vote on the second occasion. Had it not been for the SNP surge in the 2015 general election – unpredictable to say the least from the vantage point of 2011 – he would have been likely to win the seat on his third attempt.

The source argues that Lamont viewed the leadership as a 'dead-end job' and was anxious to be elected to the House of Commons. However, with more experience than Ruth, he was put forward as a stalking horse for her candidacy. The insider said there were fears Ruth would look overly ambitious if she were to announce her candidacy immediately, having only been elected that year. Instead, the argument goes, it was better to frame her leadership bid as one that was reluctantly forced on her after her preferred modernising candidate bowed out.

Certainly, it was possible Lamont could have recovered from his comments; he had said nothing that could not have been dismissed with a brief apology. And it also seems credible that he and Ruth would have had experience in hatching backroom plots together from her time in Goldie's leadership office. Yet it seems unlikely that a man as ambitious as Lamont would deliberately subject himself to public ridicule, even if it was to aid a political and personal friend. There are also easier ways to drop out of a leadership contest than sparking a row about sectarianism.

That this account of events even exists, however, is noteworthy in itself. Clearly, those in the party who were opposed to Ruth's candidacy have cast around for reasons to explain how it happened. As in the world outside politics, people who lose out often seek to blame their situation on the machinations of others, rather than any failures of their own.

Whatever the reasons, with Lamont out of the race, Ruth's supporters were now viewing her not as a good candidate but as an absolutely essential one. She had to run. High-profile backers included David Cameron and George Osborne, Scotland's only Tory MP David Mundell, as well as senior party figures. While their support would prove controversial among Ruth's opponents, it would also be crucial to her, having only just been elected an MSP.

Along with Mundell, she had also secured the favour of John Scott, MSP for Ayr, while Lamont, unsurprisingly, also backed her. While together they represented only a tiny part of the small Scottish Tory parliamentary party, they also controlled vast swathes of the membership, who lived in their constituencies and who would ultimately choose the leader. In contrast, while Murdo Fraser's parliamentary support was stronger on paper, many of his backers controlled dwindling numbers of card-carrying supporters.

When Ruth formally declared her candidacy on 4 September, she was in a strong position. It should have been the story of the day – but Fraser put a stop to that.

As Ruth prepared to announce her leadership bid, Fraser – who had already declared – would make an even bigger announcement: the Scottish Conservative and Unionist Party, which had existed in its current form for almost fifty years, should be disbanded.

It was, in Fraser's view, the only way to capture again the Scottish identity that had propelled the party to dominance in the 1950s. 'What we have to do is get many more people elected from Scottish constituencies to support David Cameron and a future UK Conservative government and the best way to do that is to create a new progressive centre-right with a Scottish identity,' an unusually casual, open-necked Fraser told the BBC on the day he announced his plans. 'I think that will be much more attractive to many people in Scotland who share our values.'

Under his plans – badged up as 'a new party for Scotland' – Fraser would dissolve the existing Tory Party and create a new centre-right grouping, albeit taking the Conservative whip at Westminster. The Scottish Unionists, the Scottish Reform Party, the Scottish Progressives, Progressive Conservatives, Scotland First, Scotland Forward, Caledonian or the Caledonians were suggested to members as potential new names.

Explaining his plans in more detail for the influential Conservative Home website, Fraser said his proposal was not out-of-step with contemporary Continental thinking among the centre-right. 'A new party, with a distinct Scottish identity and policies that are genuinely made in Scotland will demonstrate clearly to people in Scotland that we put their interests first,' he wrote. 'However, there is no contradiction between a clear Scottish identity and staunch support for remaining within the United Kingdom. Our own experience as a distinct Scottish party before 1965 demonstrates this clearly, as does the Bavarian CSU's relationship with the CDU in Germany.' He also refused to rule out opposing the devolution of major new tax-and-spend powers to Holyrood, which had long been a bone of contention among staunchly Unionist Tories.

Fraser's proposal was, like so many previous attempts at change, quickly rebuffed by party grandees. Former Secretary of State for Scotland Lord Forsyth called the plan a 'ludicrous idea', suggesting it was admitting defeat to the SNP. Sir Malcolm Rifkind, who had also held the Scottish position at Cabinet, was more welcoming. 'What is very, very healthy is that Murdo Fraser is not just raising this after he has been elected,' Rifkind said at the time.

He is saying if you want me as your leader this is the kind of way in which I wish to lead the centre-right cause in Scotland.

He is saying this is not about one individual, this is an opportunity for the people who are Conservatives in Scotland to decide what is the future of the Union and of centre-right politics. He is offering a very refreshing new start.

Others were more cautious. Aberdeen-raised Michael Gove said: 'One of the things I've learnt as a politician from Scotland but representing an English constituency is that the reality of devolution means that you should allow the party in Scotland to determine its own destiny.' Defence Secretary Liam Fox – another Scot – attempted to frame Fraser's proposals as part of a necessary soul-searching in the party. 'There is bound to be this debate inside the Conservative Party in Scotland,' he said. 'It's a necessary follow-on from the process of devolution. It's a debate which the party in Scotland needs to have and it should not be dictated by the party in Westminster.'

Certainly, the plan for a new party was the culmination of more than a decade of grappling with devolution. It was an attempt to regain the ideals of both British and Scottish patriotism that had seemingly deserted the Tories following 1965.

The shock with which the proposals were greeted is understandable. It was undoubtedly a radical solution to the Tory struggles in Scotland. That such a drastic plan was even suggested reflects how much the Tories had struggled with devolution to date. Had they developed a more organic position – and developed it earlier – such a radical reform would not be necessary. Yet the plan for a new party, coming from Fraser, should not have surprised many people. He was merely advocating an extension of views that he had held for many years and had made no secret of. They also chimed well with the mood of the national Tory

Party at the time. Cameron's leadership of the Tories, which had just led them back into office, was predicated on his 'change to win' 2005 Conservative conference speech. While the rhetoric may not have matched the reality, Cameron had successfully positioned himself as a moderniser unafraid of radical change. Fraser's plans certainly fitted with that message.

But while Fraser's changes may have been strategically sound for the party, they were tactically terrible for his leadership bid. In one fell swoop, Ruth – a young kickboxing lesbian with almost no experience of Parliament, let alone office – became the establishment candidate.

'I am proud to be a Scottish Conservative and Unionist,' Ruth said, throwing down the gauntlet to Fraser as she launched her leadership bid. 'This [proposal] is a destabilising distraction that will be welcomed by no one more than Alex Salmond.'

Fraser, the dyed-in-the-wool blue-blooded Tory, was now the radical outsider. It did not help that his plan had – as we saw earlier – been roundly rejected by the Sanderson Commission, which concluded that 'the problem is not the Party's name or logo'.

Ruth was now the candidate of both big and small 'c' conservatism in Scotland. Behind the scenes, Scottish Conservative Central Office was deeply concerned by Fraser's proposal and threw its support – controversially as it would turn out – behind Ruth. A new party, they believed, meant a new staff. Fraser had made no secret of his belief that the Tories' operation in Scotland was at least in part to blame for its poor electoral showing. If he won the leadership election, their jobs would be on the line. Under Ruth's leadership, in contrast, the status quo would be the order of the day. 'I have no interest in change for its own sake,' she told her first campaign meeting in Edinburgh, in explicitly Conservative language.

> We could spend the next twelve months discussing the internal machinations of the party. We could tie ourselves in knots. Alex Salmond would love that. Real change for the Scottish Conservatives won't come from a new name. Under my leadership, there will be no existential crisis, no wringing of hands. Instead I want people to call themselves Scottish, Conservative and Unionist.

Ruth's leadership platform, however, embodied more than just opposition to Fraser's proposal. Indeed, while the Fraser plan might have fuelled her bid, her campaign also focused on more heavyweight policy issues – including at least one that had proved fatal to the Scottish Tories over the previous decade. 'The Scotland Bill currently going through Westminster is the line in the sand,' she told her first campaign meeting in Edinburgh. 'The time for arguing about the powers the people want is over. It's time now to use the powers that we have.' In so staunchly opposing further devolution, Ruth was – it seemed at the time, at least – locking the Tories into a position perceived as being anti-Scottish.

There was now much at stake in this leadership battle – not just the future of individuals, but the future of the party itself.

As September turned into October, the contest would become increasingly bitter and fractious – particularly between Fraser and Ruth.

* * *

Ramsay Jones looks and sounds like a caricature of a spin doctor. Balding, with thin spectacles resting at the end of his nose, at first glance he looks somewhat surly. From humble beginnings as a PR for Scottish women's rugby, by 2011 he was one of the most influential behind-the-scenes figures in the Scottish Conservatives. The party's director of communications was a big backer of Ruth's and had helped convince the then BBC reporter to enter Tory politics. The pair were also close friends, having worked together in Goldie's leadership office before Ruth was elected.

Jones was warned that, as a party functionary, he had to remain neutral in the contest – but that did not bother him.

On 18 September, the 51-year-old made the 150-mile round trip from his house in Dunbar to Ruth's flat in Glasgow's West End. Just days after Ruth had announced her leadership, Jones met with her team to discuss her options. Attending the strategy meeting would lead to Jones being suspended from his job – and left Ruth's opponents outraged.

The Herald suggested that the suspension came on orders from the party's London headquarters, which would later become a bastion of Ruth mania. Jones's attendance at the meeting, however, reinforces the view that the Scottish Tory high command was deeply concerned at the prospect of Fraser's leadership.

Indeed, the Jones suspension was one of a series of setbacks and embarrassments Ruth suffered during the campaign. Just two days after she formally launched her leadership bid, her then assistant and election agent Ross McFarlane was exposed, in a video uncovered by the *Sunday Herald*, attempting to burn an EU flag amid sectarian taunting. Ruth acted swiftly, ruthlessly sacking McFarlane, whom she had employed on a part-time basis since he had helped her get elected. Yet the 'Bullingdon

Club behaviour' – as the SNP branded it – was still deeply embarrassing for Ruth, who was trying to run on a compassionate Conservative ticket.

A further cloud would be cast over her campaign after newspaper reports, orchestrated by her campaign manager John Lamont, emerged launching a personal attack on Fraser's electoral record. Fraser's camp was 'furious' with the 'below the belt' accusations – but responded in kind, making hay out of Ruth's meetings with party functionaries. In the fractured climate, probes were even said to be taking place into the veracity of Ruth's qualifications. It was ugly.

For many, this atmosphere and series of set-backs would be enough to kill a leadership bid. But Ruth was fortunate in that the party was still very much focused on its survival under the Scottish Conservative and Unionist branding. Indeed, Fraser – despite making the scrapping of the party the central plank of his campaign – was increasingly getting cold feet. 'I have never proposed "disbanding" the Party, that is a headline writer's fantasy,' he wrote to concerned members. 'I am proposing to turn what we have into a new, better Party for Scotland.'

The email, however, was widely ridiculed by his opponents, including Ruth. 'If you are going to start suggesting a whole new separate party, then you have to be very clear about what it is you are proposing,' she said. 'I've yet to see a definitive description of what Murdo is to replace the current party with.'

Indeed, while Fraser's plan was perhaps the most prudent way of returning the party to electoral success, it continued to panic the Tory establishment, who became increasingly – and publicly – opposed. Scotland's only Conservative MP David Mundell, for instance, was initially lukewarm about the idea.

'I think fundamentally changing the party name is a rather simplistic approach to the issues that we face,' he said on the day of Fraser's announcement. 'It is much more fundamental than that. It is about having a whole package of things that appeal to the electorate from policies, to the work that we do on the ground, to our approach in government.' By October, he would be militantly opposed to the 'betrayal'. 'I had intended to remain neutral in this election contest, given my unique position as our only MP, and a Government Minister, but I now believe I cannot continue to remain silent on the issue,' he wrote rather pompously for the Conservative Home website just days before ballots were distributed to Tory members. 'I believe that the prospect of the winding-up of the Scottish Conservative and Unionist Party, the emergence of another party in Scotland and the potential for a serious split is too great a threat simply to stand by and let happen without expressing an opinion.' The then Scotland Office minister would publicly endorse Ruth in the same piece, echoing sentiments he would make the same day in the speech to the Scottish Conservatives' October conference.

Fraser's plan was facing increasingly tough – and eventually insurmountable – opposition, while the grandees flocked to Ruth. Lord Forsyth – already a stern critic of Fraser's plans – was another significant backer, given the reverence in which he is held by Scottish Tories. More significant, however, were comments by Sir Jack Harvie, a Scottish businessman who has raised millions for the Tories. In an announcement engineered by Ruth's campaign team, the prominent donor said he would not give money to Fraser's 'separatist' party – and suggested the leadership hopeful and his allies should be thrown out of the

Scottish Conservatives. 'Having scandalised Scup [the Scottish Conservative and Unionist Party] by word and deed they would surely have no place within Scup in the future,' he said. 'And, for that matter, given his intention to form a breakaway party, why would Mr Fraser choose to stand for the leadership of a party he does not support or recognise?'

The intervention marked an escalation in hostilities between Ruth and Fraser in what was becoming an increasingly bitter battle. But it also added weight to concerns among the membership – who, after all, would elect the leader – about whether Fraser's new party really was the right move. It is a testament to the rising concerns in the Fraser camp that his allies were forced to produce two donors who said they would continue to back him: Robert Gibbons, the founding chairman of Highland Spring, and Robert Kilgour, a care-homes entrepreneur. It was, however, not enough – the establishment was now firmly with Ruth.

* * *

On 4 November 2011, almost exactly six months after the worst result in the Scottish Conservatives' history, Ruth was declared leader.

The 32-year-old MSP, who had only just been elected, had defeated some of the most senior figures in the party. It marked a remarkable rise for Ruth – but it had left the party deeply fractured and its future in doubt.

In her victory speech, she paid homage to the Sanderson Commission and the newly enhanced role she would be undertaking. 'This is the first time that our members have been asked to elect a leader for the whole party in Scotland and I've met our members from Selkirk to Shetland and all points in between,' she told assembled journalists after her victory was announced.

> They've been engaged, they've been enthusiastic, they've been welcoming and they're excited about our bright future too. A political party is not a leader, a political party is its membership and I want to bring our members at all levels much closer together in our party going forward and to take our party forward in unity.

The margin of victory was close – too close for Ruth's rhetorical party unity to be quickly achievable.

She had received 2,278 first-preference votes, compared to Fraser's 2,096. She eventually won on second preferences, securing 2,983 votes to Fraser's 2,417. As if the party needed any reminding of its dire situation, just 64 per cent of its 8,000 members bothered to vote in the contest at all.

The result was a bitter blow to Fraser, who had been the early favourite in the contest and clearly had a grand vision for the party's future. As he conceded, his voice and language were tinged with resent and foreboding. 'Clearly I'm disappointed that I was not able to persuade more of our members that my vision for the future is the correct one,' he said. 'But I congratulate Ruth Davidson on her victory, and she will have my full support as she tries to take the party forward.'

Others, such as former party leader and Ruth's mentor Annabel Goldie, were delighted – although Goldie did try to put some distance between herself and the new leader. 'We have a big obligation to our own party but we have an even bigger one to the Scottish public,' she said. 'I wish Ruth every success in taking the Scottish Conservatives forward. The future is exciting, I promise her that I shall not be a back-seat driver and I am confident that she is more than equal to taking on Alex Salmond.' Cameron, too, said he was 'delighted' with the result.

While congratulations also flooded in from other party leaders, it was perhaps First Minister Alex Salmond who summed up Ruth's predicament best. 'Congratulations to Ruth Davidson on her success, and I wish her well,' he began warmly.

> My own view is that Annabel Goldie was a highly successful leader for the Conservatives in Scotland, and maximised the Tory vote here. That merely underlines the scale of the task for Ruth Davidson in motivating her party – as does the number of Scottish Tory members who actually voted in this contest, and the fact that her main opponent proposed winding up the party.

Certainly, patching up a party now deeply fractured would be a tough ask. 'The hope of party grandees will be that, once the result is in, the bitterness of the election campaign can be forgotten and the party can face the bigger challenges it needs to do,' said *The Scotsman*. 'But given the amount of blood spilt in this campaign, it suggests that the wounds will take quite some time to heal.'

Ruth not only now had high-profile enemies within her own party, she also had only six months' direct experience in the chamber – and much of that time had actually been spent out on the campaign trail. On top of that, she had to face Salmond – one of the most competent performers of 21st-century British politics – across the chamber every week.

Crucially, she had also won the leadership on the tried and

tested – and failed – platform of opposing further devolution. With the independence referendum coming in just three years, she had boxed herself into a cramped and inhospitable corner.

All these factors would make Ruth's initial years of leadership fraught with plotting and setbacks. She would have to learn – and learn quickly.

CHAPTER 7

INITIAL DIFFICULTIES

Ruth had been an MSP for just two years when she imploded at First Minister's Questions. Already under pressure from her own members, in May 2013 the Tory leader stood up and demanded answers from Alex Salmond on legal advice he had received about an independent Scotland joining the EU. It was an unmitigated disaster that called into question not only her performance but also her political judgement.

Four months earlier, David Cameron had announced – amid great controversy – that he would hold an in/out referendum on EU membership if he won a majority in 2015 – a move that threatened the UK's place in Europe. Ruth, as Tory leader in Scotland, claimed Salmond had engaged in an 'embarrassing pantomime' over Scotland's place in the EU – hardly the best turn of phrase in the circumstances. Indeed, as the First Minister stood up to respond, a broad smile of something like disbelief spread across his face. He had a field day. 'I accused Willie Rennie of kamikaze tactics last week,' he said, amid increasingly loud heckles from the SNP benches.

But to talk about Europe with the phrase 'embarrassing pantomime', in the wake of a performance in the House of Commons that the leader of the Liberal Democrats ... said showed that the Prime Minister had taken leave of his senses, although the Liberal Democrats and the Conservatives are allies in the coalition government, takes the most extraordinary degree of bravado, on which I congratulate Ruth Davidson.

Amid an increasingly raucous chamber, Ruth floundered, while her own MSPs cringed. The verdict from journalists watching the scene was damning. Tom Peterkin, writing in *The Scotsman*, said her questioning was 'less than impressive' and compared her harshly with Labour leader Johann Lamont. 'Salmond's body language improved dramatically when he realised that Davidson was going to tackle him on the SNP's position on Europe,' he wrote.

For a Tory leader to mention the 'E' word at this time of all times was foolhardy, to say the least. With Davidson's party in turmoil on Europe, Salmond couldn't wait to rise from his chair to denounce the Tories. The denunciation was a demolition job that saw the SNP leader finish on a high.

Indeed, Peterkin's piece highlights the increasing sense among the Holyrood press corps that, despite showing promise, Ruth might simply not be up to the job of leading the Tories. Her performances at First Minister's Questions had been weak, and the terriers of the lobby smelled blood, with discontent among Tory MSPs becoming increasingly public. There were suggestions the parliamentary party was 'mutinous'.

These feeble performances in the bear pit of First Minister's Questions combined with a fractured party following the divisive leadership campaign would leave Ruth's authority hanging by a thread.

* * *

In the wake of her victory, Ruth tried to stamp her authority on the Tories' MSPs. It would be no easy task. Some had been members since 1999 and resented the thought of a young upstart who had been an MSP for only six months telling them what to do. Others, of course, still sported raw and painful wounds from the leadership race.

Yet Ruth misjudged the strength of opposition – or perhaps animosity – towards her. Her first reshuffle, for instance, turned into a disaster as MSPs refused to respect her authority. 'Ruth came along a little gung-ho and tried to lay down the law but she soon found out they weren't going to take it lying down,' a senior party source told the *Daily Express* at the time. Ruth had attempted to gather all her MSPs together to dish out roles – but several refused to turn up.

As tensions worsened, the unveiling of the new team had to be shelved, with senior party figures unwilling to take on the roles Ruth wanted them to. The party's education spokeswoman, Liz Smith MSP – who was also Fraser's campaign manager – 'angrily rejected' Ruth's demand that she switch to the rural affairs brief. Fraser, meanwhile, demanded a constitutional portfolio so he could challenge Salmond on independence – but was told Ruth wanted this role for herself. In an increasingly tumultuous day, Ruth then offered both former presiding officer Alex Fergusson and former leadership rival Jackson Carlaw the deputy leadership. The machinations – or, rather, lack of them – inevitably spilled into the press, further undermining Ruth's tentative position.

All the portfolios were eventually filled – in fact, every Tory MSP would eventually be given a brief. The row over the shadow Cabinet, however, was merely a taste of things to come.

* * *

First Minister's Questions is, in many ways, the public face of the Scottish Parliament. Like Prime Minister's Questions, it is the set-piece event of the political week – and Ruth was bad at it.

The Holyrood press pack call First Minister's Questions the 'bear pit', emphasising its reputation for aggressive baiting, so it is little surprise that Ruth, with almost no parliamentary experience, struggled. Her 'kamikaze' challenge to Salmond on the EU was the epitome of a litany of poor performances. The encounter crystallised concerns among Tory MSPs that Ruth was not up to the job of taking on the First Minister, according to the *Daily Telegraph*.

Even outside the chamber, she appeared unusually gaffe-prone, reflecting her lack of experience. One incident – in which a wine-quaffing SNP minister branded two Tories discussing a sick colleague in the Parliament's bar 'evil' – epitomised her lack of political nous. Then SNP Community Safety Minister Rose-anna Cunningham made the comment in the bar at Holyrood to Tory MSPs Mary Scanlon and Alex Fergusson, who were discussing visiting a sick colleague with another SNP MSP.

But fellow Scottish Conservative MSPs were left incredulous when their party press office went into 'lockdown' after the incident, instead of pressing for the minister's resignation. Indeed, Ruth instead ended up apologising to the minister involved after one of the Tory MSPs involved made the story public – although Ms Cunningham herself did eventually provide a written apology to the two Tory MSPs as well.

In another debacle, she wrongly claimed that only 12 per cent of Scottish households were net contributors to the UK economy, in a speech referring to Scotland as a 'gangmaster state' fostering a benefits culture. Her 'Mitt Romney moment', as it was branded, was seen as a lurch to the right that led to severe criticism from opposition parties and some of her own MSPs.

More bizarrely, she suffered the ignominy of being booed off the stage at gay charity Stonewall's annual awards night. To a chorus of jeers, Ruth – who had just won the Politician of the Year prize – challenged the charity on its 'Bigot of the Year' award. She said:

> Where I disagree with Stonewall is the need to call people names like 'bigot'. It is simply wrong. The case for equality is far better made by demonstrating the sort of generosity, tolerance and love we would wish to see more of in this world. There are many voices in this debate and just as I respectfully express my sincerely held belief that we should extend marriage to same-sex couples, I will also respect those who hold a different view.

The microphone was eventually taken from the Tory leader by Stonewall's chief executive Ben Summerskill, who added: 'I'm sure as leader of the Scottish Conservatives Ruth is used to being in a small minority.'

While an insignificant event on its own, it caused further embarrassment during what should have been a straightforward occasion. Indeed, amid the continuing mishaps, one SNP MSP declared: 'It is an achievement in itself that Ruth Davidson has managed to survive for a full year as leader of the Tories in Scotland.'

Certainly, Ruth's performance both inside and outside the chamber caused 'deep disillusionment' among her parliamentary group – something she eventually recognised herself. 'You don't turn around years of decline and stagnation overnight. It's a long haul and these are the months and years where we need to put in the hard yards,' she said in 2013, amid newspaper reports of growing discontent among the Tory ranks.

> We are making huge strides going forward, getting the party ready in terms of being a campaigning force, in terms of working out the policy base. We are already beginning to make progress. I will continue to work hard and continue to improve, I hope, as I go forward in this role.

She also – somewhat lamely – criticised the format of First Minister's Questions, which only allowed her two opportunities to speak.

The fact she even felt the need to defend her leadership publicly is, of course, a sign that she felt under pressure. Undoubtedly, she was correct in her analysis that deep-seated reforms would take time to affect the party's fortunes. She was trying to undo a decade's worth of stagnation north of the border, a record that could not be erased overnight. Her inexperience, of course, played a factor in her struggles. She was learning on the job – and it showed.

Yet she was not helped in her early years as leader by David Cameron. As planning got under way for the Scottish independence referendum, the Prime Minister repeatedly undermined Ruth's position and authority, even if it was accidental rather than deliberate. His casual, off-the-cuff suggestion at a drinks reception that he wasn't 'too fussed' about the timing of the referendum, for instance, went against Ruth's long-held campaign for a quick vote. The comments led to accusations that the Prime Minister had 'hung Ruth out to dry'.

One senior MSP told *The Herald* at the time:

> The real significance of this is David Cameron clearly doesn't think he has done anything wrong because the Scottish Tories are such an irrelevance we are just not on his radar. This was not wilful or deliberate or even careless. It just showed it did not occur to him the view of the Scottish party or its leader might even matter.

Indeed, Cameron was a firm ally of Ruth's, but for much of his premiership he was prone to haphazard and ill-conceived comments and decisions.

'There is absolutely no communication from London,' said another Tory MSP. 'It's ridiculous. Even the Liberal Democrats are better at this.'

Ruth of course played down any suggestions of a rift, but there is no doubt that Cameron's nonchalance undermined her leadership.

'The Prime Minister was simply repeating what he said on the campaign trail … a few weeks ago,' she said. 'That is, while he would prefer to see a referendum sooner rather than later, having a single question in a legal, fair and decisive referendum is much more important than the date on which it is held.'

The national political picture, spurred by Cameron's premiership, did not help Ruth either. The austerity agenda brought forward by the Prime Minister and his Chancellor, George Osborne – both friends of Ruth – was deeply unpopular in many parts of the country, including Scotland. The Conservatives' decision to slash public spending might have been prudent in the wake of the 2009 financial crash, but it was viewed by many in Scotland as a return to the policies of the widely vilified Margaret Thatcher. It further heightened a sense that Scotland – which allegedly had a government committed to public services – was somehow different in outlook to other parts of the UK. More fundamentally for Ruth, it reinforced the now common view that her party was 'anti-Scottish', given that she had signed up to the Cameron–Osborne agenda.

Certainly, polling from Ruth's initial years as leader reflects her deep-seated difficulties. Despite her having run on a platform to revitalise the party, its fortunes failed to improve under her leadership. For much of 2012 and early 2013, the Tories were left languishing with just 12 or 13 per cent of voters backing them. More damningly for Ruth, her personal approval was also at rock-bottom. Just 1 per cent of voters at the beginning of 2012 suggested they were 'very satisfied' with her leadership, while 19 per cent reported being 'very dissatisfied' and 21 per cent 'quite dissatisfied'.

Later polling in 2013 would hardly alter what was an uncomfortable reading of the Tory leader's popularity. Ruth had also failed to break the Scottish Conservatives free of their classic problem: being perceived as an English party. A YouGov poll in October 2012 found that just 5 per cent of voters believed she was the best person to stand up for Scotland's interests.

With poor poll ratings and rebellious MSPs, after two years at the helm Ruth's leadership of the Tories was in serious difficulty.

At her most vulnerable point, she courageously chose to reverse her central campaign platform of a 'line in the sand' on further devolution. It was a bold move – and was perhaps prompted by an apparent shift in Cameron's position. The Prime Minister had suggested he was open to further devolution in the event of a 'No' vote in the 2014 referendum, putting him at odds with Ruth's 'line in the sand' commitment. Asked whether he was prepared to give more powers to Holyrood, he told BBC News in 2012: 'I'm very prepared. I believe in devolution, and I don't just mean devolution in terms of power, I mean devolution in terms of giving people greater control over their own lives.'

That Cameron would so openly disagree with the leader of his party in Scotland again reinforces not only his casual style but also his perceived disregard for Ruth's views.

Whether or not her hand was forced, however, a commitment to further devolution would soon serve to re-establish Ruth's party as one that stood up for Scottish interests.

In a speech in March 2013 in Edinburgh, she made a passionate defence of the Union – but also announced that she would explore the option of more powers for Scotland. For the first time, it was a real return to the pre-1965 Unionist Party position. 'The debate on Scotland's constitutional future, and the referendum to be held next year, opens a new chapter in our nation's history,' she said.

We recognise that to play a part in the writing of this new chapter, the Scottish Conservatives must also turn over a new page. With the benefit of hindsight, I believe we found ourselves on the wrong side of history in 1997.

We fought on against the idea of a Scottish Parliament long after it became clear it was the settled will of the Scottish people.

Our decision not to take part in the Scottish Constitutional Convention gave the impression that Scotland's constitutional future was not a matter of interest to us, beyond keeping Scotland in the UK.

For many, the fact we were a lone voice saying 'no' in the referendum campaign simply underlined the impression we had no real faith in our own country.

It made us look as if we lacked ambition for Scotland.

But the Scottish Conservatives are not, and never have been, a party which stands in the way of the ambitions of Scotland's people.

In terms of the rhetoric, such views had been expressed by Tory leaders before, going back as far as William Hague and his attempts to frame the Tories north of the border as an autonomous party. The difference, however, would be the practical implications of Ruth's speech. While the speech did not result in direct action – political speeches rarely do – it did set the Tories on a course to explore, and potentially support, further devolution.

The Strathclyde Commission that Ruth announced – named after the Tory peer who would chair it – would be tasked with exploring options for further devolution.

It was a quite remarkable U-turn, which left many – particularly Murdo Fraser's supporters – baffled. Ruth had, after all, defeated the Scottish Conservative grandee on the basis of opposing devolution. Two years later, she was becoming a ferocious advocate of it. Fraser's faction could not be blamed if they were confused, not to mention miffed.

But the U-turn also caused significant concern among party members, many of whom had voted for Ruth because of her strong anti-devolution stance. While she had no manifesto as such in the 2011 leadership campaign, the future of the Union and the Tory Party's stance on devolution had been key factors in the campaign. Her opposition to further devolution had won the relatively unknown candidate support among a Holyrood-sceptic membership base. Yet she had now totally reversed this position.

It was a forward-thinking move, but one that only served to undermine Ruth's increasingly tenuous hold on the leadership of the party.

Indeed, Fraser used it as an opportunity to subtly attack his leader. In an article in *The Scotsman*, he praised the U-turn but also expressed his bafflement at how it had come about. He wrote, with more than a hint of vindication and dash of euphemism:

> There were those who argued that no fundamental change in party structure or political direction was required, and what was necessary was to elect a fresh new leader who would present a modern face to the electorate, and work harder to try and communicate the message.
>
> The other, much more radical, proposal involved finding a new vehicle to promote centre-right political ideas in Scotland to replace the Scottish Conservatives, coupled with a major shift in the party's historic constitutional stance to embrace greater devolution to the Scottish Parliament.
>
> There was a lively debate on these alternatives during the leadership election triggered by the resignation from that position of the popular Annabel Goldie.

He praised the realisation that this position was 'untenable' and noted that it was 'crucial' that the report be released before the independence referendum in 2014.

But he added:

A shift in policy of such a dramatic nature takes both leadership and courage.

It is never easy for anyone to accept that in the past they were wrong, and this is particularly the case in politics where opponents are quick to seize on any inconsistency of position.

So, Ruth's move was a strong one, to be welcomed and congratulated, and much of the criticism she received was misplaced. It is clearly in the Scottish Conservatives' interests to embrace the devolution of further fiscal powers to Holyrood.

The article was viewed by many as a coded attack on the Scottish Conservative leader and it is testament to how low her authority was among her own MSPs that Fraser could write such a piece without fear of rebuke.

Yet her internal opponents were also not just concerned by her performance and U-turn, but also their own future.

Ruth, in an energetic bid to push through the Sanderson Commission recommendations in full, was imposing rigorous changes to candidate selection. What had previously been a somewhat cushy – or in practice non-existent – selection process would, under Ruth, be modernised and strengthened. That meant candidates could no longer rely on their length of service being enough to secure top positions on the crucial PR list system. Instead, they would have to prove to party bosses their ability and aptitude for being an MSP. Skills in public speaking, organisation and campaigning were just some of the areas where candidates would now have to excel if they wanted the chance to secure safe seats.

This served an obvious purpose of helping to re-energise and reform the Tory brand in Scotland, which had had many of the same MSPs since 1999. 'You can't change the face of an organisation without changing the faces in it,' Ruth wrote for Conservative Home.

> Along with the willing volunteers, we too often – and in too many constituencies – had historically run little more than 'paper' candidates – doughty councillors or respected community pillars who were asked to put their name down and assured that they 'wouldn't have to really do anything.'
>
> Not only does that approach leave huge swathes of the country without any Conservative activity locally, it damages your party's returns nationally and feeds into a media narrative of failure. In a voting system, such as Holyrood's, which tops up constituencies through a regional list system where every single vote counts, it is catastrophic.

But there were more than mere electoral considerations in mind. New candidates mean a cull of the existing ones – and Ruth had plenty of enemies. A new batch, loyal to her, would make things significantly easier. She herself hinted at this in the same piece for Conservative Home. 'Currently, more than half of our MSP group are in their 60s or 70s,' she wrote in the 2016 piece. 'For a young leader, that's a huge – and very welcome – amount of experience to draw on, but it is not representative of a wider Scotland.' But she added, euphemistically: 'With a number stepping down … a host of new faces will be coming forward.'

There is no doubt that the candidate selections had an impact on changing the face of the Conservative Party in Scotland – at least in terms of competence, if not ideologically.

The selection process was now rigorous, as Ruth herself explained with a military analogy. 'I wanted candidate recruitment to be about us seeking out the best of the best. Like the old Royal Marine Commando advert, 99.9 per cent need not apply,' she said.

So I brought in outside expertise to set up a wholly new candidates' board. An HR director who'd served across several national institutions, a world champion debater to put candidates through their public speaking paces, an expert in corporate leadership to assess decision-making – people of skill and substance to run the rule over our future elected representatives. The assessments themselves changed – we set up new tests, based largely on the potential officer assessments the army carries out before Sandhurst (minus the assault course and press-ups).

For those who passed, the candidates' board has worked with them, offering training, development and sustained support.

What was the result of this new rigorous testing?

There were certainly new candidates – some of great ability – who were promoted to seats or to positions on the list where they were likely to get elected in 2016. (In a somewhat token gesture, Ruth herself would also have to be reselected as part of the scheme.) Yet she certainly went out of her way to attract people of talent and encourage them to run for the party. One such candidate was Professor Adam Tomkins – a sharp-witted intellectual and fervent Unionist. A Tory insider told of Tomkins's recruitment to the party's ranks and, ultimately, to the number one seat on the party's list in Glasgow.

> He went to the Labour Party first, when he was an academic, because he wanted to get involved in the pro-Union campaign. He rang up the Labour Party and said: 'Can I get involved?' He went to their headquarters and met [former MP] Margaret Curran and he almost had to be grateful for the time that they gave him.
>
> So he said, 'Bollocks to this, I'll try Ruth Davidson.' He went to Ruth's office and she said, 'Brilliant, how do you want to get involved?' She suggested the Strathclyde Commission and just thought, here's a talented bloke, come on in and get going.
>
> I think she's very good at bringing on – finding and recruiting – good people.

Certainly, Ruth herself suggests her new crop of candidates – fifteen of them would be elected in 2016 – have given the Tories a fresh lease of life. 'I am genuinely excited about leading this team into the coming elections – and even more excited about the difference such talented individuals can make to a parliament often criticised for the lack of strength and depth of its representatives,' she said before the 2016 election.

> We have candidates in our ranks from all backgrounds; from business, agriculture, public services, health, the armed forces, the trade unions, law, education, local government and the charitable sector.

> The candidates themselves are also a demonstration of how
> the party has changed and the face it wants to give the world.

Unsurprisingly, this is not quite the reality on the ground. While many talented Tory candidates were selected – Ruth herself took pride in now having a gold medal sprinter among her ranks, for instance – a large number of them remained traditional Conservative types. Some are more blue-collar – one of those elected in Glasgow, for example, is Annie Wells, a food retail manager. Yet more of those chosen under Ruth's new rigorous selection scheme were very much white-collar. The 26-year-old Oliver Mundell, son of the Secretary of State for Scotland, was chosen to fight a seat in the Borders. Aberdeenshire West would be fought by Alexander Burnett, who is thought to be worth around £40 million. Others among those elected include baronets and clan chiefs. The register of interests for the newly elected batch of Davidson's Dandies would, despite Ruth's rhetoric, be longer than ever.

Opposition to Ruth's leadership was, unsurprisingly, not limited to her performances at FMQs, her U-turn on devolution or her threatened deselections. As a gay, young, female leader, she also struggled to connect, at least initially, with small 'c' Conservatives.

The *Telegraph*'s Alan Cochrane, for example, was scathing about her performance throughout much of her early leadership. In one piece in early 2013, he bluntly described Ruth's policy proposals as having 'as much beef in … as there is, nowadays, in a cheap supermarket hamburger'. Vague attempts to make the party pro-devolution were branded 'a cross between a mystery tour and a non-event'. But in his diaries – later published as *Alex*

Salmond: My Part in His Downfall – he was even more critical. In a June 2012 entry, he would describe the Tory leader as 'absolutely awful'. He added:

> She is totally and utterly useless and so are her team. They haven't a bloody clue but she is the problem – big problem.
>
> Not up to the job ... and I suspect that some hacks will start asking questions. [David] Mundell said he knew she wasn't cutting the mustard ... but he claims they've got someone lined up to help her.
>
> Christ, they need it.

Such figures – prominent in the Conservative press – undoubtedly contributed to Ruth's leadership problems. Of course, it is worth noting that, as the years wore on and her leadership improved, the Tory press would be equally complicit in making her the 'darling' of their party. By 2016, for instance, Cochrane had moderated his tone – at least somewhat. He would note in his *Daily Telegraph* column ahead of the Scottish election: 'All she's got to do is prove that the Conservatives are no longer toxic. I think she can do it and if she can't, nobody can.' Yet there is no doubt that initially unfavourable press coverage of Ruth's leadership fed into the rumblings from both her party colleagues and the wider party itself.

Ruth would recognise the need to improve her performances. But she was also combative, and provided no quarter to her internal opponents. 'What annoys me is that people don't see or acknowledge the fact that, as a party, we have got our tails up at the moment. We have an issue [the independence referendum] that we can really fight for,' she told *Scotland on Sunday*, in a 2013 article written by her future director of strategy Eddie Barnes. 'No more navel gazing and no more sackcloth and ashes, because sometimes we have been, for me, too apologetic,' she would add. 'I am proud of the Scottish Conservative and Unionist party. I joined it for a reason. I believe in Conservatism.'

But with growing concern about her ability, the spectre of deselection and her U-turn on devolution, Ruth's leadership was under threat. The 2013 Scottish Conservative conference was, in many respects, the last chance for her to save her rapidly diminishing political prospects. As her Tory opponents began to break cover and launch open rebellion, she had to regain control or face being ousted.

The Conservative conference in Stirling not only set the scene for Ruth's revival, however – it was also the catalyst for the return of the Tories to the front line of Scottish politics.

CHAPTER 8

CLAUSE FOUR

'A bunch of self-indulgent Chihuahuas trying to find a lamp-post to piss against.'

So Annabel Goldie described Ruth's opponents, in character-istically forthright style, at a conference fraught with political infighting and factionalism. Her protégé was up against it.

As a sign of how tenuous Ruth's position had become, David Cameron had been parachuted in, in a bid to shore up her leadership. 'We will only succeed if we are in touch and in tune with modern Scotland, and in Ruth you've got the ideal leader,' he told Scottish Conservative delegates at Stirling's Albert Halls. 'Ruth wasn't born into the Conservative Party, she chose it. She understands that to win we've got to be a party for all of Scotland. A party focused on securing Scotland's place within a strong UK but not afraid to look at how devolution can be improved.' Going off script, he added: 'That is what Ruth stands for and I back her every step of the way.'

Other party bigwigs were also drafted in to support the embattled leader. Michael Gove praised her 'amazing achievements', while Goldie launched a ferocious defence of Ruth at a dinner for delegates. Tory MEP Struan Stevenson also rushed to support the plans for increased devolution, saying:

> The Scottish Conservatives will never have any fertile ground to plough in Scotland as long as we live on a block grant from Westminster. We are the party that can offer efficiency and low tax and a competent government but you can't do that when you are funded through the Barnett block grant.

Open talk of a coup against Ruth had certainly forced the hand of party grandees. Not only were MSPs dissatisfied with her performance to date, but party members were left fuming by her U-turn on devolution.

Her main rival, Murdo Fraser, took to Twitter after her speech to announce: 'Text for today: Luke 15 v 7'. The biblical passage in question states: 'I say unto you that likewise joy shall be in heaven over one sinner that repents more than over ninety and nine just persons who need no repentance'. The 'well-aimed and effective barb', as described by the *Sunday Post*, served to show just how weak Ruth's leadership was.

Matters were not helped when the Scottish Tory leader – with characteristic determination – ruled out any discussion or debate on the issue at the conference. Alastair Orr, the vice-chairman of the Stirling Conservative and Unionist Association, for instance, announced that he had been 'unhappy' with her performance as leader and suggested her refusal to allow a debate on further devolution made her appear 'weak'.

More significantly, Lord Forsyth – who had been an influential backer of Ruth – refused to attend the conference, despite it being held in his hometown. The Scottish Conservative Party was once again in turmoil, according to newspaper reports ahead of the conference.

For her part, Ruth was forced to deny she was hiding behind the Strathclyde Commission after she claimed devolution could not be discussed until it had reported back. She said she did not want to pre-empt Strathclyde's findings, but this did not wash with many party supporters, who wanted the chance to discuss – and presumably disagree with – the devolution plan in open session.

It was a precarious period – but Ruth was unabashed in her speech, where she set out the Conservative case for delivering extra powers. Boosted by the support of the party grandees, she launched a full-scale defence of her position. 'We are the Scottish Conservative and Unionist Party. We believe in Britain – but we put Scotland first,' she told delegates. Confronting the failure of previous Scottish Conservative policy head on, she said:

The choice is clear – we can talk to ourselves, as perhaps we have too often in the past. Or we can have an open and constructive conversation with the people of Scotland about how we can help tackle their fears and meet their aspirations. We can hold to the old ways and follow a path of slow decline. Or we can choose to do something about it – choose to turn it around. Choose to build a modern Scottish Conservative party that speaks to the aspirations of mainstream Scotland, which once again attracts the votes of people from every part of the country and every walk of life. I'm proud of our party's history, but we can't live in the past. Like you, I believe in our future; and in the future of Scotland. I believe that we must be the agents of change that Scotland needs if our country is to be all it can.

It was her Clause Four moment – the point at which she tackled internal critics and delivered a fundamental change to the party that would make it electable again. Of course, as she went on to outline new appointees to the Strathclyde Commission, the reaction was somewhat muted.

The press response, however, was more positive. The Scottish *Daily Mail* would describe the policy as the 'most significant intervention in the referendum debate to date'. Former MP Peter Duncan, writing on the Conservative Home website, was even more gushing in his praise. 'The leadership can – at one fell swoop – right the wrongs of forty years ago when the party turned its back on our devolutionist credentials,' he wrote. 'They can reverse the decline in fortunes north of the border, and finally connect with a new generation of Scots who are looking for local control, whilst retaining the best of what our United Kingdom can offer.'

In refusing to back down, Ruth, supported by Tory grandees, saw off her rivals and held on to the leadership. The party membership, while disgruntled, was powerless to effectively oppose the changes.

The looming independence referendum also played heavily on rebels' minds and helps explain why Ruth was not openly challenged. Despite their bitter disagreements and disappointment at Ruth's leadership, it was not a time for a bloody coup. In many ways, and somewhat ironically, the Tories' devotion to the Union prevented them from fighting harder against Ruth's devolution plans, or at least using them as the basis of a leadership challenge.

As a result of the Stirling Conference, Ruth had regained control of the situation and was imbued with a newfound confidence, particularly at Holyrood. Reporting one session of First Minister's Questions at the end of 2013, Tom Peterkin would write in *The Scotsman*:

> Overall one couldn't escape the impression that Ms Davidson got the better of [Mr] Salmond at FMQs – an outcome that would have been almost unthinkable a few months ago … An improved record at First Minister's Questions has been accompanied by some impressive contributions to parliament more generally … After a rocky start, there are small signs that Ms Davidson is growing into her job.

The Strathclyde Commission would report back a year later – by which time Ruth's standing had much improved. But it was those recommendations – and Ruth's wholehearted embrace of them – that fundamentally changed the party's fortunes.

Lord Strathclyde's conclusions, which would go on to become Tory policy, emphasised the two classic strands of Conservatism in Scotland – patriotism for Britain and for Scotland. 'These proposals are our own,' he wrote in the introduction of the rather thin, 24-page document. 'They are offered to the Party in the spirit in which they were commissioned – to provide a Unionist perspective on devolution and a direction in which constitutional policy can develop. Our aim is to make Scotland the best it can be.'

His report made several proposals, the most notable and radical of which was the devolution of income tax. The Scottish Parliament should be able to set the rates and bands of the tax, he argued – a measure that was introduced by the Conservative government in 2016. It also suggested the devolution of some benefits, as well as the establishment of a committee to support further devolution.

Lord Strathclyde explicitly justifies these changes in historic Unionist terms.

He states:

> The genius at the heart of the Anglo-Scottish Union of 1707 is that it allows both nations to blossom within a shared state. The Union was not and never has been an incorporating Union, re-quiring Scotland to assimilate as if she were nothing more than a northern region of England – or even an English colony. On the contrary, the Union is founded on the principle that Scot-tish institutions maintain their distinctive identity. Throughout the Union this has been true for the Church, for education, for Scots law and for the Scottish legal system. And, since devolu-tion, it has been true also of the Scottish Parliament.

Much of the language in the report is political – it was published, after all, just months before the independence referendum. Lord Strathclyde takes a number of swipes at the SNP, pointing out instances where they have overtly recognised the benefits of the Union. This reflects the tensions and worries among those op-posed to independence at the time the report was written. But it does not detract from the fundamental point of the Strathclyde Commission – that the Tories had embraced devolution for the first time. Years had been lost in the political wilderness by their failure to come to a coherent position on devolution, but finally they had an answer. It was largely forced by the prevailing cir-cumstance of the independence referendum. But, however it was achieved, it represented a watershed moment for Ruth's party and was in no small part down to her leadership.

Launching the report in Glasgow, she said:

What we have at the moment is like a tricycle, what the Scotland Act 2012 brings in is a bike with stabilisers, and what this builds on is taking the stabilisers off. So it does allow MSPs to take decisions not just over the rates of taxation that we levy, but it also allows them to vary one or more. It allows them to introduce a new band of income tax. It allows them to find the formula that best allows the work that the particular government of the day wants to carry out and has a mandate for in Scotland. I think that flexibility shows a responsibility.

David Cameron hailed it as 'a clear, coherent and Conservative blueprint for the next stage of Scotland's devolution journey'.

The reaction to the report too was broadly positive. Writing in his blog for *The Spectator*, journalist Alex Massie said:

It is, as you would expect, an unimpeachably Unionist document but one that applies Tory philosophy to devolutionary politics. And not before time. The Tories are not responsible for the circumstances in which contemporary Scottish politics is arranged but they are, at long last, responsible for their response to those circumstances.

After a generation of craven self-abasement and denial they have emerged from their cave and have, at long last, something to present to the Scottish electorate.

They have something to say and, by jove, they actually intend to say it. Astonishing scenes.

He added: 'However improbably, this makes the Tories the party of devolution now.'

Retrospective accounts have been equally glowing. Anthony Seldon and Peter Snowdon, writing in their book *Cameron at 10*, stated that the Strathclyde Commission delivered 'fresh impetus' to the Better Together campaign. They added: '[The Strathclyde Commission] recommends giving Scotland further devolution and attracts widespread praise'.

Alice Thomson, writing in *The Times*, suggested that Ruth Davidson and Lord Strathclyde 'may save the Union' with their recommendations. Former Tory MSP Brian Monteith, writing for Conservative Home, suggested Ruth's party had 'gazumped' Labour by becoming the party of devolution. He added, making reference to the recommended devolution of tax-and-spend powers to Holyrood:

> Critics in the Conservative Party have branded the policy as a consolation prize for Alex Salmond. But in truth it is a straightjacket, because it means that so long as he or the SNP (or indeed Labour) are in power in Scotland, they will have to match their spending promises with an explanation of how they will fund them. Relying on spending the block grant is no longer enough.

The Scottish Conservatives, of course, were not unique in presenting proposals for further devolution – both Labour and the Liberal Democrats had already published similar documents. What makes the Strathclyde Commission remarkable, however, is that it was requested by a Tory leader and came to be embraced by the majority of her party. Of course, as we have seen, many of the ideas contained in the commission's final report were not particularly new or innovative. On the contrary, many in the party – and not just Fraser – had been arguing for greater responsibility over tax-and-spend policies in the Scottish Parliament. But, until Ruth tackled the issue in 2013, debates over devolution in the Tory Party had been deeply fractious. The party had flip-flopped and paid lip service to greater powers and autonomy for its own party, without ever embracing a coherent or sustained position. But now they had taken a clear and concise stance, which was official party policy. And, while opposition remained among the party membership and some grandees, the threat of the break-up of the Union itself undoubtedly focused the minds of Tories and limited the dissent that had previously racked the party so deeply.

Ruth's revival – and with it the Tories' revival – was not just down to policy, however.

Towards the end of 2013, Ruth took a significant step on the path to detoxifying the Scottish Conservatives. It was a journey that began even before she entered politics – but it would allow her to make her most eloquent speech and reaffirm her leadership.

The Marriage and Civil Partnership (Scotland) Bill, which would legalise same-sex marriage in Scotland, was a free vote. This was politically convenient for Ruth in particular, with the notion of same-sex marriages being most controversial among the Conservative ranks. Indeed, when the legislation was finally passed, eight of the MSPs who opposed it were Tories, with seven coming from the SNP benches and three from Labour. Given there were only fifteen Tory MSPs however, that means more than 50 per cent of Ruth's party opposed the bill.

Of course, the legislation attracted significant attention from the public. More than 77,000 responses were received by the

Scottish government during a consultation before the bill was brought before MSPs, although the legislation in itself was not that radical by today's standards. It allowed freedoms for religious groups who did not want to conduct same-sex marriages; both the Catholic Church and Church of Scotland opposed the legislation. Similar laws had already been passed in other countries too, including England and Wales.

But that did not diminish the significance of the event for Ruth, who dropped her attack-dog demeanour in favour of impassioned rhetoric. 'The debate is not easy and it was never going to be – when areas of love meet the law and when belief, commitment and faith collide with legislation, the waters will always be difficult to navigate,' she began with a flourish.

> Today, I speak on behalf of only myself. I have no doubt that this could be the most personal speech that I will ever make in the chamber. I believe that marriage is a good thing. I saw the evidence of that every day growing up in a house that was full of love. My family had the stresses and strains that are common to all, but there was never any doubt, question or fear in my mind that our togetherness was in any way insecure.
>
> I do not want the next generation of young gay people to grow up as I did, believing that marriage is something that they can never have. With this bill, we have the opportunity to change that, and to change the attitudes and stigma that being lesbian, gay, bisexual or transgender can still evoke, and that can cause so much harm.

It was a barnstorming speech that was welcomed in the press, as well as by fellow MSPs. *The Scotsman*'s Tom Peterkin said it 'received much praise for the honesty with which she tackled an issue which meant much to her as an openly gay politician'. Her eloquence even earned her an inflammatory reprimand from the Westboro Baptist Church, a famous anti-gay hate group based in America.

Yet, despite her eloquence, Ruth would admit that she felt deeply conflicted about the vote because of her faith. Predictably, the MSPs who opposed the bill did so on religious grounds. 'I am not ashamed to say that on returning to my parliamentary office after the vote, I cried deep sobbing tears of relief and re-lease and joy and pain and pride and dozens of other emotions all mixed up together,' Ruth said after the bill passed. 'In truth, I didn't really know why I was crying – I hadn't expected to – but I couldn't stop for a full five minutes.'

The attitude of her own church in the proceedings had, how-ever, caused her some disappointment. She said: 'I believe in the freedom of the church to make decisions regarding when, how and to whom they convey sacraments such as marriage. I would dearly love my own church, the Church of Scotland, to offer same-sex marriage ceremonies, but I fully respect its autonomy in making that choice.'

Ruth – ever the moderniser – is hopeful her church will one day conduct same-sex ceremonies. 'I believe I'll see it in my life-time, absolutely,' she said in an interview in 2016. 'I certainly hope so. The Church has come a long way very fast. It still has a long way to go but it's absolutely going in the right direction. I'm very hopeful I'll be able to see gay church weddings in my lifetime.'

As well as being a personal journey for Ruth, however, her support for equal marriage was a significant step in modernis-ing the Tories in Scotland – and making them electable again.

With her party split on the issue, it was her own passion and eloquence in the debate that were crucial. While Tory votes mattered little in either passing or blocking the legislation, her speech helped show the Conservatives in Scotland in a new, compassionate light.

Same-sex marriage was a popular idea among Scots, who have a tendency to think themselves more socially liberal than the rest of the UK. In the aftermath of Ruth's speech, polling suggested 30 per cent 'strongly supported' equal marriage and a further 26 per cent 'tended to support' it. A significant minority – 35 per cent – did oppose the legislation. But crucially for the Tories – and Ruth – more than three-quarters of those aged between eighteen and twenty-four supported the act. It might have alienated some older voters, but Ruth's support helped reinvent – or at least reintroduce – the Tories to a significant portion of increasingly politically engaged youngsters in Scotland. Journalist and former Tory MP Paul Goodman wrote: 'Scotland's Conservative leader is certainly a moderniser, who pitches her appeal to Scotland's mainstream mass of moderate voters. Support for same-sex marriage is considered to be a touchstone for modernisation and she is for it, too.'

Indeed, as Ruth's stature grew, so too did her willingness to push ahead with that modernisation of the party and break from the past. On the death of Nelson Mandela, she offered stern criticism of the Tories for failing to do more to stand up to apartheid South Africa. 'Many members of my party did not recognise apartheid for the grave violation of human dignity that it was and did not back the struggle to end it,' she said. 'It is a stain on our party and those members have found themselves on the wrong side of history. For someone a generation behind, it is almost incomprehensible to me how their judgement could have been so wrong.' This was again a shrewd move to reinvent the party by a woman who was still at school when Mandela was released from Robben Island in 1990.

In terms of policy, this mattered little, but it again served to change perceptions of the Scottish Conservatives. The Tories under Ruth's leadership would not be a bunch of wealthy, white closet racists, as some caricatures would portray them, but rather modern, outward-looking and friendly. The Mandela speech also offered Ruth the chance to publicly rebuke a part of Thatcher's legacy without actually having to criticise any of the reforms the former Prime Minister had initiated.

In her leadership, Ruth had, by her nature and personality, already served to re-energise her party. With these moves, she sought to reinvent – or rather rebrand – it as a new, modern force, separated from the past. The results would not be instant, but the Tories were beginning to move away from the images of stuffiness, realpolitik and unmitigated laissez-faire capitalism.

Further, through the Strathclyde Commission, Ruth had recaptured the essence of Scottish Conservatism that had been lost in the decades following their 1955 triumph. The Tories could now claim to be a party that embraced both Scotland and the UK. They were positioned as a Scottish party first and foremost once again, but one that believed in Scotland's place in the UK.

This pivot occurred at just the right time. With the SNP winning a majority in 2011, they would now have a mandate to hold a referendum on independence. The fallout from the vote would have major ramifications for UK and Scottish politics – and for Ruth herself. It would be a tense fight – but one Ruth was more than keen for.

VICTORY AT ...

CHAPTER 9

VICTORY AT ANY PRICE

D on't look triumphalist – or so Alex Salmond's advisers tried to warn him. Today of all days, however, that was going to be a tough ask. For, on that blustery October day, the First Minister had just put pen to paper and signed the Edinburgh Agreement.

Scotland would have a referendum on independence, putting the constitutional future of the UK at stake for the first time in hundreds of years. Under the 2012 deal, at some point before the end of 2014, one question would be put to Scots – eventually, should Scotland be an independent country? – with all parties agreeing to respect the binding result.

Or at least that was the idea.

The Edinburgh Agreement was the culmination of Salmond's political life and a quite remarkable achievement. The SNP had previously – during its minority tenure between 2007 and 2011 – tried to get a referendum bill passed, but it fell without a majority. Now, the Nationalists encountered no such difficulty.

Despite the efforts of his advisers, the First Minister is positively beaming in photographs of the signing at St Andrew's House, the seat of the Edinburgh government. His rhetoric, too, was somewhat high on drama. 'It is ... a historic day for Scotland and I think a major step forward in Scotland's home rule journey,' he told a press conference after the signing of the agreement. '[It] means that we will have a referendum in two years' time which will be built and made in the Scottish Parliament on behalf of the Scottish people. I think that is a substantial and important step forward.'

If Salmond was beaming, David Cameron was dark.

The Prime Minister had recognised that trying to stop a referendum would be futile – but his acquiescence was nevertheless begrudging. It would, of course, have been a kamikaze move for a UK Prime Minister to try to stop the vote. Some argue that perhaps he should have done so – that the UK is too important to be risked on the whimsical up-and-down of party politics. Such a move would, however, have been a gift for Salmond and the SNP, who are experts in driving the wedge between Edinburgh and Westminster. The – no longer just faux – outrage had Cameron refused Salmond's request would have been palpable. Bringing forward a referendum bill was, after all, a manifesto pledge for the 2011 election, where the SNP had broken the Holyrood system and secured an outright majority on their own.

Cameron was right to give his consent, but, with just one MP and, in 2012, little sign of a Tory recovery in Scotland, he was at best disinterested. Indeed, Salmond was skilled at jumping on the Prime Minister's casual carelessness that – some would later suggest – brought additional difficulties to the Union campaign. 'I always wanted to show respect to the people of Scotland,' Cameron said, somewhat mundanely, after the deal was signed. 'They voted for a party that wanted to have a referendum, I've made that referendum possible and made sure that it is decisive, it is legal and it is fair.'

Tory grandees, however, were less than impressed with the deal, which they felt gave too much away to Salmond. Lord Forsyth – never one to hold back in his interventions on Scottish politics – branded Cameron 'Pontius Pilate' for signing the accord largely on the SNP's terms. He added: 'Salmond has been able to get what he wants. If that's called a negotiation, that's stretching the language. It sounds like a walkover to me.'

For Ruth, the signing of the Edinburgh Agreement and the slow march towards a referendum was a welcome distraction. As we have seen, with her leadership on the ropes, the spectre of the break-up of the UK was, in many ways, a political gift. In 2012, however, there was no real risk of Scotland actually voting for independence. Salmond's project languished in the polls. The referendum, it was often said in those heady days, would not even be close. Pro-independence support was stuck at around a third of voters for much of 2012 and 2013. A slight bump in favour after the Edinburgh Agreement was signed was still not enough to really lift support for Salmond's campaign. Polling expert Nate Silver would suggest there was no chance of Scotland voting Yes. But over the next two years an impassioned – often aggressive, even violent – campaign would develop. And every month the polls edged closer and closer. It was easy to see, as time wore on, why Salmond wanted the longest campaign that was feasible.

The referendum may have begun as a welcome distraction for Ruth, but it became a life-and-death struggle not just for her party, but also for her country.

* * *

Despite the Conservatives' being the party most associated with the Union, it was clear that a successful referendum campaign would require the support of Labour.

Ed Miliband's party were the dominant electoral force in Scotland in the run-up to the referendum. With vastly more members and volunteers, the support of Labour would be crucial to the No campaign's ultimate victory.

The cross-party Better Together campaign, as it would be called, was opposing the Yes campaign. Better Together was largely a Labour-led enterprise, sharing many staff and expertise. There was a role for Tories, of course, but the upper echelons of the campaign were managed by senior Labour figures. The day-to-day operation was run by Blair McDougall, a highly regarded former Westminster Labour special adviser and party strategist. Alistair Darling, the former Labour Chancellor and Edinburgh MP, was the public figurehead of the campaign. Articulate, experienced and well known, he would play a crucial role over the next two years. Emphasising Labour's dominance, Darling and Scottish Labour leader Johann Lamont took centre stage at the Better Together launch, with Ruth and the Scottish Liberal Democrats' Willie Rennie taking more minor roles. With Yes support gaining ground in the latter stages of the campaign, former Labour Prime Minister Gordon Brown would be called on to bolster Better Together's flagging support.

This strategy was prudent. The three main Unionist parties were, effectively, facing off against the SNP in the referendum. The pro-UK campaign needed unity if it were to succeed. Naturally, Labour, as Scotland's electorally dominant party, would take the lead in this. But such a move also kept the Tories somewhat out of the limelight. Salmond's greatest wish was to make the referendum a Conservatives versus Scotland contest. He felt such a scenario would irk enough Scots to cajole them into voting Yes. Keeping Labour at the forefront of the campaign, albeit under a cross-party umbrella, was largely successful at avoiding such a scenario.

Yet Labour's necessary dominance in the campaign did not relieve Ruth of her responsibilities.

On the contrary, dyed-in-the-wool Tory voters would be the stalwarts of the campaign – and they needed to be galvanised. This would be Ruth's key responsibility for much of the campaign. 'Our United Kingdom is under threat,' she would tell activists in Stirling. 'Separatists continually talk the UK down and blame London for supposedly holding Scotland back. We all know that is nonsense. We know Scotland benefits from being part of the most successful political union of modern times.'

Indeed, articulating the case for the UK helped Ruth return the Tories to a 1955 footing. It was a theme she would regularly return to in the run-up to the referendum. One such example is a speech she gave 100 days before the vote:

The people of Scotland should have good reasons to be passionate about wanting to remain within the United Kingdom family. That is why it's imperative in these final weeks of campaigning to offer voters a positive vision of how our nation can progress and have a bigger say within the UK.

A no vote in September is the patriotic choice to deliver the best of both worlds in Scotland. A no vote ensures more powers for the Scottish Parliament, but still guarantees we can keep the pound. It keeps Scotland at the heart of the fastest-growing economy in the Western world, while independence would turn Scotland's biggest market into its biggest competitor overnight.

This patriotic theme – tinged with economic concern – was her go-to argument for the referendum campaign.

It was a strong Conservative argument that resonated well with her supporters. 'The Tories have been punch bags for so long that some have simply accepted that is their role – but Davidson urged the party to reclaim its patriotism,' wrote *The Spectator*'s Alex Massie, reviewing Ruth's 'muscular and unapologetic' conference speech in March 2014.

That speech contained a blistering attack on Salmond's view of the Union. '[He] hasn't realised that this land is our land,' she told admittedly subdued supporters.

This Union is our Union. And every one of us has their own personal reasons for wanting it to stay. Our United Kingdom belongs to all of us. We've built it together. We've traded together. We've fought together. We've lived together. We've loved together. We've settled and built our lives together. This land is our land and we will allow no one to break it apart.

The British Empire, of course, was gone, but she was still able to invoke a sense of patriotism to both Scotland and the UK.

Ruth invoked different arguments for backing Better Together than her political partners in the organisation. Labour – and indeed the Liberal Democrats – backed the pro-UK campaign on largely economic grounds. They were not Unionists per se. Rather, they believed remaining in the UK was the best way to deliver social justice and workers' rights. This argument centred on the business case, so to speak, for remaining within the UK. Scots, for example, enjoy higher public spending per head than their counterparts in England and Wales. The uncertainty of an independence vote would also hit workers' pay packets the hardest. That an independent Scotland might only be sustainable as a low-tax haven added weight to the argument that the break-up of the UK would benefit business leaders, not workers.

There was a great deal of merit to these economic arguments – and they would make up the backbone of the pro-UK rhetoric during the campaign. The Yes side would of course counter with somewhat exaggerated stories about NHS privatisation in England – a particularly effective ploy – as well as the possibility of perpetual Tory rule from London. Social justice, they argued, could only really be protected by an independent country free from the clutches of Westminster. In the view of Better Together, however, the bottom line was that the economic facts showed the Union helped and protected working people.

Ruth – and indeed other Tories – made similar arguments on the campaign trail. But social justice and workers' rights were not the central Tory tenets for backing the Union. Instead, the referendum campaign allowed Ruth to articulate a patriotic – but crucially Scottish – case for the UK. As noted above, she was frequently critical of the 'separatists [who] continually talk the UK down'. The SNP, Ruth argued, did not really want Scotland to be part of something great, something bigger than itself that gave it a place on the world stage. The Union, to use a cliché, allowed Scotland to punch above its weight. Thus, Ruth believed, if you loved Scotland, you must love the UK too.

It was a powerful argument – but not one without its flaws. Many people were and are deeply concerned about Britain's place in the world. Its status as a nuclear power, for instance, causes consternation among many – if not a majority – of Scots, who have to live alongside Trident-armed submarines at Faslane. Certainly, Ruth's arguments were more likely to speak to Conservative voters concerned about power and prestige than those outside her party. But it was nevertheless a deeply personal argument for Ruth, given her time spent both covering British troops as a reporter in Kosovo and later in the army herself. Those experiences had imbued her with a sense of being part of something greater, which became her chief weapon in articulating the case for the Union at its time of peril.

While these arguments did not instantaneously return the Conservatives in Scotland to the heady heights of the mid-twentieth century, there is some evidence it laid the groundwork. Data collated by Professor John Curtice's What Scotland Thinks project shows that from the signing of the Edinburgh Agreement to the referendum itself in 2014, support for Ruth's party broadly improved from around 11 or 12 per cent to 14 or 15 per cent. Non-Conservative supporters also trusted Ruth's voice during the referendum debate.

More importantly, as Ruth herself would point out, the Scottish Conservatives – or at least traditional Tory viewpoints – were once again helping to shape political discourse in Scotland. 'For the first time in my lifetime, the Scottish Conservatives have good reason to claim that we stand foursquare aligned with the values of the majority in Scotland,' Ruth wrote for Conservative Home in the run-up to the referendum.

It's been a long time since we've been able to make such a claim and have it taken seriously. But, in what is a transformative time in Scottish politics, all the evidence suggests that the ambitions and values of our party and the ambitions and values of people in Scotland are moving in the same direction.

More than 80,000 people, for instance, joined 'Conservative Friends of the Union' – a remarkable number that went well, well beyond the circa 10,000 membership of the party in Scotland. The Friends – despite being a free to subscribe group – also helped raise around £250,000 in small donations for the Better Together campaign. Such was its success that it was touted as a potential model for party membership across the country.

Mark Wallace, writing for Conservative Home, said:

> Focused, issue-based campaigns like the independence referendum are good opportunities to do this kind of work. When such issues are live, various tracts of the electorate become more motivated than normal, and if they find the Conservatives are on the same side as them then that experience can help to overcome mistrust or stereotypes which would otherwise prevent them from ever considering voting Tory.

In 2014, a thousand Tories and Friends of the Union would be herded into the Edinburgh International Conference Centre for the Tories' spring conference. Ruth explained this resurgence of interest – if not yet actual electoral support – explicitly as a revival of traditional Scottish Tory values. '[The surge in support] illustrates how the campaign has energised our cause, reviving long-held principles, and compelling people who have never previously been involved in politics to act in order to defend what we hold dear,' she wrote in a piece for Conservative Home.

All this is good news for Conservatism in Scotland. But more importantly, the campaign has given us the chance to re-engage people who we haven't been connecting to for far, far too long. Conservatives across the country are now making the sensible, serious and progressive case for a strong Scotland in the UK.

Barnstorming attacks on Salmond also helped galvanise many of her supporters. After the First Minister's 2012 SNP conference speech in Perth – where he described the Tory government in Westminster as 'incompetent Lord Snooties' – Ruth accused him of a 'cynical attempt to drive a wedge between the people of Scotland and their nearest neighbours in the UK'. She added: 'It was a performance beneath the office of First Minister and showed a man incapable of taking responsibility for his own actions, never mind being trusted to establish a new nation state.' Such an attack might have been ironic from an Etonian like Cameron, but Ruth was able to deliver it with gusto.

As well as boosting her party, the referendum campaign also brought Ruth closer to her political rivals, particularly Labour's Johann Lamont, who would constantly query why she was a Tory.

* * *

But Ruth's responsibility in the campaign was as much about what she didn't say as what she did. A chief concern for the Better Together campaign was making it too Tory, so Ruth was often left to keep her head down and not put a foot wrong, which she did effectively.

As columnist Tim Montgomerie put it in the run-up to the vote, the SNP would 'try and put the Tories on the ballot paper' during the referendum, in a bid to capitalise on the perceived unpopu-larity of Cameron's party. Salmond, for instance, was desperate to debate the Etonian, English Prime Minister during the campaign, in a bid to frame the debate as Scotland versus the Conservatives. (In the end he had to settle for Alistair Darling – twice.)

Likewise, in more minor debates, the Scottish Tories did not feature either. Of four head-to-head clashes broadcast on STV's *Scotland Tonight*, all would feature Sturgeon versus one of either Labour or the Liberal Democrats.

The strategy of Ruth avoiding taking a lead in the campaign was not only prudent at the time: it would also prove electorally beneficial for the Tories later on. Scottish Labour became the chief face of the anti-independence movement, which was often accused – whether justly or not – of 'talking Scotland down'.

It is notable, though, that it was Labour people who headlined at Tory events and not vice versa. When the dust had settled, it was Miliband's Labour and not so much Cameron's Tories who would feel the wrath of Yes supporters.

Of course, Ruth did not make deep inroads by the 2015 general election, but the fact that Scottish Labour had alienated much of its support in the 2014 referendum would be a pivotal factor in Ruth's triumph in 2016.

*   *   *

Despite not being the most prominent face of the campaign, Ruth was still able to enjoy some major successes, which would ultimately prove crucial to the eventual Better Together victory. One such issue was the EU – particularly, whether or not an independent Scotland would automatically be a member of the bloc. With typical bluster and gusto, Salmond insisted that an independent Scotland would be a member, despite several people speaking to the contrary, including the President of the European Commission and the Prime Minister of Spain. He claimed this position was born out of legal advice he had received, but baulked when it was demanded this advice be published. Catherine Stihler, a Labour MEP, had made a freedom of information request to try to get the advice released. The Scottish government still refused, despite the Information Commissioner ruling that the advice should be released on appeal. With the opposition now scenting blood, the matter was taken all the way to the highest civil court in Scotland. But just as it was about to make its ruling, Nicola Sturgeon – then Salmond's deputy – made a speech in Holyrood in which she admitted that, in fact, there was no advice. It was a major embarrassment for the SNP, particularly given the bid to stop the release of the non-existent advice had cost taxpayers thousands of pounds in legal bills. Support for independence dropped points in the polls as a result.

Ruth skewered the Nationalists over the fiasco, which came just after two of their MSPs had resigned after it was controversially confirmed an independent Scotland would join NATO, overturning the anti-nuclear party's decades-long stance on the issue. 'On Friday it was proved beyond all doubt that the Scottish National Party is a party without principle, voting for a policy that it does not believe in, and today the members of that party with principle voted with their feet and walked out,' Ruth began, referencing the resignations.

However, NATO is not the only international body that is tying the SNP in knots. We found out today that, despite desperate claims of knowing the answers and despite thousands of pounds of taxpayers' money spent in courtrooms to keep information from the Scottish people, the SNP has never taken advice on a separate Scotland's place in the European Union. It does not know whether we would be spending pounds or euros. However, it is worse than that – when I and other party leaders tried to exact the truth, we were shouted down.

Ruth – despite her earlier difficulties in challenging Salmond on the EU – was absolutely in her element, focusing on the themes of competence and evidential government that dominate her political mantra.

The Tory leader taunted Sturgeon with her own words that arguing an independent Scotland would not be an EU member is 'utterly absurd'. 'It is not absurd and the Deputy First Minister does not know. Monetary policy, EU membership – when will she stop trying to hoodwink the public on the big issues?' It was a sterling performance to which Sturgeon could only rather lamely reply that Tories should not go on about 'principle'. The debacle would continue to dog the SNP campaign for independence.

Ruth, however, was one of the few politicians who – initially, at least – stopped short of accusing Salmond of being deliberately misleading over the incident, reflecting, perhaps, her more measured role in the campaign itself. But she would return to the issue again and again throughout the campaign with typical unrelenting style – later unfavourably likening Salmond to famously untruthful US Presidents Richard Nixon and Bill Clinton.

Such tactics, however, did not find favour in all quarters. Andrew Nicoll, writing in *The Sun*, was particularly disobliging. 'The only thing that saved [Salmond] was the clumsiness of the attack, with Tory Ruth Davidson coming close to tasteless abuse in jokes about Richard Nixon and Bill Clinton – jibes that flopped and left the First Minister free to hit back,' he wrote. 'Ruth Davidson was more like Presidential candidate Mitt Romney, [Salmond] said, but Romney only sneered at 47 per cent of the voters and she had dismissed 88 per cent.' Nicoll went on to conclude, however, that the EU membership debacle had left Salmond looking 'dodgy'.

Certainly, the decision by David Cameron to hold the EU referendum – which was announced during the Scottish campaign – somewhat blunted Ruth's attacks. As Salmond said during a January debate in Holyrood: 'It is obvious to any reasonable person now that the uncertainty on Scotland's position in Europe comes from the Conservative Party, led by the nose by Eurosceptics and the compromises that David Cameron has had to make to hold on to his job.'

The SNP's debacle over EU membership, however, was just one in a number of incidents that left the pro-independence case looking shoddy at best. Ruth's attacks helped reinforce the image that, contrary to their public statements, the Yes campaign actually had little idea what an independent Scotland would look like. While the issue of EU membership – let alone NATO membership – might have seemed like a niche issue for voters in 2014, Ruth and the wider Better Together campaign tied it in to a coherent narrative of incoherence among the Nationalists. There is nothing voters – and indeed businesses – like less than uncertainty. Ruth was adept in showing that the case for independence was uncertain in spades.

*   *   *

The referendum campaign effectively began when Salmond and Cameron signed the Edinburgh Agreement, allowing for two years of debate. The key issues, however, were already known and discussed. Currency, economic strength and defence – as well as EU membership – were the main battlegrounds of the campaign.

Better Together's focus on economic factors led to accusations that the pro-Union side was relying on 'Project Fear' to win votes. As we have seen, this mantra largely came about because of Labour and Liberal Democrat attitudes towards the Union. They did not make a nationalist case for the UK, but an economic one.

Many Tories – including *The Spectator*'s Fraser Nelson – were critical of the strategy. He wrote: 'This argument was poison: strong enough to damage the enemy and (just) win the referendum. But it made the case for the Union seem appallingly weak, and based on scaremongering.'

There is something of a consensus among Scottish Conservative staffers – and beyond – that the doomsday tactics not only worked but also were accurate. The collapse of the oil price in particular would have delivered a devastating blow to the already precarious finances of a would-be independent Scotland. But it was Labour's Alistair Darling, as head of the Better Together campaign, who was chiefly responsible for delivering the economic arguments that most resonated with voters. On the question of currency, for instance, it was the former Chancellor who repeatedly landed the body blows. 'The people of Scotland are entitled to know what is the position going to be if we were to vote for independence,' Darling said in his matter-of-fact tone, which sharply contrasted with Ruth's more rhetorical arguments.

You cannot assume that the rest of the UK will simply fall into line with what Alex Salmond wants. If we don't get that currency union, what is the alternative? What's Plan B?

Now, he has a Plan B, because no one but a fool would go into a negotiation if they hadn't got a Plan B. So let us hear it. We want to hear it in this White Paper because if we don't hear it then absolutely nothing he says will have any credibility whatsoever.

It was this argument that would ultimately win the day for the Union, but Ruth nevertheless deserves credit for galvanising supporters in her party throughout the campaign.

* * *

But in the weeks leading up to the vote there was a growing sense that the Yes campaign might just edge it. A poll for the *Sunday Times* immediately before the ballot had even put Salmond's campaign ahead. As the vote neared, the momentum had definitely shifted away from the Unionists and to the separatists.

Yet party sources have suggested Ruth remained unflappable and certain of the cause throughout. Even as others became increasingly concerned – most notably Scottish Liberal Democrat leader Willie Rennie – Ruth remained convinced of the basic soundness of the Better Together arguments. The patriotic case for the UK – mixed with the cold, hard facts of the economic reality of an independent Scotland – might not have had the glamour of the Yes campaign, but that suited the Tory leader's style just fine.

She, however, was the exception rather than rule, as a score of grandees became increasingly panicked as the vote neared.

The Yes campaign was perceived to be gaining ground on Better Together, leading to an increasingly popular view in the No camp that something radical had to be done. The nuclear option was eventually undertaken by Cameron, Clegg and Miliband, on the front page of the *Daily Record*.

The Vow, as it would infamously become known, was a pledge from all leaders to provide further devolution of powers in the event of a No vote and regardless of who won the election the following year. It was in many ways a cynical attempt to offer voters the best of both worlds: greater powers within the cushion of the UK. The extent to which it influenced the campaign is debatable and, while symbolically significant, it is unlikely to have changed the minds of many voters. Some Yes supporters, however, were naturally angry at what was perceived as a last-minute bribe by the Unionists.

The front-page vow itself contained little detail on what would actually be devolved, or when. As Joe Pike revealed in his book *Project Fear*, the pledge was designed in a largely cack-handed manner. The Chancellor, George Osborne, was ambushed on screen by Andrew Marr in the run-up to the vote. The TV presenter was wielding an *Observer* front page that suggested more powers were on the way if Scotland voted No. Osborne stood the story up, leading to a last-minute scramble to pull together some kind of post-referendum devolution deal.

From Better Together's point of view – with the campaign increasingly distraught at the prospect of defeat – it was probably a success, at least in the short term. But Ruth was – in the words of one senior party insider – 'fucking furious' with Cameron over The Vow. While she had been consulted over the pledge, she was strongly opposed. The Scottish Tory leader – rightly – argued that

The Vow would play right into the Nationalist narrative. SNP leaders would be able to suggest that they did not lose on the question of independence, but rather the vote was one about more powers.

Ironically, Cameron himself had recognised this danger as far back as 2012, in his negotiations with Salmond leading to the Edinburgh Agreement. The then Prime Minister had defeated the SNP leader in his demand for there to be two questions on the ballot paper – one on independence and another on devolution. Unionists felt it was important the contest be a binary one, until it looked like they might lose. One senior insider, who was with Ruth when The Vow was being discussed, said:

> It was the only time she got angry during the campaign. She felt that this would allow the SNP narrative to get going again. So rather than us voting on independence, what we had was a scenario where the Nats would be able to turn round immediately and say we were offered this bribe of new powers and now it is not going to be delivered and x, y and z. She was very angry about that. There were some interesting scenes in the Better Together office.

When Downing Street raised the prospect of The Vow, Ruth asked them to play it down, if they had to do it at all. 'We were consulted on it,' the insider said.

> But we felt very strongly that it was not necessary and that we should not make it a big thing. Genuinely, we felt it would let the Nats off the hook. Unfortunately, that is exactly what happened, and it allowed this SNP narrative to get going within hours of the result.

There was, of course, little in The Vow that every major party had not promised previously. As a document – there was no actual physical specimen, just a newspaper front page – its commitments were suitably vague so as to allow all parties to accommodate their various pre-referendum devolution pledges.

As we have seen, one of Ruth's key reforms was her embrace of the Strathclyde Commission, which she not only set up but had wholeheartedly endorsed but a year before the referendum vote. It is therefore noteworthy that she was so angry about a commitment to follow through on devolution. As an organised and determined campaigner, her anger would have in part stemmed from the panicked way in which the commitment was produced. Undoubtedly, the timing of The Vow was poor, allowing it to be easily dismissed as both desperate and cynical. It may have helped the No campaign in the final stages, though research suggests there is no evidence to support this theory. On the contrary, Ruth was probably right in her view that it was an unnecessary move. The Tory leader was also correct in her assumption that it would allow the Nationalists a get-out clause in the event – to her mind, inevitable – that they lost the referendum.

Away from the tactics of the campaign, however, Ruth's view of The Vow reveals her concerns about devolution. While she had embraced the Strathclyde Commission, she had begun her public career in politics as a committed anti-devolutionist, which may suggest that her backing the Strathclyde Commission was as much about securing her leadership of the party as it was a change of heart on her part. Supporting some form of extra devolution was also a political necessity in the run-up to the referendum and, while Ruth publicly supported it, she clearly had reservations in private. Many of the Conservative Party's membership in

Scotland – not to mention the rest of the UK – also continued to have deep-seated reservations about devolution, and Ruth may have been reflecting these views. It was after all just over a decade after the creation of the Scottish Parliament that voters returned a pro-independence majority at Holyrood that could threaten the future of the UK with a referendum. In that context, the appetite for giving Holyrood more powers, among dyed-in-the-wool Tories at least, would have been low.

* * *

On 18 September 2014, 55 per cent of Scots voted to remain part of the UK. There was a palpable sense of relief as the results flowed in. At the close the silent majority had come out for the No campaign.

The mood at the Better Together election party in Glasgow's Marriot Hotel was increasingly jubilant. Fuelled by excessive amounts of wine, it bore some resemblance to the last days of Rome. Ruth, however, remained extremely calm throughout the night, according to her director of strategy, Eddie Barnes. 'I don't think she had a moment's wobble, really, about the whole thing,' he said.

> There was no kind of whooping for joy, it was just relief. But one of the things she was worried about was all the booze that was in the room and her view very much was, we should get this cleared up because it looks bad. She was focusing, as always, about the practicalities.

Despite her prudishness, for Ruth, it was a crucial victory. Not only was it a cause close to her heart, it had also helped galvanise her ailing Scottish base. The mantra of patriotism for both Scotland and the Union was part of the political discourse once again. The Scottish Conservatives had returned home.

More practically, the Conservatives had made a prominent commitment to further devolution, despite Ruth's anger. Crucially, her views on The Vow would remain private. In public, she continued to support the idea of greater devolution to Scotland – at least until more powers were delivered. Such a dichotomy between the public and private views of a politician is perhaps not uncommon, but it shows how politically expedient Ruth is willing to be. In this instance, she was forced to shelve her private views in favour of protecting both her own leadership and the success of the Better Together campaign.

Of course, such pragmatism was not without its benefits. Many of the powers that would be devolved coincided with Ruth's Strathclyde Commission recommendations, adding further weight to the Scottish Tories' return to the ideas of 1955. Coming in the aftermath of Ruth's referendum campaign, which had helped reignite the ideas of patriotic Unionism, the new devolution settlement helped shake the stubborn mantle that the Tories north of the border were 'anti-Scottish'.

More practically still, Salmond – defeated and deflated – was now gone from office, soon to be replaced as First Minister by Sturgeon.

In the immediate aftermath of the vote, however, there were also difficulties already coming to the fore for the Tory leader. While many were nursing sore heads in Glasgow, David Cameron spoke outside Downing Street to hail the result. It was a speech that went down badly, both with Better Together and with Ruth herself. The Prime Minister used the occasion to announce greater devolution – a process, he said, that would include so-called English votes for English laws, or EVEL.

The policy was logical – it had in fact been supported by the SNP for many years, until an about-turn when the Tories announced they now supported it – but it was clear this was not the time to raise it. One Scottish Tory insider said it was a 'pity' the policy was announced at 10 a.m. after the referendum result, when instead Cameron should have given a speech that was 'all about the United Kingdom and not about England, or Scotland'. Ruth herself would admit in an interview with Politics.co.uk that Cameron 'from a Scottish perspective ... could have timed it better'.

EVEL would continue to cause problems over the next year, strengthening the SNP's post-referendum narrative. 'There is no question that the great disrespect shown to Scotland in these proposals is likely to have more people asking whether Westminster is capable of representing Scotland's interests at all,' Nicola Sturgeon would say in 2015. Indeed, the SNP would go on to suggest the lack of progress caused by tying Scottish devolution to EVEL could trigger a second referendum (it did not), while Labour were equally scathing about the 'betrayal' by the Conservatives.

Of course, these points of constitutional mechanics may have resonated little with voters. But it provided a classic example of the Nationalist ability to weave an anti-Westminster narrative. Taken alone, such small points may seem of little consequence, but when viewed as a whole, they would have an increasing impact on post-referendum Scottish politics. Indeed, it is striking that the Conservative Party – and particularly Cameron – once again managed, either by accident or by design, to so casually misread the Scottish political mood. Ruth herself, while recognising the dangers of the SNP narrative, was unwilling – at least publicly – to distance herself from Cameron's plans for EVEL. The result was the SNP's narrative on the issue was strengthened.

*   *   *

Just days after the 2014 referendum, Ruth took to the stage for the party's national conference in Birmingham. Her speech was full of relief, but also hope for the future. 'The Nationalists have been telling anyone who would listen for years, that if people looked – really examined – our United Kingdom, they would see a country born of history that should be returned to history,' she told the enthusiastic Tory crowd.

A Britain in decline that oppresses the very people who make it up. An anachronism on Europe's northern shores, still dreaming of a globe painted pink and a place where that which divides us is greater than anything we have in common. We were told if people just opened their eyes, they would see a nation state with its best days behind it; a product past its sell-by date, a sinking ship with independence the only lifeboat.

Well, we did look. We did examine. Scotland as a country embraced the political arguments of this campaign like no other. Propositions were tested, conjectures dissected, claims analysed and questions of identity – both national and personal – weighed and measured.

Never in modern British history has any democratic event seen such levels of participation. And when all the ballots were cast, all the votes were counted – the result was clear.

In many ways, the speech was an extended version of her referendum campaign stump. Yet Ruth also recognised the profound need to make a new case for Unionism. As she would point out in the same speech, 1.6 million Scots had backed independence in the belief that they would be better off going it alone. Such sentiments were a tacit acceptance that, while her pro-UK referendum arguments had resonated with Tories, they had little impact among other Scots.

Indeed, Ruth accepted that while the 'Project Fear' narrative of pure economics had won the 2014 campaign, it would not be enough to save the Union indefinitely. 'This referendum sent a tremor through the fabric of this nation and the echoes of that tremor will last a lifetime,' she said, presciently. 'We have to address the fact that – Yes or No – people in Scotland want change. The status quo is smashed, there's no going back, and the old rules do not apply. And that is a challenge. But it is an opportunity too.'

In the weeks, months and years that followed the vote, she would be proved right on both counts.

CHAPTER 10

THE UNIONISTS?

A t 2.42 p.m. on 20 November 2014, Ruth stood to be elected as the First Minister of Scotland.

The tried-and-tested tactic was doomed to fail, of course. Nicola Sturgeon, running to replace the newly resigned Alex Salmond and backed by the SNP majority, was certain of victory. Yet Ruth, with characteristic pluckiness and defiance, pressed ahead anyway. Addressing her fellow MSPs, who formally elect the First Minister, she made an impassioned case for the Union. 'One issue has dominated the political landscape for the entirety of this session of Parliament, and the Deputy First Minister, who is seeking to ascend one rung, finds herself on the opposite side of the issue from the majority of people in this country,' she said.

> So today, I offer an alternative, as someone who wants Scotland to prosper as part of our United Kingdom, not outside it, and as a member of this Parliament who wants it to work better, using the powers that it has to improve public life in

Scotland, and the powers that are coming to limit the financial burden on families across our country.

It was a bold and buoyant contribution, which reflected Ruth's growing stature and confidence in both Holyrood and the wider country.

Indeed, the jest and good humour with which she took her inevitable defeat and Sturgeon's victory is further evidence of this. As David Torrance notes, Ruth's performance was 'infused … with the humour required for such a quixotic bid'.

'After a hard-fought contest for the position of First Minister, in the end my opponent just shaded it. I promise that I will not demand a recount,' she told cheery MSPs, before joking that Margaret Thatcher, Britain's first female Prime Minister, was a 'personal role model' for Sturgeon, the first female First Minister.

The political situation across the country, however, was more serious for Ruth than the jovial scenes in the chamber might suggest. The referendum had been won and Salmond was gone – but there was little else to celebrate.

Far from being crushed by their defeat, the Nationalists grew in strength. Sturgeon – full of charm and charisma and defiance – was largely responsible for this. But the surge in support for the SNP, which was rapidly becoming apparent across the country, was also a result of regret and disappointment at the No vote at the referendum. In the months that followed the vote, membership of Sturgeon's party would rise to over 100,000, making it the third biggest party in the whole of the UK – despite Scotland representing only about a tenth of the population. The SNP would describe the rise as the 'incredible legacy of democratic engagement from the referendum', but for other parties it was more ominous.

The general election, set for May 2015, just months after the No vote, would be Ruth's first major electoral test as leader. Of course, as leader of the Scottish Conservatives, she had less to lose than the Labour Party. The Tories had just one seat north of the border – the Borders stronghold of David Mundell – compared to Labour's forty-one and the Liberal Democrats' eleven. Yet, following five years of coalition government and polls predicting a second hung parliament, it was thought Ruth's ability to win seats in Scotland could prove decisive. Ruth and the Tories had a fight on their hands – and Scotland would prove key.

*   *   *

In the 2015 campaign, Ruth came into her own. Projected onto the national political scene, she became known outside Scotland to many people for the first time. Her bonhomie in the face of seemingly insurmountable odds added to her reputation as a political character.

In contrast to Labour's anguish amid polls suggesting the SNP would whitewash the election in Scotland, Ruth maintained a buoyant visage, with the famous image of her riding on a tank perhaps the best example of this trait. 'I don't know what threats our country, our region, the world, is going to face over the next thirty years and I don't think Nicola Sturgeon does either,' Ruth said, astride a turret, surrounded by journalists and photographers. 'That's why I think we should listen to the defence chiefs who are writing publicly today about how this is a cornerstone of our defence here in the UK.'

The image would become one of the archetypal pictures of the campaign in Scotland and beyond. Yet it also had a deeper meaning. While Ruth would persistently insist Thatcher was, by 2015, a political irrelevance in Scotland, the similarities were clear. The Iron Lady had herself been pictured riding a tank in West Germany in 1987 – a photo opportunity to deliver much the same message about the importance of national defence. While the chiffon scarf and '80s trench coat had disappeared – Ruth was wearing a Barbour jacket and wellies – the symbolism was equally striking.

Ruth was even described as 'Scotland's Iron Lady' – a moniker, *The Independent* dryly pointed out, she could probably do without. But there was some truth to it. Thatcher, with her commitment to neoliberalism, had reinvigorated a Tory Party, in England at least, still reeling from the loss of empire. The Prime Minister had given the Conservatives a purpose again. Ruth, while politically quite different from Thatcher, was embarking on a similar project to reinvent, if not realign, the Scottish Conservatives. The building block for this revival would, unsurprisingly, be Unionism.

Other appearances were equally colourful, if less Thatcherite. Ruth, for instance, chose to push her party's pensions policy at a run-down and near-deserted Mecca Bingo, where she even tried her hand at calling the numbers. She was photographed holding a fish, playing the bagpipes and driving a steam train. As Joe Pike points out in *Project Fear*, it was a way 'to promote a fun, positive message for her party as their vote came under pressure'. Of course, as any spin doctor worth his salt knows (and Ruth has good ones), people remember far more of what they see than what they hear. If you create a good image, not only can you get to the top of the news agenda, but you can also stick in voters' minds.

Yet, while Ruth's photo calls helped boost her profile, it was her performance in TV debates in the run-up to the election that were the key component of her campaign. The Tory leader's performances – in contrast to her struggles just a few years before in the Holyrood chamber – were widely well received, even by her opponents. Scots, polled by Lord Ashcroft, believed she appeared more trustworthy and honest than embattled Labour leader Jim Murphy – even though most had no intention of voting for either. '[Ruth] was excellent – genuine and conducts herself well. But I could never vote for her policies,' said one of those polled, according to *The Independent*.

Ross Clark, writing in *The Spectator*'s Coffee House blog, was full of praise. 'It takes something to stand before a Scottish audience, where the Tory brand isn't just toxic but radioactive, and earn applause for making the case to reintroduce prescription charges,' he wrote after one of Ruth's performances. In the Scottish Tory leader, he added presciently, the party has a 'potential star'.

Of course, Sturgeon would fire onto the national stage with a commanding performance against national party leaders, prompting famous Google searches of 'Can I vote SNP in England?' Her shooting down of UKIP leader Nigel Farage in one session was generally viewed as a key point in an otherwise quite drab national campaign, while her assertions about 'ending austerity' also proved popular.

Yet there is little doubt that Ruth did more than hold her own against the First Minister in the debates north of the border. Her commanding performance even led Cameron – interviewed on the BBC's *Woman's Hour* – to hint he thought she could lead the party across the country. 'Well, indeed. I don't put a limit on her ambition, I think she is extremely effective,' the Prime Minister said, when asked whether he saw her as a potential successor.

Ruth, of course, threw cold water on the suggestion – but her similarly robust statements in the past have proved malleable with time. 'There's not a vacancy and certainly not one that I'm interested in,' she said when asked about Cameron's comments.

> I think leading any national UK party is possibly one of the loneliest jobs around. I'm quite happy where I am. I have plenty of things I want to accomplish both in and out of public life, but I have to say leading the Conservative Party has never been one of them.

Nevertheless, it is a mark of how far Ruth's star had risen during the referendum campaign and beyond into the general election that she even had to deny it.

Much of the Conservative Party strategy in the run-up to the election was based around attempts to build Ruth's profile north of the border. It was thought her middle-class, 'ordinary' background would help dispel assumptions about Tories in Scotland. This was most prominent in her party election broadcast in February 2015, which would receive widespread attention – and be mostly remembered – for featuring Ruth with her partner, Jen Wilson, for the first time.

The Tory leader had previously been relatively protective of her partner's private life, with party press officers only confirming her age. But in the slick video, Ruth is pictured first at home with her parents, before being seen walking and drinking in a pub with Jen. At the close, Ruth, Jen and Ruth's parents take a selfie amid the backdrop of a setting sun.

While the imagery – drinking instant coffee, for example, while chatting away with her mum – was designed to give a sense of normality, Ruth's language provides a clear insight into her political style and appeal. 'All through school and university, I always had jobs washing dishes and waiting tables,' she said in a voiceover accompanying the clip, entitled 'Join the Conservative Family'. 'I went to my local school in Buckhaven and we were never particularly near the top of the league table. We were always pretty close to the bottom when it came to exams.'

She adds, with a cheery smile:

There's a myth that the Conservatives are just about the people who have already made it in life. We're not – we're about people who want to make it in life, who want to get on, let their children have a better quality of life than they had. And there is nothing more natural in the world than that.

The overt symbolism of Ruth – with her partner – was designed to back up the assertion that the Scottish Conservatives were not the draconian, socially conservative, anti-progressive party people might think. It was a clear break from the days of Thatcher and Section 28 – which Ruth had so vehemently opposed. But it was also, through that image, an implicit attempt to break other stereotypes of the Tories in Scotland post-Thatcher. The Conservatives, Ruth wanted to tell voters, were no longer the party in favour of privatisation, welfare cut-backs and the poll tax.

The presence of Ruth's parents, Doug and Liz, is also noteworthy. The pair, who grew up in deprived areas of Glasgow, are pictured in their own home, enjoying a tranquil middle-class existence that would have seemed out of reach when they were growing up. The imagery was subtle, of course, but it played into

Ruth's key message – that the Tories are a party for people who 'want to make it in life'.

Unconsciously, the picture of a happy family also reinforced a message of togetherness. In the aftermath of the divisions of the referendum campaign, here was a diverse group of people pulling together through their familial ties. They were diverse, but they worked together.

Such themes would increasingly run through her 2015 election campaign. In one prominent campaign advert, Ruth said: 'I'm voting for a break for low-paid workers. I'm voting for schools that end inequality. I'm voting for more nurses in our hospitals. I'm voting for a local police force. I'm voting for a fairer Scotland. We've got more in common than you think.'

There was scant detail behind the rhetoric, which rather jarred with an election campaign south of the border that was largely focused on cutting the deficit and controlling public spending. Of course, she was not running for a seat herself and had only a passing say on UK government policy. For Ruth therefore, the 2015 general election was more about setting out her stall for future contests. The work of the campaign was about setting out the narrative – namely that the Tories were no longer toxic and were avidly pro-Union.

And such messages were well-received by much of the press in Scotland and beyond. Rachel Cunliffe, writing for CapX, said: 'Ruth Davidson is a leader who calls into question what the average voter thinks they know about the Conservative Party.' She added: 'With her state school education, working class background and time in the Territorial Army, [Ruth] can argue for school choice, hard work and personal responsibility without sounding disingenuous and condescending.'

Despite her successes though, the outlook for Ruth's Tories – like other non-SNP parties in Scotland – was bleak. Polls were persistently showing massive support for the SNP across the country, predicting an almost clean sweep of Scottish seats for the Nationalists.

And Ruth was not without her own – albeit minor – slip-ups, suggesting at the launch of her party's campaign in Edinburgh at the end of March that a Tory majority 'didn't look likely'. While this was a break from the traditional political tactic of talking up your chances during the campaign, however, it was perhaps not the 'hand grenade' described in the *Daily Record*.

Speaking on the campaign trail, she remained upbeat about her own party's chances, suggesting they would increase their vote on 2010, even if she tempered expectations somewhat:

> But in some ways I can work as hard as I can, my candidates can work as hard as they can, they can put out all the positive messages, but how those votes break down into seats is very much in the lap of the electorate, not in the lap of the campaign organisers.

Then Scottish Labour leader Jim Murphy suggested the SNP surge would ensure Cameron won the election. 'There is no gloss that can be put on these polls. This is bad news for Scottish Labour but great news for the Tories,' he said. 'David Cameron will be rubbing his hands with glee when he sees these polls, because any seat the SNP take from Scottish Labour makes it more likely the Tories will be the largest party across the UK.'

Far from winning fresh seats in Scotland, however, it was clear Ruth faced a struggle merely to cling on to the one seat they already had. Mundell had a solid, but not insurmountable, majority of just over 4,000 – a bedrock that could easily be wiped out in the SNP surge. Ruth herself – prudently, it turned out – declined to predict how many seats her party would win, telling the BBC's Andrew Neil that the 'scars of 2010' – when the party had predicted returning twelve MPs only to be rewarded a solitary one – were still being felt.

Behind the scenes, party strategists hoped they might be able to clinch traditional Tory heartland seats from the Liberal Democrats, such as Aberdeenshire West and Kincardine, and Berwickshire in the Borders. Eddie Barnes, Ruth's director of strategy, said it took the Scottish Conservatives some time to realise the full scale of the coming SNP surge.

> There was an STV poll that had the SNP on about 50 per cent and we all thought – bollocks.
>
> But as the campaign went on there was a growing realisation – from about January onwards – that something was happening. I spoke with a number of Tory grandees and told them that the SNP could get more than twenty seats – and they said, 'Don't be ridiculous, you're talking nonsense, the Westminster election cycle will revert, people will realise they're electing a Westminster government and they know the SNP is powerless.'
>
> But then we got into April and we were out campaigning, and people were saying it was a maelstrom – a tornado. At that point we realised it was about survival, totally about survival.

Barnes said that the Tory campaign had to quickly revert from targeting new seats – in places like the north-east and Borders – to saving Mundell.

We had three seats in play – realistically – which were David's seat, John Lamont's seat [Berwickshire, Roxburgh and Selkirk], and West Aberdeenshire and Kincardine.

It became clear that Aberdeenshire was going to be out of reach from a couple of weeks out. At that stage, we were thinking, if we can hold on, that's a good result.

Despite focusing their campaign on the Borders – Mundell and Lamont were fighting neighbouring seats – it was thought the incumbent might have been defeated and the new candidate elected.

'It looked like it was David's seat that was going to go and that John would win,' Barnes said. 'David was increasingly of the view that he had lost in the run-in.'

But while the Tories electorally faced an increasing struggle to survive in Scotland, political developments north of the border would still play a crucial role in the campaign. With polls across the country tight – suggesting another hung parliament – the press was rife with speculation about the make-up of future coalitions. Ruth was scathing about her party's former partners, the Liberal Democrats, whom she branded 'headless chickens still running around the chicken coop, not a brain cell in sight, and about to get stuffed'.

But it was fear of a Labour–SNP deal that proved the most potent – and damaging – coalition prospect during the campaign. South of the border, the Conservative Party – under the direction of election supremo Lynton Crosby – ran advertisements featuring Labour leader Ed Miliband in Alex Salmond's top pocket. The message was clear – vote Labour and you could end with the SNP, if not in No. 10 then very possibly in No. 11.

Concerns about Miliband's alleged weaknesses – and his initial refusal to rule out such a deal – left English voters spooked. Ruth herself would suggest: 'The election may be another three months off and yet Nicola Sturgeon and Ed Miliband are already halfway down the aisle.' A Nationalist–Labour pact, Ruth claimed, would see 'the SNP pulling the strings'.

In an interview with BBC's *Good Morning Scotland*, she was even more frank. 'Ed Miliband is weak. He's a weak leader that can't control his own party,' she said. 'The idea of Ed Miliband as Prime Minister with, I don't know, Stewart Hosie [then SNP deputy leader], Alex Salmond, as Deputy Prime Minister scares the bejesus out of me. I don't think Ed Miliband would stand up to the concessions that Alex Salmond would wring from him.'

Cameron was equally forthright in his promotion of this scare tactic, saying:

If you want to avoid a Labour government propped up by the SNP – which is not just a possible outcome, but frankly a very possible outcome because Labour can't cross the line on their own – if you want to avoid that because, like me, you worry about having the government being held to ransom by a bunch of people that don't want our country to succeed, indeed they don't want our country to exist, then the answer is to vote Conservative.

These arguments even became something of a manifesto pledge – albeit an implicit one – for the Tories north of the border. 'We have tackled the problems we inherited,' their 2015 manifesto stated. 'We held the referendum on Scottish independence. It was the right thing to do, and the question of Scotland's place in the United Kingdom is now settled.'

Of course, the strategy had another, potentially more damaging, effect. As well as scaring English voters, talking up the prospect of a Labour–SNP coalition government allowed Scots to vote for the Nationalists without feeling they risked letting the Tories back into government. Hoping for a coalition administration, left-leaning Scots could vote for the SNP rather than Labour, but still aim to rout Cameron. This, of course, served the Tory cause in England well, because without Scotland's Labour MPs, the prospect of Miliband actually winning the election would be nearly – if not totally – impossible. Scottish politics, then, would be crucial in providing Cameron with the seats for his majority – just not by electing anyone north of the border.

Despite its effectiveness, the strategy caused bitter resentment among many, leading to accusations that the Tories were willing to create a crisis in the Union just to win the election. Alex Massie, writing in *The Spectator*, branded the Salmond–Miliband poster 'stupid', adding it was 'increasingly evident … that no one at Conservative Campaign Headquarters really cares that much about the Union'.

Tory grandee Michael Forsyth was even more scathing. In an interview with *The Guardian*'s Nicholas Watt, he described the Conservative election campaign as 'short-term and dangerous'. The former Secretary of State for Scotland warned: 'The Tories are entering into a dangerous, destructive embrace of the Nationalists, which is bad for Scotland, it is bad for the UK … This will end up with the destruction of the UK.' He added:

> We've had the dilemma for Conservatives, which is they want to be the largest party at Westminster and therefore some see the fact that the Nationalists are going to take seats in

Scotland will be helpful. But that is a short-term and danger-ous view which threatens the integrity of our country.

Others supported the tactic, with Iain Martin, writing for the *Daily Telegraph*, suggesting it was 'one of the most powerful weapons' the Tory campaign had.

Certainly, it forced Labour into a change of strategy, with Miliband being forced to rule out a deal. He told *The Guardian*:

The SNP are not going to have leverage in a government led by me. If it took coalition with the SNP to have a Labour government, there is not going to be a Labour government. I could not be clearer than that. My Queen's speech will not be shaped in any way with the SNP in mind.

The SNP, for their part, were keen to play up talk of a pact. 'After the election, every Westminster politician will have to come and face the reality of the electorate's judgement,' former party leader Alex Salmond told Radio 4's *Today* programme in April 2015.

There is no disrespect or disgrace in any politician coming to terms with the democratically expressed position of the electorate.

All politicians, those of us who are lucky enough to be elected, chosen by the people, will try to do their best as they see it in the interests of the people who elected them.

Sturgeon – the current party leader – was positively dismissive when Miliband ruled out an SNP coalition. 'I'm just facing up to reality. A minority government can't govern without support from other parties. Either Ed Miliband will accept that or he won't,' she said. At a rally in Inverness, she tried to argue – in a move that Jim Murphy said made him want to laugh – that Miliband was not progressive for ruling out a pact with the SNP. 'No one who is truly committed to delivering progressive politics would contemplate for one minute ushering the Tories back into office, rather than work with the SNP,' she said.

Of course, SNP strategists were playing the same game as the Tories. By talking up the prospect of a coalition, they encouraged people to vote for them over Labour, while retaining the prospect of getting Cameron out of No. 10.

In the end, as we know, a coalition would not be needed. But there is little doubt that the prospect of a Labour–SNP coalition played heavily on voters' minds and influenced the outcome of the election, both in Scotland and the rest of the UK.

Ruth faced tactical voting problems of her own. With an SNP victory looking increasingly likely, Tory strategists became deeply concerned that their traditional voters might 'hold their noses' and vote Labour in a bid to block out the nationalists. Such was the fear in the Conservatives' Edinburgh headquarters of this occurrence, Ruth took the bold step of directly warning her supporters off trying such tactics. In a letter to 100,000 supporters, she warned against such a move in bold language, playing on the fear of a second referendum and independence. 'Last year I fought to keep our country together. This year I'm fighting for that too,' she wrote. 'So this year – like last year – I'm asking for your support. I'm asking you to vote for the only party which can keep us on the right track, that's the Scottish Conservative and Unionist Party.'

Members believed this was a prudent move, with one telling the *Daily Telegraph*:

She's right to firm up some spines and we should do all we can in that regard ... Quite a lot of our traditional supporters are considering what to do in the election. They don't like the idea of voting Labour but they might hold their noses and do it to stop the Nats.

Though he added: 'But asking Tories to vote Tory does smack a little of desperation.'

Ruth's only MP, David Mundell, also joined in the efforts to dissuade people from voting tactically. 'Clearly, there is a basis for support for the Conservatives in Scotland,' he told *Holyrood* magazine during the campaign. 'It doesn't matter if you're in the most unwinnable seat in Scotland, it's important that you register that vote and demonstrate the body of people who don't support a left-wing consensus with two parties who are trying to out-left each other.'

In the end, however, tactical voting was the least of the Tories' worries; by the end of the campaign, they were in no state to be challenging for seats in most areas of the country. But there was no doubt the election would be dramatic and unpredictable in Scotland. As Mundell put it: 'It really will be a tsunami, and I have to be on high enough ground. There are many Labour and Lib Dem MPs who are on the beach.'

Ruth was in BBC Scotland's election studio when the exit poll was released. Sandwiched between Scottish Labour's then deputy leader Kezia Dugdale and Scottish Liberal Democrat leader Willie Rennie, it was clear it was going to be a long night. Pollsters were – fairly accurately, it turned out – predicting the SNP would win fifty-eight of Scotland's fifty-nine constituencies. Secret Tory hopes of grabbing two more seats quickly evaporated, replaced with anguish over Mundell's result. It would be Labour and the Liberal Democrats who would suffer most in Scotland, but it was still a torrid night for Ruth, who is personal friends with Mundell, one of her key and early backers.

The Tory MP – in any usual election – should have been on solid ground. His majority was 4,194 – a significant increase from 2005 – and there was no clear challenger. The SNP came fourth in the traditionally pro-Unionist seat in 2010. Mundell had also forked out significant sums in his bid to hold his seat. His spend of more than £46,000 was the highest of any candidate in Scotland. Yet as the night wore on, Ruth became increasingly panicked he could lose.

Lurching between the BBC TV studio and her hotel across Glasgow's Pacific Quay, Ruth received box-by-box updates from Mundell's team at the count. Still, despite her worries, she maintained upbeat publicly. On learning of the result of the exit poll, she dryly remarked: 'I remember 1992. Exit polls can get it pretty badly wrong. I'm going to wait until 3 a.m. or 4 a.m. before I start making predictions.'

In the end – despite prophecies, including his own, to the contrary – Mundell would just hold on, winning a majority of 798. His relief after the count was palpable, even if he continued to tout campaign sound bites. 'I think it is quite clear in this constituency people did want an MP who represented their views in relation to the future of our United Kingdom and I do think the economy did play an important part as well,' he said. 'I think people wanted the stability that a Conservative or Conservative-led government would bring.' The Tories had avoided replicating their 1997 wipe-out, but only just.

Mundell, previously a junior minister, would go on to be

appointed Secretary of State for Scotland. With just one MP north of the border but an overall Conservative majority at Westminster, he was the only candidate.

But Eddie Barnes said there was widespread relief that the Tories had not gone backwards in the general election: 'To just cling on in the face of all that left us pleased. The nightmare scenario – in the current climate – would be to have a Conservative government at Westminster and no Conservative MPs in Scotland.'

As the scale of the SNP victory became apparent – they would win fifty-six of Scotland's fifty-nine seats – Ruth, unsurprisingly if somewhat lamely, defended her party's performance. While it was Labour and the Liberal Democrats who bore the brunt of the SNP tsunami, the Tory vote share also fell. 'We know that between a fifth and a quarter of our natural supporters voted tactically in what was one of the strangest, I think most overwhelming elections we've ever seen north of the border,' she said. 'It was an absolute tsunami.'

Yet it was in many ways a tidal wave created by the Tories. There is no doubt that cynically talking up the prospects of a Labour–SNP deal both encouraged votes for the Nationalists in Scotland and hurt Labour in England. It was a dangerous, short-term strategy from a party that is supposed to have the Union at its core. And yet similar – if not the very same – tactics would become the template for Ruth's Holyrood surge the very next year.

In the immediate aftermath of the result, she was unusually taciturn in her analysis, perhaps reflecting that she never thought her party's tactics would prove quite so effective. 'This [an SNP victory] would clearly put stresses and strains on the United

Kingdom unlike the stresses and strains that we have previously seen, however, the Union has been put under strain before and has endured,' she said on election night.

Asked later on *Newsnight* if the result was the 'death of Unionism in Scotland', she was more robust, saying: 'I don't think so – we had a big conversation, we had a referendum, we had our say and it was a clear decision in terms of staying part of the United Kingdom.' Such rhetoric would come to form the backbone of Ruth and the Scottish Conservatives' response to the general election result north of the border.

Despite arguably employing tactics that encouraged the SNP victory, the Tories would argue they were still the only party that could protect the Union. Ruth's speech at her party conference later that year would tacitly hint at this idea, talking up the SNP threat her party had helped create, while reiterating support for the Union. Acknowledging that the election result had emboldened the SNP on independence, she said:

It's worth remembering, Conference, that last year if just 200,000 people had changed their votes, our country would now be suing for divorce. The United Kingdom would have ceased to be. We must never come so close again.

The SNP are already calling for a re-run and the storm has not passed. But our future as a family of nations within a nation state can be better secured. We can rise to the challenge of nationalism by building a stronger and more flexible union ... A practical plan for the Union delivered by the party of the Union.

Continuing the theme, Ruth threw down the marker for her strategy for the Holyrood election the following year. 'As the

RUTH DAVIDSON

head of our campaign, I have made it clear to my team that I want to target the regional list vote next year,' she said.

And for so long as the SNP refuses to rule out another referendum, our message for voters looking to cast that second vote is clear. Whichever party you support, use that vote intelligently. And if you're one of the two million people who voted No in last year's referendum, use it as your intelligent vote for the Union. And be assured of this – every cross in the Scottish Conservative box is a vote backing Britain and defending Scotland's place in it.

Ruth might have failed to improve the Scottish Conservatives' performance in the general election. But, with the future of the Union very much back on the agenda, she was not going to let the opportunity pass her by again – and the SNP were going to help her.

CHAPTER 11

STRONG OPPOSITION

'It is clear the SNP are on course to win the Scottish election.' It might be an odd quote to start a political campaign if you are not Nicola Sturgeon – but it is how Ruth chose to launch hers in 2016. She was not, she said, campaigning to be First Minister. She was not asking people to vote the Conservatives into power. She was not hoping to win. Ruth's strategy was to be the 'Strong Opposition' to the SNP. And it certainly seemed prudent.

Unlike Scottish Labour, who (at least publicly) clung to the notion they might win despite trailing by thirty points or more in the polls, Ruth knew she would lose. She knew too that Scottish Labour – her main rivals in the race for opposition – were struggling. Still reeling from losing forty of their forty-one MPs in May, the party were leaderless for much of the summer after Jim Murphy was forced out, having lost his own East Renfrewshire seat on a 24 per cent swing to the SNP. By the autumn, his deputy Kezia Dugdale had been elected leader. While both charming and able, she had only been elected as an MSP in 2011 and was something of an unknown quantity to the electorate

– except hardcore SNP voters, many of whom loathed her after her controversial role in Better Together. The election of Jeremy Corbyn as the national party leader only added to a sense that Labour were lost in high, turbulent seas – a perception reflected in polling too. There was, Ruth would argue, therefore a 'vacancy' as Leader of the Opposition in Scotland.

It was a high-risk strategy. The notion that the Tories could beat Labour in Scotland – a scenario that had not occurred since 1959 – was unthinkable. Failure to achieve her stated aim would leave Labour with an open goal to claim some form of victory out of what would be – whatever the circumstances – a pretty dismal result. But Nicola Sturgeon's government's performance had compounded a sense in Scotland that the SNP's dominance needed to be firmly checked, particularly in potential Tory heartlands. A number of ongoing and costly foul-ups reflected a growing concern about the 'arrogance' of the Nationalists. And with more powers on the way to the Scottish Parliament, these problems could only grow, Ruth argued. She recognised too that, with the SNP entrenched, voters might still fancy a change of the political landscape, just not of the government. Scotland needed a strong opposition – and Ruth was certain she could convince voters the Scottish Conservatives were the party to provide it.

* * *

The massive devolution of major new powers to the Scottish Parliament in the aftermath of the referendum had been largely ignored, relegated and forgotten amid the SNP's 2015 general election triumph. Despite being perceived by some Yes supporters as a last-minute bribe from Westminster, the Conservatives under Ruth – as we have seen – had actually started to support more devolution, albeit for less than two years and despite her private reservations.

The Vow – as it became known after the *Daily Record* front page – was a commitment from all three national party leaders to devolve new powers to Scotland, regardless of who won the 2015 election. The cross-party Smith Commission, set up in the wake of the 2014 vote, would articulate the basis of this further devolution – largely focused on devolution of taxes and welfare. Income tax would be devolved along with air passenger duty, and Scotland would receive half of all VAT receipts, finally moving Holyrood towards becoming a Parliament that would have to raise as well as spend money. Martin Kettle, writing in *The Guardian*, described Smith's devolution plan as offering to 'radically change the nature of government in Scotland'.

The proposals, which took longer than expected to pass through Westminster, eventually achieving royal assent just before the 2016 Scottish election, bore remarkable similarity to those proposed by Ruth's controversial (in Tory circles at least) Strathclyde Commission – and the Tory leader wasn't slow to make that point. 'This deal is very close to the Strathclyde Commission report the Scottish Conservatives set out in June, with a few notable enhancements,' she proclaimed, on the day the recommendations were announced. It was, Ruth said, a key point in the history of devolution and the Scottish Parliament – and, crucially, one delivered not by Labour or the SNP, but the Tories. 'Our commitment at the start of these negotiations was that our Strathclyde Commission plans would be a "floor not a ceiling" on our ambitions,' she added, perhaps somewhat misleadingly. 'We have delivered on that pledge. This is a package designed, built and delivered by Scottish Conservatives and Scottish Conservative ideas. The Strathclyde Commission has become the foundation for the Scottish Parliament's new financial future.'

Of course, it is disingenuous of Ruth to suggest the proposals were entirely the work of the Conservatives – every party had two members on the Smith Commission. Yet she also argued that the Scotland Act 2016 (the bill that encompassed the Smith Commission recommendations) was 'devolution delivered'. It was, she maintained, the final set of powers that should come to the Scottish Parliament. This is not, given her private view of The Vow, surprising. Clearly, Ruth had maintained the deep-seated reservations about further devolution that had propelled her to the leadership over Murdo Fraser in the first place. Supporting devolution in 2013 had been another act of political pragmatism ahead of the independence referendum. It had got the Tories onto a pro-devolution footing, but only so far as it would be electorally useful – she was not, now or ever, a committed devolutionist. Reflecting her views, after the act was passed she hailed Holyrood as one of the world's most powerful 'sub-state legislatures' – a comment ridiculed by Nationalist politicians.

Whatever her views on the devolution settlement, however, she would use it to shrewdly frame the debate ahead of the Holyrood elections around the competence of the Scottish government. With the Scottish Parliament now facing the option of taking more or less money out of people's pockets, she reasoned, voters would take more of an interest in the effectiveness and prudence of the administration. This was, of course, bread-and-butter ground for the fiscally conservative Ruth. 'This is a plan which, for the first time since devolution, brings real accountability and real responsibility to the Scottish Parliament,' she said. 'Future Scottish governments will have to look Scottish taxpayers in the eye when they are spending their money. Successive administrations have been able to claim credit for public spending, and then blame Westminster when it runs out. That now ends. The powers are there to do as they please.' She was throwing down the gauntlet to the SNP primarily, but also to her rivals for opposition, Scottish Labour.

Ruth's message of power with responsibility resonated beyond the devolution deal, which would eventually become law in March 2016, just weeks before the Scottish Parliament elections. A series of high-profile administration blunders, which particularly affected Tory heartland issues, reinforced the need for effective government – and an effective opposition. One such issue was the delivery of Common Agricultural Policy (CAP) payments, a power already devolved. Changes to the system had required a new computer service to deliver farmers their money. Months followed months of delays as it became increasingly clear that the new IT system simply did not work. Farmers were left without crucial payments (at the time of writing, many have still not been paid), while the taxpayer was left with a ballooning bill amid successive attempts to get the computer system working. The debacle, in the end, would cost taxpayers at least £178 million in IT bills. For Ruth, however, the foul-up was a godsend. Not only did it reinforce her message about effective administration, but it also spoke to traditional Tory rural areas, many of which had turned SNP in previous elections. Ruth, hammering home the issue at First Minister's Questions in February 2016, said: '[Nicola Sturgeon] has lost the trust of rural Scotland. She has overseen yet another government IT fiasco, and farmers no longer have confidence in her Rural Affairs Secretary.'

The message – that the Scottish government was incompetent, even arrogant – was clear. Other decisions, such as a ban on GM crops in Scotland, lent weight to Ruth's appeal to traditional Tory rural voters. Indeed, the so-called Tartan Tories would start returning to Ruth's party for the first time in many years during the 2016 election. These voters, generally based in rural areas, had gradually switched their support from the Scottish Conservatives to the SNP as they felt the Tories had become increasingly 'English'. The Tartan Tories – many of whom do not actually support independence – enjoyed SNP policies and government. Regressive measures such as the council tax freeze, enacted by Salmond's Nationalist administration, appealed to voters naturally sceptical of taxation. Yet they became increasingly disillusioned with the party as it began – particularly under Sturgeon – to adopt more left-wing, pseudo-socialist rhetoric, if not actual policies. Ruth's reinvention of the Tory brand therefore allowed them to return to their natural home. By supporting devolution, she had cast off the 'anti-Scottish' image – and she also offered palatable policies on taxes, namely that they should be lower. This general style, accompanied by a focus on rural issues and good governance, greatly enhanced the Tories' prospects in many areas of Scotland away from Edinburgh and Glasgow.

Another area where Ruth excelled during the campaign was over the Scottish government's hugely controversial named person scheme, which would see every child under the age of eighteen given a state-appointed guardian. Advocates of the policy believe it will help stop neglect and abuse, but Ruth and her colleagues viewed it as an unnecessary intrusion into family life. With the policy due to be rolled out in the summer after the election and public opposition growing, Ruth was able to harness that resentment to push her message on competence. 'Only now are parents waking up to how big an intrusion this is,' she said at one campaign stop. 'Let's press the pause button on this. Let's not introduce it in August. Let's get back round the table and find a way to best allocate resources to the young people who are in vulnerable and at-risk situations who need it the most.'

Her opposition to this issue won her many plaudits, not least in the right-wing press, which was effusive in its opposition to the scheme. Yet it does represent another example of Ruth's political expediency and, where necessary, her willingness to gloss over her own party's history to score political points. When the policy had actually passed into law, two years before the election, Ruth's Scottish Conservatives had abstained. She would claim on the campaign trail that her party had always opposed the specific named person act but could not vote against it because it was bound up with other legislation the party was in favour of. This was the case, but it is worth noting that there was scant mention of the named person scheme at the time. Certainly, there was nothing like the hue and cry from the Tories that was raised during the election campaign. Ruth had, however, realised that there was substantial opposition to the scheme – and not just among her core vote, but across the country. Opposing it, no matter how late, added a valuable asset to her campaign message. Such issues proved key in the run-up to May's Scottish election.

Coupled with this hard-nosed attitude towards the government's effectiveness was an attempt to appear a mature and rounded leader. Despite her relatively young age, Ruth aimed to rise above both the SNP's Sturgeon and Labour's Dugdale. Amid their often fiery exchanges – and sometimes petty squabbles – at First Minister's Questions, Ruth took on a statesmanlike – almost motherly – air, suggesting the pair should 'just calm down for a minute'. With her baptism in the bruising referendum and general election, Ruth had now developed the competent, coherent and often passionate debating style that would bring her to prominence nationally. Voters liked her at her fieriest, of course, and this would feature regularly too. In the shouting match that regularly passes for political discourse in Scotland, Ruth was one of the loudest. This played into her 'Strong Opposition' mantra. While it may not be the case in reality, voters appeared attracted by Ruth because she, quite literally, seemed to oppose the SNP in the strongest and loudest terms.

Of course, all was not rosy in outlook for the Scottish Tory leader. The SNP continued to retain the commitment of more than 50 per cent of voters in some polls, while Sturgeon's personal approval was also through the roof, despite an increasingly chequered record in government. But Ruth, of course, was not running to be First Minister, but Leader of the Opposition. Here there was cause for optimism, with the Tory leader persistently outpolling her Labour rival. Almost half (45 per cent) of voters believed Ruth would make a better Leader of the Opposition than Dugdale (24 per cent) when don't knows were removed, according to a YouGov poll in *The Times* in April 2016. Similar numbers believed the Tory leader would also be better at holding the SNP to account, while Dugdale's ratings dropped to 18 per cent. There was comfort for the Labour leader in the fact that she was viewed as being more in touch with working people, but on pure competence Ruth was again leagues ahead, with 47 per cent of voters believing she was competent compared to just 18 per cent for Dugdale.

When considered in the context of recent Scottish politics, these numbers are hardly surprising – indeed, it could be argued that Ruth should have been doing better. In contrast to Dugdale, who had been leader for only a year or so, Ruth had been in the job since 2011. She also, as Scotland's most senior Tory, had enjoyed greater exposure in the referendum campaign. Certainly, Tory strategists were concerned that Ruth's personal poll ratings did not translate into major polling shifts. Labour was often slightly ahead of the Tories in both the constituency and the list vote – with only one poll ahead of the election putting the parties neck-and-neck. Yet it was clear Ruth's strategy of trying to hold the government to account and rise above the tittle-tattle debates of Holyrood was having an effect. Her own personal appeal too would become a central plank of the Tory campaign. The Tories' slogan – which also featured on ballot papers – was 'Ruth David- son for a Strong Opposition', carefully fusing both the personal and political message of their election.

As psephologist Professor John Curtice points out, Ruth had made 'discernible if unspectacular' progress with voters. 'Last September [2015], when no less than six polls were conducted to mark the first anniversary of the referendum, the party was being credited on average with 14 per cent of the constituency vote in Holyrood vote intentions,' Professor Curtice wrote in the months before the 2016 election.

In contrast, when the same six polling companies polled again in January or early February this year, the party's average share stood at 17 per cent. Meanwhile, even though already dismally low, over the same period Labour's average share of the vote slipped from 22 per cent to 20 per cent. So while the Conservatives may not have caught Labour up, they were now reckoned on average to be no more than three points behind.

The electoral expert, however, also sounded a note of caution, reflecting the difficult odds facing Ruth's seemingly modest ambition to become Leader of the Opposition. 'Not that a 17 per cent share could necessarily be regarded as evidence that Scots Tories were finally emerging from the depths to which they first descended in the 1997 UK general election,' he wrote.

It is, after all, no more than the share of the vote they obtained on that inauspicious occasion when it lost all of its Scottish MPs. Indeed, it is no more than the 17 per cent they won in the 2007 Scottish Parliament election, hitherto the party's best performance in a devolved contest. In short, while not wholly unrealistic, the party's aspiration to overtake Labour said more about the weakness of their opponents' position than it did about the strength of their own.

SNP leader Sturgeon agreed with this assessment, suggesting that the Tories' rising vote share was not necessarily down to Ruth's brilliance. 'I think [the resurgence of the Tories] says less about Scottish politics than it does about the state of the Scottish Labour Party,' she said in an interview with the author in the final days of the campaign.

This apparent closeness of Labour and the Tories in the polls is much more a feature of Labour's collapse than it is of any real resurgence in the Scottish Tories. I don't want the Scottish Tories to have a strengthened position in Scotland – I've opposed Conservatives and what they stand for all of my political life. But I do really despair of a Labour Party that doesn't appear to be able to take for granted that they will beat the

Tories. It really does beg the question for me – what is the Labour Party for?

There were doubts, though, about whether or not Ruth's running as a 'Strong Opposition' was prudent. One poll by Survation for the *Daily Mail* reported only 12 per cent of voters were more likely to vote Conservative given their stated aim of coming second. Perhaps unsurprisingly, 35 per cent said it made them less likely to vote for Ruth.

Matters worsened when a leaked internal party document – or 'explosive dossier', according to the *Daily Record* – revealed that the Scottish Conservative manifesto would not represent a plan for government. The document, allegedly left either accidentally or deliberately on a Parliament photocopier, said: 'The manifesto will not be presented as Our Plan For Scotland, but more as a prospectus to show what the Scottish Conservatives stand for, how we have changed and what we will pressure the Scottish government on in the next parliament.' Indeed, Ruth herself would admit as much in the document's foreword, in which she argued she was applying for the only 'vacancy' available. She wrote:

This is not a normal foreword, nor is this a normal manifesto.

That's because this isn't a normal election.

In a normal election, all of the parties set out their stall for what they would do in government – what their priorities are for action, what laws they would pass and what policies they would deliver.

As much as I would like to imagine myself First Minister in a few weeks' time, with my new Cabinet around me; I know that this is not the job the majority of Scotland's voters have in mind for me on May 5th.

It is clear that the SNP are on course to win the Scottish election.

Instead, I'm applying for another job. Because there is an important vacancy in Scottish public life that I, along with my team, are best placed to fill.

And that is the vacancy for a strong opposition. It is a vacancy that has been lying open now for nine years, with Labour leader after Labour leader failing in the post.

Given Ruth's stated target of opposition, this lack of ambition was perhaps to be expected, but it caused ructions among some in the Tory ranks. In widely reported comments, the chairman of the Selkirk Conservative and Unionist Club Jim Terras wryly suggested 'policies or a detailed manifesto would help' in the election campaign.

Ruth, of course, was characteristically robust, if a little inarticulate, in her off-the-cuff refutation of the story. 'Maybe Jim doesn't read papers but I can't say we haven't been putting ideas out there,' she said. 'We will have a full manifesto bursting with ideas. We have been the only people holding the government to account on some of this stuff.'

Certainly, Ruth was instrumental in coming up with – and then delivering – the 'Strong Opposition' strategy. 'There was an opportunity to leapfrog Labour, but obviously no chance of beating the SNP,' explained her director of strategy, Eddie Barnes. 'So gradually throughout the autumn, the strategy emerged of focusing on being a strong opposition, rather than the government.' Ruth, Barnes said, was an early proponent of the tactic, but admitted that other party figures needed convincing:

I remember when we were toying with these ideas and my immediate reaction was, who goes into an election campaign saying they're going to be the opposition? There was that initial gut reaction, that certainly I – and I think probably others – had, that this feels odd.

But I think most people then realised that this would work – that it was the right thing to do. I think most importantly it was realistic and that's what wins you trust with people. That was the beauty of our campaign, we were being straight with people. Ruth was instrumental in crafting that message.

* * *

Ruth's campaign to be Leader of the Opposition began with a pledge to offer a 'real alternative' to the SNP. With more than a hint of the Orwellian about her and with 150 days to go until the poll, Ruth said: 'With Labour in such disarray, many people are worried – deeply worried – that Scotland is becoming a one-party state.'

But she also returned to the themes of Scottishness and patriotism that she and her party had rediscovered in the years since 2014. 'I don't need to go to London and have David Cameron do a photo op signing a wee piece of paper to tell me that I'm in charge. And he doesn't need it either,' she said. 'Ours is a party that now gets devolution and has transformed itself to reflect entirely our modern union. This is a Scottish election. So, this is our campaign. It's our plan, policies and ideas. Made in Scotland. For Scotland.'

As well as talking up Scotland, Ruth continued to press her personal commitment to 'compassionate Conservative' values.

Her policy to increase NHS spending was one instance where she fused her own experience with Tory values, telling the Scottish Conservatives' spring conference of her accident as a child. Such themes – based around her own personal experience, her own normality – would be constantly returned to throughout the campaign. Clearly, her background in Fife, having attended Buckhaven High, were viewed as a fitting antidote to the classic image of the Etonian Tory.

Indeed, if the 2015 general election had been about getting to know Ruth, this contest was about trying to understand how and why she was a Conservative. Gone were the cheery, off-the-wall photo calls, although she was once pictured riding a buffalo. Instead, she spent much of the campaign travelling the country, speaking to voters at street stalls and on doorsteps. The focus of her campaign was, as she herself articulated, on issues – not what the Tories would do differently, of course, but how they would make the Scottish government do them better.

There were, however, two exceptions to this rule.

The first – and most obvious – was tax. With the devolution of income tax, political debate in Scotland came to include fiscal responsibility – or lack of it – for the first time. The Parliament would have to raise what it spent. Labour believed this provided an opportunity to move away from the constitutional issues that had dogged Scottish politics – and their party in particular – over recent years. Dugdale went so far as to describe it as Scotland's first 'tax-and-spend' election, an unusually pejorative term on which to base a campaign. It was, however, designed to unmask the SNP as an anti-progressive party, by showing voters that the Nationalists would not raise people's taxes to invest in public services. Her plan was to raise income tax by 1p across the lower and higher bands – and restore the 50p top rate of tax – to invest particularly in education, but also other public services.

For Ruth, however, the new powers also offered a chance to articulate her Tory views on tax. Scots, she argued, should not pay more than their counterparts south of the border. On the contrary, as one would expect, she suggested taxes should be lower in Scotland, to encourage investment and growth. This policy was quietly dumped when the numbers failed to stack up, meaning public services in Scotland could not be sustained if there was a tax cut. Ruth was undoubtedly a Tory on tax policy, but only so far as it would not erode her compassionate Conservative brand. She would still, however, argue against tax being higher in Scotland than the rest of the UK. 'There is no justification – none at all – for demanding a higher tax burden on Scottish families than there is on people elsewhere in the UK,' she would tell Tory conference, to a warm reception. 'You might as well hang a sign that says Scotland is closed for business. The sign at the border shouldn't read: "Give us your money", it should read: "We welcome your business".'

Such views, however popular with rank-and-file Tories, were, perhaps unsurprisingly, not widely shared across the country. Polling suggested around 40 per cent of voters would tend to support tax rises to pay for public services, with around 20–25 per cent tending to oppose such a move. Notably, tax rises on the highest earners were even more popular, reflecting the age-old truth that voters always want more money spent on public services as long as it is not theirs.

But despite Labour's efforts to focus on both the SNP's and Conservatives' tax plans, the constitution continued to dominate the campaign – and Ruth already had her tactics, and her

pedigree, worked out. Dugdale's dilemma was that about a third
of Labour voters had backed independence against their party's
wishes. Those voters, it was thought, would be unlikely to back
her party again while it continued to support the Union. Yet,
Dugdale also had to avoid alienating those who had voted No
in 2014. It was – and remains – a difficult, if not impossible, bal-
ancing act, and during the 2016 campaign the Labour Party ultimately failed to adequately resolve it. As Dugdale put it, shortly
after being elected leader of the Scottish party:

> I want people who voted both Yes and No to see that the
> Labour Party is the vehicle for progressive change in this
> country, which is why I am completely comfortable and, in
> fact, would encourage people who voted Yes in the past to take
> a look at our party and see that it has changed.

She would not try to 'shut down' internal debates and insisted she
was happy for members and even MSPs to campaign against the
Union in the future. It was an understandable move – replicated
by the Liberal Democrats – but one that also sowed confusion
among both rank-and-file members and, more importantly,
ordinary voters concerned about the prospect of independence.
Further flip-flopping throughout the campaign, such as suggesting she might support a second independence referendum in the
event of Brexit, added to the perception that Labour might at the
very least flirt with Yes voters in a bid to win power.

Ruth, on the other hand, had no such difficulties. As you
would expect, fewer than one in ten Tory voters had crossed their
ballot papers for Yes. While she did not have a plan for government, she did have a firm plan – at least rhetorically – to oppose a

second referendum on independence. 'We will seek to scrutinise and oppose where necessary – most obviously over the SNP's proposed plan to reheat the independence referendum,' she said ahead of her party's 2016 election manifesto launch. 'The need to make the case for our UK has never been more important.'

Some – including those in the Labour Party – would argue that such rhetoric showed an incredible brass neck, given the Tories' perceived role in boosting support for the Nationalists in the 2015 general election. But for Ruth, it was a brutally effective, if cynical, tactic, aided in part by Sturgeon's need to appeal to hardcore pro-independence supporters during the campaign.

Certainly, despite the lack of policies in the Scottish Conservative manifesto, the future of the Union featured prominently. In fact, it was on practically the first page, albeit couched in terms of weak government. 'Scotland voted No by a clear margin in 2014,' the first policy point stated.

> Events since have suggested that, had it voted Yes, the country would be starting life with an annual deficit of £15 billion, the highest on the entire European continent as a proportion of GDP. The decision we made to vote No has ensured that hospitals, schools and transport networks continue to be maintained. It is vital for future generations that we continue to make the case for our United Kingdom.
>
> The referendum on independence pulled families, colleagues and communities apart. Scotland spoke and the question should now be settled for a generation. However, the SNP has said it wants to pursue its separation campaign for the next five years.
>
> This is a clear breach of the Edinburgh Agreement, which tied both sides in the referendum to 'respect' the result. Worse,

it will create further uncertainty in Scotland and will prevent better government.

The Scottish Government should focus on the issues that affect us every day – improving our health service, creating better schools, and building a more secure country for us all.

Instead, reading standards have declined, our farming communities have suffered from the SNP's IT fiasco, and the move to a centralised police force hasn't worked.

Scotland needs a Scottish Government focussed on the things that matter. A strong, principled opposition will fight every day to get the SNP to focus on running the country.

This was followed by a three-point plan to preserve the Union, which included a pledge to launch a 'positive' drive to promote its benefits. There was, however, little of substance to these ideas. The chief proposal was opposition to a referendum – and it did not go much further beyond that.

Yet the Union's role in Ruth's success should not be overstated. While it was important, her mantra of being a 'Strong Opposition' went beyond a single issue. Her campaign message was focused on holding the government to account across a range of areas, of which – as we have seen – independence was but one.

*   *   *

In contrast to her previous performances, Ruth somewhat struggled during the two TV debates of the Holyrood campaign. In an unusual misstep, she merely shrugged when quizzed about the bedroom tax by Dugdale. It was a bad look for someone who had made much of her compassionate values. Dugdale herself said after the debate: 'Ruth Davidson's callous shrug of the shoulders when asked about the bedroom tax tells you all you need to know about the Scottish Tory Party. They are just the same old Tories.'

Other parties naturally chose to highlight some of Ruth's more controversial (in Scotland, at least) policy areas. While it was not the secret plan the SNP claimed – it was in the Tories' manifesto – proposals to reintroduce prescription charges in some areas were controversial. Likewise, the Tories' bid to end free university tuition proved equally contentious. Yet both were bold, honest, Conservative policies, which reinforced Ruth's image as a straight-talking leader.

Perceptions of her performance on the campaign trail too were broadly positive. David Torrance, writing for *The Independent*, said:

> The key is likeability and credibility. Ms Davidson … is a talented media performer, and her profile – both in Scotland and the rest of the UK – has been high since the 2014 referendum. Now, in the past popularity hasn't been enough (Ms – now Lady – Goldie was also an appealing character), but given Scottish Labour's dire performance, Ms Davidson's credibility is also growing.

But Kieran Andrews, writing in *The Courier*, was more scathing.

> It [Ruth's campaign] is unashamedly negative.
>
> Pushing to be a 'strong opposition' and focusing your campaign on what you are against – independence and named person legislation, primarily – is gutter politics.
>
> But there is now a cigarette paper between the Tories and Labour in the polls, so there's a strong argument it is working.

Dugdale herself described the Tory leader's campaign as 'appalling'.

Certainly, Ruth spent much of the campaign attacking her chief rivals – Labour – rather than the SNP. In one particularly withering speech at Stirling University, she said:

> They [Scottish Labour] will try to smear us as usual, of course. Though in the Labour Party's case, they don't even do that very well. Just the other day, they issued a press release which tried to attack me by using a big reveal describing me as – wait for it – just another Tory. Headlined for immediate release: – The leader of the Scottish Conservatives is a Conservative. [That is] Scottish Labour summed up in one useless press notice: one part negativity to two parts total incompetence.
>
> I ask you: do we really have to suffer five more years of this third-rate party, blundering about, punching wildly, and never landing a blow? A Labour Party which still doesn't get it – and seems to blame the Scottish people for no longer voting for it?

One person, however, was conspicuous by his absence from the campaign: David Cameron. Unlike Labour leader Jeremy Corbyn, who met with Dugdale once – slightly awkwardly – in Edinburgh, the Prime Minister did not visit Scotland in the run-up to the election. Speculation immediately mounted that Ruth thought her long-time mentor was too 'toxic' and could damage the Tories' chances. Perhaps, but the Conservative leader's absence also helped reinforce Ruth's position as the Tory chief north of the border. While she was extremely close to Cameron, she recognised that to win over voters, the Scottish party needed to appear independent of Westminster. As she herself explained: 'It's my name on the ballot paper so I will be handling the Scottish election.' Eyebrows were raised, but publicly distancing herself from Cameron almost certainly helped – rather than hindered – win over floating voters and Labour supporters concerned about the future of the Union.

*   *   *

As the election campaign drew closer to its decisive day, Ruth gave one last rally at Edinburgh's Botanic Gardens. On the cusp of her constituency, the peaceful locale jarred with the fiery occasion, as Ruth continued the theme of hammering her opponents – Labour. She was in a confident mood, buoyed by both internal and external polling suggesting her target of becoming the official opposition was within her grasp. 'Who do you want holding that Scottish government to account?' she asked a motley crew of Tory activists.

A Labour Party weakened by division, low on batteries, reduced to its smallest team ever? How does that work? Or a fresh team – my team – this team, ready, united; ready to serve and raring to go?

Well, I say this – Labour, you've had your chance. Twice. Move over and let someone else have a go. Let me get stuck into them.

Ruth's new team was certainly on display. Epitomising her candidate cull, Ruth was supported in speaking by two would-be MSPs (they would both be elected for the first time the very next day), Ross Thomson and Annie Wells. Representing the new era, both hailed from working-class backgrounds and spoke in Thatcherite tones of the need for individual betterment.

Alongside the new arrivals, the party's only MP, David Mundell, encouraged members to give their all in the final push for votes. The campaign, he said, did not end until polls closed at 10 p.m.

For Ruth, it would be the most anxious and extraordinary twenty-four hours of her life. This was the moment she would either succeed or – like the line of leaders before her – fail to revitalise the Scottish Conservatives.

CHAPTER 12

THE RESURGENCE

'On polling day, I am woken by day three of a tension headache firing tentacles up the back of my neck and the base of my skull then burrowing into the cortex beneath,' Ruth wrote in *The Spectator* of the early stages of only her second Holyrood election day and her first as leader.

> My back throbs thanks to the ire of a decade-old spine break that has never fully healed. I spit blood mixed with toothpaste into the sink. My skin has broken out into the kind of volcanic fury not seen since my teenage years and my nails are bitten down to stumps.

It is a typically honest and graphic description, reflecting the fear and trepidation with which she greeted the vote.

While she was primarily concerned with a good result across the country, Ruth also faced a personal battle in her target constituency seat of Edinburgh Central. Having dumped Glasgow – where she previously, and controversially, stood on the list – the

Tory leader was hoping to unseat the SNP in a constituency where her party had previously come fourth, with Labour second.

It was therefore not just a personal contest, but something of a bellwether for how the Tories were performing nationally. Should she appear on course to win, it would reflect a serious Tory surge. Conversely, anything other than a close-run contest would indicate that her bid for opposition lay in tatters.

There was cause for optimism. The constituency contains the capital's affluent New Town – an area of natural Tory voters – and had been strongly pro-Union in the 2014 referendum. The Green Party was also standing in the seat – one of the few constituencies they would contest. As Scotland's only other mainstream pro-independence party, the Greens might, Tory strategists hoped, draw votes from the SNP, who had won the seat in 2011 with a wafer-thin majority of only 237 votes.

Unusually too, the contest was a nearly all-female one, the only male candidate being a no-hoper from the Scottish Libertarian Party. The SNP's candidate, Alison Dickie, was a former school teacher running to replace fellow Nationalist Marco Biagi, who was standing down. She said the near all-female line-up made the Edinburgh Central contest more 'mature'. 'I hear about what's happening elsewhere and you can see there is a lot of old-style male fighting,' Dickie told Ian Swanson of the *Edinburgh Evening News*. 'We've had enough of negative politics. We're doing it quite respectfully. It has been a positive thing.'

Ruth herself had held many campaign events in the constituency – but could not avoid returning to national campaign themes. Potholes, pavements and bin collections were big local issues, according to Ruth – a holy trinity of bugbears that voters will raise in probably every constituency in the country. When talking about national issues, however, she was far more confident.

*   *   *

Ruth's election day began with a trip to St Mary's Parish Church's Café Camino, her polling station. Smiling broadly alongside partner Jen Wilson – an increasingly regular sight on the campaign trail – the Tory leader slid past a gaggle of photographers to cast her vote.

Except she had actually voted by post weeks before – meaning she was forced to duck behind a pillar to avoid being seen failing to go into a booth. With the amateur theatrics dispatched, she spent some time outside the polling station trying to register her support.

This was not a particularly scientific process. In typically military language, she wrote in *The Spectator*:

> I spend my hours as a sentry at various polling stations in [the] seat I hope to win, campaigning with my fixed air-hostess smile and saying a cheery 'good morning' every three seconds as voters filter past. I try to keep score. The ones stopping to chat are a mental mark in the 'for' column. Those who ignore me and stare at their feet are in the 'against'. Going by the mental maths it's close, but the Presbyterian Scot in me knows it's worse to hope. It's the hope that kills you.

Yet as voters trooped to the polls across the country, that is all she – and her party, after years in the wilderness – could do.

Initial signs were quite positive for the party, not that Ruth had a clear picture yet. Get-out-the-vote efforts were proving effective in many Tory target areas, particularly the north-east of Scotland. Here, it was hoped the Conservative vote would increase significantly on the 2015 general election, the PR list system giving voters the opportunity to vote according to their true preference, rather than voting tactically to keep out a rival. In other areas, such as Fife, turnout was much lower than expected, which spelled trouble for the SNP and its drive to secure 'both votes'.

As ever, while Tory Party internal polling suggested they should be confident, the question of whether voters would actually turn up was key. As night approached, along with the close of the polls, the campaigning became particularly frenetic as activists from all parties tried to get their last voters to the polls. As the clock struck 10 p.m., Ruth and the Tories faced an anxious wait – but their mood was generally positive. The Tory leader, along with her senior staff, slowly made their way to the Royal Highland Centre as the results began coming in. Ramsay Jones – who was now working for Cameron as a special adviser – shuffled around the count, anxiously checking his phone, his glasses perched delicately on the end of his nose.

The initial results sent in were mixed for the Conservatives, but broadly positive. Scottish Labour were – rightly – convinced they had won a target seat of Edinburgh Southern, while the Liberal Democrats had won in Orkney with 67 per cent of the vote. Following the debacle of Alistair Carmichael and the so-called Nikileaks memo, it had been thought they might face a voter backlash in the former Scottish Secretary's seat. Both results, however, suggested that the SNP were struggling to achieve the overwhelming dominance they had in 2015. Similar results followed that pattern – the Liberal Democrats, for instance, took

Edinburgh Western – but the Tories' strength, so concentrated in far-flung rural areas, meant their positive results would be among the last to arrive.

Ruth herself, however, would not have to wait so long. As she watched between a cigarette huddle outside and the buzz of the count floor, the Edinburgh Central tally was rapidly nearing completion.

Coming in at around 4.20 a.m., the win, on a near 10 per cent swing from the SNP, was the first great result of Ruth's night – but one she approached with characteristic humility. Always retaining an officer's concern for her troops, she was reluctant to appear too buoyant before other results were called. But she did allow herself one egregiously cheesy grin for the cameras, looking somewhat like a schoolgirl who had just won her first poetry competition.

'This is indicative of how voters can change and make a considered choice,' she said after her victory was announced.

I am under no illusion that everybody who voted for me in that seat is a true-blue, dyed-in-the wool Tory, and neither are they in places up and down Scotland. They are people who want us to do a very specific job, and that is to hold the SNP to account.

In the end, she had gained more than 15 per cent on the Tories' showing in the same seat in 2011 – and an admittedly slim majority of just over 600. As the result was read out, the count was overtaken with chants of 'Ruth, Ruth, Ruth'. No single moment could better sum up her campaign – and the Tory strategy that accompanied it.

If she was personally cautious and humble in victory, her opponents were less so. The SNP were undignified in defeat in Edinburgh Central, immediately blaming the Green Party for Ruth's victory. There may be some truth that their decision to run there – they did not contest every constituency – split the SNP vote. But such a view underestimates the tremendous effort the Tory campaign put into Edinburgh Central. Ruth appeared at photo calls in the constituency so often that one source in a rival party suggested she might have broken electoral broadcasting rules.

A short while later came the news that Alexander Burnett had won Aberdeenshire West – another gain from the SNP. The aristocratic Burnett won with a majority of 900 – a substantial figure given the Tories had never held the seat before. Shortly afterwards, it was announced Ruth's party had gained Dumfriesshire from Labour, who had held it for seventeen years, with Scottish Secretary David Mundell's son Oliver winning more than 13,500 votes. These victories marked the success of the Tories' focused and intensely localised campaigning. In their target area of the north-east of Scotland, for instance, they were the only campaign to employ a dedicated press officer to push the party's message with a specific regional focus.

Despite these constituency successes, however, it would be the list votes – which take the longest to work out – that would deliver Ruth her victory. With the last result counted and calculated, they would hold twenty-four list seats, returning, for the first time, two MSPs in staunchly left-wing, anti-Tory Glasgow. This was a particularly noteworthy, albeit small, success, given the second city of the empire had historically been vehemently anti-Thatcher.

Elsewhere, they would jump from two to four MSPs on the North East regional list and make gains in the Highlands and

Islands. One victorious candidate, solicitor Liam Kerr, thought his chances of success so unlikely that he had scheduled to fight a trial the week after the election. The case had to be swiftly passed to a legal colleague.

Indeed, it was on the proportional list vote – as opposed to the first-past-the-post constituency vote – that the Tories would supplant Labour. The irony of the Conservatives – perhaps the most vehement opponents of proportional representation at Westminster – winning via that very system was not lost on many. It had, however, been a deliberate tactic of Ruth's party to pursue list votes. The PR system, unlike the constituency vote, negates the need to vote tactically and the Tories undoubtedly benefited from people perceiving they could vote for them without wasting their ballot.

As Ruth returned home with partner Jen, her party now counted thirty-one MSPs – more than double the number achieved when she herself was first elected, just five years earlier.

*　　*　　*

'Peak Nat', a triumphant Ruth declared the day after the election, 'has passed.' Now without a majority – and facing a Conservative opposition for the first time – the SNP, the Tories argued, were on the slide.

Central to this argument was the perceived lack of a mandate for a second referendum on independence. Speaking three days after the result, Ruth said:

What was really significant about the result is that we managed to stop them having a majority. They slipped back. Peak Nat has passed. They didn't put a clear mandate for a referendum in their manifesto, unlike in 2011, and now they don't even have a majority. That takes that second referendum off the table for five years. It gives Scotland the stability that it requires.

Such views were, to say the least, short-sighted. Yes, Sturgeon had failed to return a majority, winning sixty-three seats, two short of the required total. But the Scottish Greens – who support independence – had won six seats, meaning a pro-independence majority remained. On the point of the manifesto, Ruth was correct – but only for a matter of weeks. In fact, the SNP manifesto had argued that the Scottish Parliament should have the right to hold another referendum if there was 'a significant and material change in the circumstances that prevailed in 2014, such as Scotland being taken out of the EU against our will'. The EU referendum would take place little more than a month later.

In the aftermath of the election, Ruth's efforts to focus on being an effective opposition were also mentioned but, given the tenor of the campaign, they were also vague. 'As a minority administration, I believe the SNP will be forced to listen, to learn and to improve,' she said after the count. 'I am very, very proud that our performance has helped to bring this about.'

Yet she remained cautious about her party's prospects – and hinted, correctly, at the notion that people had voted Tory out of fear for the Union, rather than support for her. 'I'm really aware that people who are not Conservatives voted for us,' she told the *Daily Telegraph* on 7 May. 'They didn't do it because they love the Conservative Party. A lot of people felt conflicted. I've a duty of responsibility to do the job we promised them we would do.'

Of Ruth's thirty-one MSPs, a remarkable twenty-four were

newly elected. There was little time for the new batch to settle, though. Despite having faced three elections in two years, there was a fourth rapidly approaching on the horizon. It was a contest that had been largely – and understandably – ignored during the run-up to the Holyrood vote. Indeed, the only time the EU referendum was ever really discussed in the campaign was in the context of it providing a *casus belli* for a second plebiscite on independence. But it was now just weeks away.

The EU referendum was a vote that would, in many ways, come to define Ruth as much as the independence campaign two years earlier. She was facing both a personal and a political battle – one that would project her across the country and raise her profile once again. Yet it would, ultimately, wreck her hard-won credibility as the defender of the Union.

Ruth, the Tories and the Union were stronger than ever on 6 May. By 23 June they would be on the brink of collapse.

CHAPTER 13

DISASTER

'As everyone knows, last night's decision was not the outcome I campaigned for in this referendum,' a beleaguered Ruth announced on the morning of 24 June 2016, hardly believing she was saying these very words. 'It was not the result I sought and I am deeply saddened that this is where we are.'

The UK had voted to leave the EU. For most commentators, it was an unexpected – and dramatic – result. For Ruth, as her statement suggests, it was far more than a shock. In one night, her chief political allies – Cameron and Osborne – had been swept from office. The Cameroon brand to which she had so avidly subscribed was firmly on the scrapheap. And a second Scottish independence referendum was not just on the table, but, in the words of First Minister Nicola Sturgeon, 'now highly likely'.

The very centrepiece of the electoral campaign that had propelled Ruth to success at Holyrood – her pledge to fight any attempt to hold another independence referendum – was, in just over a month from the Parliament vote, coming unstuck.

Perhaps most concerning, it was her own party that had delivered the *casus belli* – the material change in circumstances – the Nationalists had been so eagerly angling for.

Ruth – just weeks after achieving the seemingly impossible – was once again in a fight for her political life. The EU referendum result had changed everything.

* * *

Ruth was – unlike many in her party – a genuine pro-European. The Tory leader of course had reservations about the Continental bloc but was, on the whole, supportive. Speaking in Brussels in September 2015, Ruth said she would back remaining in the EU regardless of any deal the Prime Minister signed. Indeed, almost as if to reinforce the point – to prove she wasn't bluffing – she actually made the speech before Cameron had even begun negotiating with EU leaders on any kind of special relationship.

By laying out her support for the EU so early, Ruth had in effect guaranteed her support for the Continental bloc, regardless of what deal – if any – was agreed. As Eddie Barnes put it:

> She has spent the last five years defending unions. Of course, the EU was never going to be as important to us as the UK Union, but nonetheless she saw the benefits of the EU. It is an extension of the same argument.
>
> I think layered onto that was the Unionist argument, because we knew exactly what was going to happen if we lost, which is what has happened. It has allowed the Nationalist grievance machine to start up again.

Certainly, Ruth was not as passionate in early support for the EU as she was for the UK Union. Yet the similarity of the arguments she employed is striking. 'To me, the cost–benefit analysis is clear,' she said in the same September 2015 speech in Brussels. 'The advantages we gain from EU membership clearly and categorically outweigh any disadvantages that come with it. So for my part, I will be backing our national interest and urging Britain to stay within that reformed EU.'

Ruth was clear – perhaps incorrectly – that this referendum would be unlike the Scottish one in 2014. It was not a matter of nationalism, she argued, but rather one of national interest, of economic and diplomatic logic. 'For me this isn't a question of personal or national identity,' she said in the same speech.

> This isn't about who I am or who anyone else is either.
>
> I come at this from the point of view of someone who wants Scotland and the United Kingdom to prosper in the modern world and – with our allies – create a freer and fairer planet for others to prosper too.

But while she insisted her support was based on cold, hard economic fact, she also offered personal reasons for backing Brussels. Her family's prosperity, she said, was the result of her father, Doug, being able to trade with Europe, first in textiles, then in leather goods and finally in whisky.

Ruth's support for the EU did cause anxiety among Eurosceptics, who viewed her as a formidable opponent. Writing for Conservative Home, Mark Wallace described her support for Remain as a 'concern' for Leave supporters, given she was 'an undoubted asset' to the pro-EU side. He added:

The Remain camp is largely populated by tired Blairites, now driven from their natural habitat by Corbynite hordes, fringe obsessives who are unwilling to brook any criticism of their beloved project and discredited Jeremiahs, who wrongly predicted disaster if we failed to join the Euro. The addition of someone who is none of those things, and instead is an optimistic politician who has a feel of the modern world about her, is undoubtedly of benefit to that cause.

Of course, her support for the EU was not as controversial as it would have been among the more Eurosceptic Westminster Conservative faction. In the Scottish party there are hardly any of the 'swivel-eyed loons' that so often barrack and block Tory leaders in the House of Commons. As the EU referendum loomed, just six out of Ruth's thirty colleagues would announce their support for the Leave campaign.

This strength of pro-Remain feeling was largely down to the timing. Ruth was, post the Holyrood election, in an unassailable position in the party. Many of those elected were first-time MSPs and were perhaps reluctant to publicly disagree with their leader on the first major issue that came up for debate.

Yet it would be unfair to say that, in other circumstances, the Scottish Conservatives would be more anti-European. As the EU referendum result in Scotland showed, there is just less public Euroscepticism north of the border. Cosmopolitan cities like Edinburgh and Glasgow pride themselves on being welcoming and inclusive, and support for the EU is generally rolled into this liberal outlook. Elsewhere, in places like the Highlands, Brussels had provided huge amounts of cash to support projects designed to grow the economies of more secluded areas.

There were, of course, many in Scotland who opposed the EU – and who had done so for a long time. Fishing communities, particularly in the north-east of Scotland in towns like Peterhead, had suffered greatly under the Common Fisheries Policy. Many blamed Brussels for the slow decline of the industry. Indeed, scores of fishermen for the region would take part in Nigel Farage's pro-Brexit flotilla down the Thames in the run-up to the vote. It is also worth noting that many more hardcore Nationalists remain sceptical of the Continental bloc. This is a position consistent with their desire to be independent, as opposed to the argument of Sturgeon, who wants to take Scotland out of the UK but into the EU. Nevertheless, there was no question that Scotland was – despite these groups – generally Europhile.

The general mood among Ruth's party in the run-up to the vote was therefore one of apathy. There was the weariness from the election campaign to contend with, while many party staffers were focusing on embedding themselves in Holyrood and had little stomach for door knocking, especially in a Scottish summer. In light of the 2014 campaign, senior Scottish Conservatives were also confident that so-called Project Fear tactics would work. Warnings of economic disaster for an independent Scotland were, party sources argued, the best campaign tactic. They were confident that the same strategy would win again in the EU referendum.

The Tories were not unique in this. While Scottish Labour had made efforts to conduct voter ID for the EU referendum during the Holyrood campaign, there was a general consensus that Scotland would vote Remain without much effort. Polls suggested as many as 75 per cent of voters north of the border backed staying in the EU. This was London's fight, the argument went, and one we don't need to engage with.

Ruth – and Sturgeon – however, would enjoy no such luxury. The First Minister – the anti-austerity darling of the 2015 election debates – would be called on to tackle the Leave campaign first. Going head-to-head against Boris Johnson, Andrea Leadsom and Gisela Stuart, Sturgeon was the standout performer on the Remain side.

In truth, though, that debate was somewhat flat. Johnson, up against three women, did not implode, as some may have expected. As a man known for his bombast and eccentricity, there was an assumption – if not a hope – that he might do something outrageous, but it was not to be. As a spectacle, it is chiefly remembered for the emergence of the catchphrase 'as a mother', oft used by both Andrea Leadsom and Gisela Stuart, which would become the resonant *bon mot* of the Leave campaign.

In contrast, Ruth faced a much more difficult challenge. While Sturgeon had appeared when the Remain side was confident of victory, Ruth was called on when it was at panic stations. Polling showed an increasingly tight race, while there was a growing perception that warnings of a Brexit-induced economic Armageddon were falling on deaf ears, or even turning off voters.

There was a further point too, that while Scotland might be a Remain heartland, it was itself a key argument in the referendum debate. As the *Sunday Times* revealed, even Boris Johnson, as he tried to decide which side of the debate to back, highlighted the threat to the Union as one of Remain's great strengths. With the SNP threatening a 'material change in circumstances' could trigger a second vote, the future of the Union was at the very least implicitly threatened by the Leave campaign.

UKIP leader Nigel Farage went even further with an interview with the *Press and Journal*, suggesting he would deliberately court Nationalists for the Leave side, with the prospect of causing another constitutional vote. When asked by the paper if he would look to appeal to independence supporters who might be inclined to vote tactically to leave the EU in order to force another referendum on the future of the Union, Mr Farage said: 'Yes, absolutely.' He added, in characteristically bold terms: 'We will win our one and they won't even get a chance of winning their one. I think it would be great fun because the margin would be huge this time with oil at $35 a barrel.'

Certainly, the Scottish faction of Vote Leave – the official campaign to quit the EU – were quietly confident they could pick up votes among the SNP. Such a strategy was bolstered further by some of Sturgeon's party grandees openly campaigning against Brussels. The most notable, former deputy leader and MP Jim Sillars, highlighted the 'glaring contradiction' between wanting powers back from Westminster and being happy to send them to Brussels. In the end, Vote Leave campaigners estimate around a third of SNP supporters backed Brexit, be it for ideological or purely cynical reasons. They were, it has been reported, joined by former Nationalist Cabinet minister Alex Neil, while it is thought a further five or six SNP MSPs may also have voted Leave.

South of the border too there was the potential for Scotland to play a more decisive role in the campaign. A poll published by *The Herald* in May suggested that twice as many UK voters were concerned by the prospect of Scottish independence compared to the number concerned by Brexit. This statistic reflects the ultimate ideological issue that divided the two referendums. As Hugo Rifkind pointed out in a piece for *The Spectator*, if Scotland had voted to leave the UK, it would have a tangible impact. Voters would wake up and discover their country, as they had known it all their lives, no longer existed. Such a dramatic change in circumstance would undoubtedly have played on voters' minds and, ultimately, forced the more cautious to plump for a No vote. In contrast, the EU was a less tangible entity. Voters could 'take back control' without really experiencing anything immediately different. The economic consequences over the long term would be severe, but the UK would continue to exist, with bureaucrats in Brussels left to deal with the fallout.

While not heartening for the Remain campaign, there was a sense that a popular figure like Ruth might be able to turn support for the UK into support for the EU in the referendum. As we have seen, she had form for such arguments. She was able to make the economic arguments for the UK during the 2014 referendum, but also a passionate and patriotic case for the Union. Of course, in that contest, those arguments were largely aimed at the already converted Conservative base. But during the EU referendum, it was Tory voters who needed to be persuaded to vote Remain.

The national debate at Wembley was therefore billed as a decisive contest – and one where Ruth would take centre stage. Eddie Barnes, Ruth's director of strategy, said that the Remain campaign were keen from the start to get the Scottish Tory leader to appear, despite flagging energy. 'Bit by bit, Ruth's profile had been building nationally over that last year to the extent that people like Andrew Cooper [a Remain campaign strategist and pollster] championed her very much,' he said. 'So when they were looking around for people to take part in the debate, she was a clear choice because they were going after that demographic of

Labour voters, who she does well with.' That left Ruth as the 'go-to choice' for the pro-European campaign, Barnes said. 'The fact that she had experience of these massive debates was also an asset,' he added. 'She did the SSE in the 2014 referendum campaign and she was the only person on that panel who has debated in front of thousands of people. That counts for a lot in what can be a terrifying atmosphere.'

It was the then Chancellor George Osborne – and the then Prime Minister David Cameron – who were given the task of approaching Ruth to take part in the debate. Barnes said: 'She had a private meeting with [Osborne] and also Cameron; he sounded her out in late May. They were really keen to make sure that she got involved, which she was more than happy to, obviously.' Despite suggestions in the press that Ruth was anxious to take on Boris Johnson, Barnes said this is 'confected'. 'She wanted to make the case and the arguments – she was one of the first out of the traps to make the case for the EU and she wanted to continue doing that.'

*   *   *

'This isn't the Boris show,' Ruth declared, in front of 12,000 voters at the BBC's debate.

She was not wrong.

The Wembley Arena debate cemented Ruth as a national political figure and a force within the Conservative Party. Alongside newly elected London Mayor Sadiq Khan, Ruth made the passionate case for Remain and was deeply combative towards the opposite numbers from her own party. One of the most brutal scenes of the contest, which took place just days before the national vote, came when Ruth attacked Andrea Leadsom. The Leave campaigner told the audience that 60 per cent of British laws come from Brussels. But Ruth, savaging a minister from her own party, hit back:

> I can't let it stand that you tell a blatant untruth in the middle of a debate days before a vote. Thirteen per cent of our laws, according to the independent House of Commons library, that number is 13 per cent. In the last five-year parliament it was four, it was four bills out of 121 that came out of Europe. I think that there is a real question here.
>
> You are being asked to make a decision that is irreversible, we can't change, we wake up on Friday and we don't like it and we are being sold it on a lie because they lied about the cost of Europe, they lied about Turkey's entrance to Europe, they lied about the European army, because we've got a veto over that.
>
> They put these in their leaflets and they've lied about it here tonight too and it's not good enough.
>
> You deserve the truth – you deserve the truth.

It was a brutal denunciation of the Leave campaign that won Ruth plaudits far and wide. The anger in her voice, which resonated around Wembley and beyond, had echoes of the 2014 campaign. Ruth was always one for robust debate but, as with Salmond in the EU during the Scottish referendum, she became furious when she felt opponents were misleading voters.

Her turn of phrase during the debate was also, in many ways, textbook 2014. She focused not just on the economy but also, as we see above, the irrevocability of a Leave decision. This was an attempt to cajole voters, of course, but it was also an attempt to get them to take the vote seriously, despite the EU often being a figure of fun in the British press. Indeed, because of Ruth's general bonhomie, when she is serious, even stern, it has a greater impact.

Susie Boniface, writing in *The Guardian*, described her as 'the star striker' of Wembley. Jane Merrick, in the *Telegraph*, was similarly full of praise, describing Ruth as the 'outstanding winner' of the contest. The *New Statesman* said that Davidson – and the equally popular Sadiq Khan – had added a much-needed 'punch' to the Remain side. Even the Leave-supporting *Spectator* warmed to Ruth's 'insurgency-style attacks'.

It was, however, all to be in vain.

While Scotland voted resoundingly to Remain – although the 62 per cent figure was not as high as many thought it would, or should, be – the UK as a whole voted to Leave.

Ruth had positioned herself on the losing side, although right up until the votes were actually counted, she still believed Remain would win. 'I wouldn't say she was complacent but she was pretty confident Remain would win,' said Barnes.

It was a funny night because it was five o'clock or six o'clock and one of the Remain camp people was texting her information, pointing out that the London vote was down in terms of turnout with a crazy rain shower. They were worried about the weather in London not being good because it was such a crucial area. But I think even at 10 p.m. – with the exit poll and Farage conceding defeat – Ruth thought it was fine.

Much of her election night was spent giving media interviews in Glasgow – and it was as she was about to go on air that the first result came in. 'She was literally being miked up to go nationwide when the Sunderland result came through,' Barnes said. 'That was an "oh shit" moment. Newcastle was an "oh fuck". Suddenly it became clear it was going pear-shaped.'

Despite the seriousness of the result, Ruth's first concern was what Sturgeon would do next. The future of the Union was always at the forefront of her mind. 'We watched the results come in until about 3 a.m., when we realised it was a done deal,' Barnes said. 'From then on we were straight into quickly getting into the repercussions.'

Not only would her closest political allies now bow out, but independence would return to the forefront of political discourse in Scotland.

She would need all her guile and determination to get back on top.

* * *

On the morning of 24 June, two of the most unthinkable things in Ruth's brief career in politics happened – almost simultaneously.

Sturgeon took to the stage of Bute House and – just weeks after the Tories had resurged on the basis of keeping the UK intact – declared independence was, once again, back on the table. She said: 'I intend to take all possible steps and explore all possible options to give effect to how people in Scotland voted – in other words to secure our continuing place in the EU, and in the single market in particular.' The First Minister added: 'I think an independence referendum is now highly likely but I also think it is important that we take time to consider all steps and have the discussions, not least to assess the response of the European Union to the vote that Scotland expressed.'

Not only was Ruth's ideological nemesis in resurgence, but her political ally David Cameron later resigned outside Downing Street. Ruth tried to appear stoic about the situation, but the depth of her despair was palpable. It was telling in itself that she made only a public statement on 24 June and gave no interviews, despite the seriousness of the situation. 'I spoke to the Prime Minister and offered my thanks on behalf of the party in Scotland for his service to this country,' she said, with language reflecting her long-standing belief in politics as public service. 'He has served Britain honourably for these last six years and I know he will discharge his duties these final few months with the same diligence and love of country that has marked his tenure.'

Privately, she was said to be 'absolutely gutted' that her friend was leaving office. A source said: 'She was very, very upset. She could understand it, but she was very upset about it.' Cameron was very 'phlegmatic' during their conversation, according to the source, while Ruth also spoke with George Osborne. The source added: 'She thanked Cameron for everything that he had done – it was quite emotional.'

While she reserved warm words for Cameron, the same could not be said for Sturgeon, who was publicly warned against a second referendum on independence. 'Like the First Minister, I am disappointed with the result,' she said.

Like the First Minister, I want to see stability prioritised in the days ahead. But I do not believe that a second independence referendum will help us achieve that stability nor that it is in the best interests of the people of Scotland. The 1. 6 million votes cast in this referendum in favour of Remain do not wipe away the two million votes that we cast less than two years ago.

And we do not address the challenges of leaving the European Union by leaving our own Union of nations, our biggest
market and our closest friends.

Behind the scenes, the Scottish Conservatives were shocked by
how far Sturgeon had pushed the possibility of a second referendum on the day of the result. Barnes said: 'To be honest, Sturgeon went much further than even we were expecting in terms of
actually declaring there was going to be legislation [for a second
referendum]. We had anticipated she was going to be cranking it
up immediately, but not quite so explicitly.'

After Sturgeon spoke, Ruth and Barnes held a crisis meeting
at the Scottish Conservative Party's headquarters, in Edinburgh's
New Town, to work out a strategy. That strategy would, naturally,
focus on opposing a second referendum on independence. But
it would also take on subtler points about ensuring the wishes
of Leave voters – as well as Remainers – were respected. It was
hoped that, despite the vote, Scots would actually recognise the
importance of the Union more than ever. Without the EU, of
course, they now had only the UK.

In the days ahead, however, polling numbers looked worrying
for Ruth and Unionists more widely. A snap *Sunday Post* poll
put support for independence at 59 per cent after the EU result
was announced. Other surveys would follow suit, although none
breached Sturgeon's 60 per cent target. The First Minister had
previously suggested that sustained – meaning three months,
she would admit – support for independence among about two
thirds of Scots would lead her to consider holding another ballot.

As talk of independence raged in the north, Ruth also had to
secure her base in the south. The now-former Prime Minister

Cameron had been a key ally and supporter over the past six years. Ruth's support base in Westminster risked being eroded completely.

Having savaged Boris Johnson and Andrea Leadsom in the Wembley debate, the prospect of either becoming Tory leader – and with it Prime Minister – was bad news for Ruth. Indeed, the *Daily Telegraph* even suggested that, such was the animosity between the Scottish Tory leader and the former Mayor of London that she was even contemplating breaking up the Tory Party if he won the race to succeed Cameron. The plan – which was described as 'doing a Murdo', in relation to the 2011 leadership contest and the proposal to form a new party – was denied by the Tories' press office. But it seems likely that it was being considered at the highest levels of the Scottish party. The damage that might be caused by Johnson, who is deeply unpopular among much of the Scottish population, as premier was considered too much to bear.

Much like the 'line in the sand' on devolution, the proposal to split from Westminster reflects how pragmatic Ruth is willing to be to protect her party's fortunes north of the border. Indeed, this was now a marked characteristic of Ruth's political career. Personal allegiances regularly ebb and flow in politics – Ruth is not unique in this. But she is often seemingly willing to take radical – indeed, entirely contradictory – positions if circumstances change. In part, this is prudent strategy. As part of her military training, she would have been schooled in altering tactics to deliver victory. In public politics, of course, it is difficult to regularly change course without leaving yourself open to accusations of being unprincipled.

In this case, the proposal to split the party never came to

fruition. It was quickly consigned to the dustbin, along with Johnson's leadership hopes. Ruth herself, now desperately short of allies, also sought to patch things up with Johnson. The pair met for a drink in Westminster, with a source describing them afterwards as 'very good friends'. This, while representing good public relations for Johnson, was questionable. Fiercely loyal, it is unlikely Ruth would privately quickly forgive the former London Mayor for his perceived betrayal of Cameron over the EU referendum. In public, however, she was as anxious as Johnson for any perceived difficulty to be patched up.

Nevertheless, Ruth still had the Tory leadership battle to contend with. With her political allies decimated, it was a testy and trying contest for the Scottish Tory leader. Initially and inevitably, she had to deal with speculation that she herself might run. There was never any serious chance of this happening. She was not an MP and, despite her popularity, was still a relatively unknown quantity among many of the backbenchers suddenly propelled to prominence. Further, she was on the losing side in the EU battle and had just won an election in Scotland.

There may be a time in the future for Ruth to move south, but this was not it. Her strong preference was for the Work and Pensions Secretary, Stephen Crabb. Her allegiance to him is unsurprising. The Welsh MP had a similar background to Ruth: born in Scotland, comprehensively educated, Christian and, generally speaking, on the moderate wing of the party. Indeed, both were, in some ways, insurgents in the Tory Party, given their unprivileged backgrounds and relative youth and modernity. Of course, they would disagree strongly on gay marriage, although Crabb would later suggest he was wrong to vote against it.

Ruth favoured him enough to describe him as her 'political

soulmate' – about as strong as an endorsement can get. Before the leadership contest had even begun, she effused praise for him. 'I think there's a few really, really competent and impressive people who demonstrate warmth as well as intelligence and I think that's quite important in politics,' she said of the Welsh MP.

Not that her compliments went unreciprocated. In 2015, Crabb would claim – not incorrectly – to have 'much in common with Ruth'. With a turn of phrase that neatly encapsulates the Scottish Tory leader, he added: 'In the kind of political street fights we have both been through in Scotland and Wales, we know that you can't get away with any weak and woolly brand of politics. You have to be passionate. Your head screwed on, yes, but also with a full beating heart.'

In many ways, a political alliance between the pair was predestined and Ruth's strong support for Crabb when he announced his leadership bid is unsurprising. Her influence could be clearly seen on his campaign, which had the future of the Union as one of its key themes. While it is not known how much influence she had on his short-lived campaign, given their friendship it is likely she would have provided both advice and counsel.

Despite Ruth's backing, however, Crabb would finish a disappointing fourth in the first round of the Tory leadership contest, falling behind Michael Gove, Theresa May and Andrea Leadsom. Johnson had already withdrawn. His rather rapid defeat was made notably more dramatic by the revelation that he had been 'sexting' a girl around half his age. Friends suggest Ruth – never anxious to judge someone else's personal life – was 'concerned' but not angry. Her reaction was more one of disappointment than rage.

With her 'soulmate' now not just defeated for the leadership but driven out of the Cabinet, Ruth was running out of options.

Rather than trying to influence the outcome, her chief concern now was to ensure that – second time round – she backed the winner. Ruth had won hard-fought gains in Westminster – such as the right to attend Cabinet meetings – from Cameron, and needed and wanted to keep them.

As the contest hit hyper-drive – Gove would be the next contender knocked out – Ruth threw her weight behind Theresa May. In the circumstances, it was a logical move. While the Scottish Tory leader and Home Secretary were hardly ideological bedfellows, they had more in common than Ruth and Leadsom. As well as the general perception that she simply was not up to the job, the latter had of course been savaged by Ruth in the EU referendum debate just weeks before. Leadsom had also angered Ruth during the referendum campaign with her repeated use of the phrase 'as a mother'. Ruth felt the phrase was both exclusive and superfluous. When Leadsom went further – suggesting to *The Times* that she would be a better leader than May because the latter does not have children – Ruth publicly, and emphatically, called her out, saying there was a 'gulf in class' between the two candidates. Would the Scottish Tory leader have supported Leadsom if she had felt there was any chance of Leadsom winning the contest? (Well, there wasn't.) What's clear is that Ruth felt it more important to speak up for the inclusive and modern Tory Party that she believed in, rather than let pass a silly public comment by a leadership contender.

Ruth herself was full of praise for May. Announcing that she was backing the then Home Secretary, the Scottish Tory leader said May had the 'steel' to go 'eyeball to eyeball' with Sturgeon, as well as German Chancellor Angela Merkel. Ruth, of course, already knew that the fight for the Union was about to restart in Scotland, and was anxious to ensure the new leader was up to the task. Indeed, in May, Ruth would have a leader who was less laid-back than Cameron – and who, she hoped, was unlikely to make so many of the casual blunders the former Prime Minister had in the run-up to the 2014 contest.

Perhaps more out of hope than belief, she added:

[May] has got a huge capacity for work, she has got all the leadership skills, she can see the way other people have looked at the Tory Party and not liked what they've seen, and they know the way in which she wants to change the party so that it is a party for everybody, not just a party for one section of society.

When Leadsom withdrew, it was clear Ruth's political instincts, at least second time round, were correct. May was now Prime Minister – and Ruth had backed her at just the right time.

A Scottish Tory source even suggested the new Westminster leader was considering trying to crowbar Ruth into her Cabinet as Scottish Secretary. The job, which was eventually held by incumbent David Mundell, would have been difficult, if not impossible, to conduct while Ruth remained an MSP. She would also have been reluctant to take on the additional work, given her enhanced role in Holyrood and the resurgence of Nationalist sentiment in Scotland. Yet it is a testament to how quickly she had established herself with May that such things were even being discussed.

Certainly, despite the furore of those choppy weeks, Ruth was still confident enough to be able to poke fun at her opponents. After May's election – or rather appointment – the Scottish Tory leader held a lunch in Westminster where, in typical good humour, she dissected recent events. To laughs, she said she was delighted to still be in office when everyone else was 'resigning, getting knifed, bottling it, withdrawing, failing, declaring, or falling on their sword'.

Referencing the ongoing challenge to Jeremy Corbyn's Labour leadership that emerged after the EU referendum, she continued: 'That's the difference between our two parties: Labour is still fumbling with its flies while the Tories are enjoying their post-coital cigarette. After withdrawing our massive Johnson,' she added, to more laughs.

Leadsom was also targeted, with Ruth ridiculing the Brexiteer's CV claims during her leadership bid. While she had publicly patched things up with Johnson, she clearly still had venom for Leadsom. 'Before politics, not only was I a BBC journalist but I singlehandedly saved the British banking system during the Barings collapse,' Ruth joked. 'A little-known fact was that I was the original Misha the bear at the 1980 Moscow Olympics, and that was the same year I won Eurovision. Which, speaking as a mother...'

That she was able to make light of the turbulent period is a testament to her own self-confidence and, perhaps more so, her relief that she herself had in fact survived the EU referendum.

Despite the bonny exterior however, all was not entirely well in Ruth's relationship with the Westminster party – and May in particular. The Scottish Tory leader was given the primetime spot of introducing the new Prime Minister at conference. Such a position – which Ruth had held previously under Cameron – is indicative not just of her own success, but of the credibility May felt Ruth lent her.

In many ways the speech was positive, as one would expect.

Ruth attacked May's opponents and insisted she would make an excellent Prime Minister. Yet she also sought to put clear blue water between the pair, in quite stark terms. Ruth's speech followed the announcement that businesses could be forced to publish lists of foreign workers in their employ, a policy that came about after it became increasingly apparent that curbing free movement of people from the EU was more important to voters than access to the single market.

'Internationalism abroad must find its echo at home,' Ruth told the packed audience in Birmingham.

> As we have difficult – but necessary – debates on how we manage borders in future, let us not forget that behind discussions of numbers and rules and criteria, there lies people and homes and families.
>
> And for those who have already chosen to build a life, open a business, make a contribution, I say this is your home, and you are welcome here. The Conservative Party I know is optimistic in spirit and internationalist in outlook – we are an outward-looking people, and so we must remain.

The comments were certainly not on message with the theme of the conference. The rhetoric itself was almost a carbon copy of Sturgeon. Indeed, the speech was probably a tacit attempt to quell the growing angst in Scotland about the direction that the UK government was taking over Brexit. But it was also, once again, a defence of Ruth's particular brand of Conservatism – compassionate and inclusive. That she felt the need to so publicly defend it is reflective of the fact that, post-EU referendum, such sentiments were largely yesterday's politics.

Ruth actually met May backstage immediately after her speech, as the Prime Minister was about to go on. May was said to have congratulated Ruth on the 'great speech', but it is unclear if she had actually heard it. Ruth was said to have responded 'and good luck to you, Prime Minister'.

Of course, distancing herself from more unpopular Tory government policies was a tried and tested tactic of Ruth's. She had done it, for instance, on George Osborne's plans to cut back tax credits. There was a sense, though, that this moment was different.

Her speech also contrasted with that of the Secretary of State for Scotland – and her friend – David Mundell, who chose to toe much more of a party line. He used warm tones to describe the new Prime Minister – and his only reference to Brexit was also positive. 'We can't and won't provide a running commentary on exiting the EU, but I want to be absolutely clear,' he told the Birmingham audience. 'We will negotiate as the United Kingdom, leave as the United Kingdom, and face the future together as the United Kingdom. A Team UK approach. Because the UK is Scotland's vital union.' This scripted and uncritical view is unsurprising, given his Cabinet position. But Ruth's views, given her status as Scottish leader, surely carry more weight.

Ruth – a proudly moderate Tory – was profoundly concerned about the direction of her party. While she was clearly delighted the leadership vacuum had been filled relatively smoothly, Ruth was uncomfortable about the tone and tenor of the new government.

And it was not the first time Ruth had chosen to publicly disagree with her new boss. Before the EU referendum had even taken place, May called for the UK to scrap the European

Convention on Human Rights (ECHR). It was a controversial view – at least outside the Conservative Party – and one Ruth roundly rebuffed. 'I take a slightly different view from Theresa May – I think we should recognise that the ECHR was in large part drafted by people from Britain, and it's British values that are enshrined there,' she told Pink News.

> In terms of a Scottish context, the ECHR is written into the original Scotland Act, so it would be up to the Scottish Parliament to decide whether we changed the basis of that. There's nothing at a UK-wide level that would be able to change that without Holyrood's consent. I think it's a little bit more complicated than Theresa May is trying to push out there.

How this relationship will develop in the future, only time will tell, but Barnes argues that Ruth's relationship with May will grow in the coming years. 'Ruth knows the Prime Minister much better than she knew Cameron at the start of their premierships,' he says.

> She's obviously had five years with plenty of meetings with Theresa May and they've got to know each other quite well. They had a private meeting the day before she became PM in the Cabinet Room, where they were able to talk about the priorities and they very much have a good relationship.

But despite those early assurances, Ruth is unlikely to be as comfortable with May as she was with Cameron.

* * *

The EU referendum result was not, of course, the only political shock of 2016. The election of Donald Trump as President of the United States horrified many people – including Ruth.

Scotland – or rather the Scottish government – has little or no international relations capacity at present, so it is perhaps understandable that Ruth was quite damning in her criticism of the Republican. Without any potential fallout from prejudging the election, Scottish politicians were free to express their views without fear of diplomatic repercussions. (Not that such fears stopped many in Westminster commenting either: Boris Johnson, for example, responding to Trump's campaign-trail claim that some areas of London had been completely radicalised, announced: 'The only reason I wouldn't go to some parts of New York is the real risk of meeting Donald Trump.')

Trump, however, has enjoyed a lengthier relationship with the Scottish political class than he has with politicians in the rest of the UK. The billionaire owns two golf courses in Scotland and was once close with former SNP leader Alex Salmond. But the pair had an acrimonious and public falling out over wind farms being built off the coast of the Trump International Golf Links in Aberdeenshire.

The Republican's long-running battles over his business investments in Scotland meant that many – Ruth included – were used to The Donald's bluff and bluster, long before he entered the international political scene. Taking to Twitter in December 2015, and showing the benefits of her English Literature degree, she would use Shakespearian language to brand Trump a 'clay-brained guts, knotty-pated fool, whoreson obscene greasy tallow-catch'. Appearing on comedian Matt Forde's television show, she would reference – with typical good humour – Trump's infamous comments about sexually assaulting women, which had emerged during the campaign, advising pet owners to 'look after that cat and not let Donald Trump anywhere near your pussy'. (In the same programme, she would have the audience in stitches when she replied to Forde's question about her puppies with an innuendo-laden, 'Well, thanks for noticing.')

In an interview with the author during the 2016 Scottish election campaign, Ruth went further on her views on US politics. 'I'm utterly a Blue Dog Democrat,' she said, referencing a political caucus in the United States that identifies as conservative Democrat.

> I am fiscally conservative but socially liberal, and that's where they are. It is about comparability. The whole political discourse in the United States is so much further to the right than it is in the UK that I don't see any real comparability. I would back almost anyone over Donald Trump.

Ruth, of course, was not unique in this criticism, but it could be argued that such remarks reflect that her political judgement is not fully matured. She could, as noted earlier, speak without fear of diplomatic repercussions. But had her role been different – as an MP in Westminster, for example, with a direct say over foreign policy – her comments would be considered misplaced. It is once again an example of how Ruth's natural, conversational style, while effective, also contains risks.

Nicola Sturgeon, of course, had already gone further and stripped Trump of his role as a Scottish business ambassador after he pledged to ban Muslims from entering the United States. The First Minister branded the future President 'obnoxious and offensive', while Labour's Kezia Dugdale went to actively campaign for Trump's rival, Hillary Clinton. All of them – including Ruth – would wake up on the morning of 9 November 2016 to a result none had wanted or expected.

Trump's victory presented the biggest diplomatic difficulty for Sturgeon, of course, given her position. The First Minister said, without a hint of irony, that the outcome of the vote must be 'respected'. She added: 'We value our relationship with the United States and its people. The ties that bind Scotland and the US – of family, culture and business – are deep and long-standing and they will always endure.'

But Ruth, as one of the most senior Conservatives in the country and with the special relationship seemingly on the line, also had to moderate her tone. Speaking after the election, she expressed her disappointment, but also her hope for the future. The Scottish Tory leader also linked the Republican's election to the Brexit vote months earlier, saying:

It's not the result I wanted but we now have to hope that President Trump turns out to be a different man to candidate Trump.

Mr Trump tapped into the disaffection we are seeing across the world right now due to economic uncertainty. That's not something we can ignore. Those of us who believe open, Western values are the best way to provide economic security for people now have to redouble our efforts to show they deliver for people.

How the relationship between the Conservatives and Donald Trump will continue is, of course, impossible to tell. Initial overtures appear to suggest that, post-Brexit, May and her

Conservative allies – that include Ruth – are anxious for a good relationship with the President.

But Ruth's early criticism of Trump is a good example of how her political judgement can sometimes let her down. It reflects, perhaps, that, at thirty-nine years old, she still has things to learn in politics.

*   *   *

Aside from Ruth's relationship with politicians south of the border and across the Atlantic, the far more important question of the future of the Union remained. The uncomfortable truth was that the Tories had brought the Union into disrepute. In the first instance, the politically expedient tactic of talking up a possible SNP–Labour coalition in the 2015 general election helped the Nationalists to their landslide victory in that vote. The influence of fifty-six MPs in Westminster can be debated, but what is clear is that their overwhelming victory – supported in part by Tory tactics – allowed the SNP to regain momentum and relaunch their separatist narrative when it should have been ebbing away. Secondly, in the 2016 Holyrood election, Ruth continued to play the SNP at their own game, talking up fears over the future of the Union that, in almost every sense, her own party had let flourish. As we have seen, this was an effective tactic, but a self-serving one nevertheless. Finally, Cameron's decision to hold the in/out EU referendum, again under pressure from his own MPs and to protect his majority from a possible UKIP surge, gave the SNP the predicate needed to actually launch a second separatist campaign. Of course, the current situation is not entirely the fault of the Conservatives. But it is largely as a result of these actions that the question of independence has not – and now, for the foreseeable future, will not – disappear.

Indeed, one of the main promises of the Better Together campaign – that a No vote in 2014 meant Scotland could keep its EU membership – had proved, at best, short-lived. Ruth herself was open to the charge. In a TV debate on 2 September 2014, the Scottish Tory leader said: 'I think it is disingenuous of [Scottish Green Party co-convener] Patrick [Harvie] to say that No means out and Yes means in, when actually the opposite is true. No means we stay in, we are members of the European Union.'

Such comments, it goes without saying, are now deeply contentious. Pro-Yes supporters have seized on them to support the narrative that the No campaign deceived Scottish voters into backing the Union. Recriminations are, of course, typical when a side has been roundly defeated, but there is little doubt that the Tories' actions – not just on the EU, but also on issues such as EVEL – have added weight to these arguments.

In the aftermath of the vote, Sturgeon pledged to do all she could to – using the SNP's language – protect Scotland's place in Europe. 'It is vital … that we seize the chance that we have, before those negotiations start, to ensure that Scotland's voice is heard as widely as possible: in London, in Brussels, and by member states across Europe,' she told fellow MSPs in one of the earliest Holyrood debates following the EU referendum.

The Prime Minister gave me a commitment on Friday morning on the full engagement of the Scottish government and to ensure that the interests of all parts of the UK are protected and advanced. Today, I seek the Parliament's authority to hold the Prime Minister and his successor to that commitment.

It was, given the circumstances, a modest – and generally acceptable – demand. Politicians from across the political divide, including Labour and the Liberal Democrats, gave their support to the First Minister. Yet Ruth struck a more combative tone, viewing Sturgeon's demands as a thinly veiled move to drive Scotland towards a second independence referendum. After outlining where she supported the SNP administration – in relation to, for instance, membership of the single market – Ruth added: 'I cannot ignore the fact that, within hours of the vote becoming clear, the Scottish government had pushed questions of independence to front and centre.' In doing so, Ruth was clearly seeking to solidify her base and return to the offensive after several weeks of being on the defensive. Those arguments would develop over the coming weeks and months into something more coherent.

A second independence referendum, Ruth's argument goes, presents more of a risk to the Scottish economy than Brexit. Uncertainty will reign and confidence will be hit if there's a spectre of a second ballot hanging over Scotland. In one such speech on the subject – there have, of course, been many – Ruth said:

> The unstoppable bandwagon of late June now appears to have been parked in a lay-by. We have had five years of uncertainty and rancour over our constitutional status, now added to by the EU referendum result. As a result, most people in Scotland now do not want to add to that any more – yes, they remain troubled by the EU result, but that is not translated into support for further constitutional upheaval in the form of yet another referendum on independence.

There is some evidence to support this point of view. A YouGov poll for *The Times* in January 2018, for instance, suggested that half of Scots oppose having a second independence referendum in the next five years, while 50 per cent of those polled would still back a No vote. Those figures have changed very little since September 2016, when pollster Matthew Smith wrote:

> The appetite for a second referendum will disappoint the SNP ... with YouGov's latest Scotland survey finding just 37 per cent of Scots backing a second independence referendum and 50 per cent opposed. Should they be successful in forcing another vote, the results would be almost identical to last time, with 54 per cent of Scots voting against independence and 46 per cent in favour.

Professor John Curtice, however, is more upbeat about the general polling picture for the Yes campaign. In March 2017, he said:

> The nationalist movement in Scotland has never been stronger electorally. Meanwhile, from its perspective the outcome of the EU referendum appeared to be a perfect illustration of their argument that for so long as it stays in the UK, Scotland is always at risk of having its 'democratic will' overturned by England.

But, pointing to polls showing rising Euroscepticism north of the border, he too sounds a note of caution.

> However, the commitment to the EU of many of those who voted to Remain does not appear to be strong enough that they are likely to be persuaded by the outcome of the EU referendum to change their preference for staying in the UK.

Meanwhile, there is a risk that linking independence closely to the idea of staying in the EU could alienate some of those who currently back leaving the UK.

Nevertheless, the Brexit vote has continued to dominate Scottish – and UK-wide – political discourse. The Scottish Conservatives have established a Brexit committee to advise the party on the possible implications for Scotland on leaving the EU. Ruth explained its role thus:

> I am ... announcing today that the Scottish Conservatives will form our own expert group to assess the risks and opportunities of Brexit for Scotland.
>
> As well as two of my MSPs – one who voted Remain and one who voted Leave – I am delighted to say that the group includes a panel of leading figures including Sir Iain McMillan, the former head of CBI Scotland, and Gavin Hewitt, the former chief executive of the Scotch Whisky Association and, prior to that, Her Majesty's Ambassador to Belgium, Finland and Croatia.
>
> I will ask them to report to me on how best they believe Brexit can deliver for Scotland and – crucially – for the entire United Kingdom.

Not only is its remit vague – to say the least – but the committee seems immediately hamstrung by Ruth's refusal to consider any kind of separate deal for Scotland.

Certainly, Ruth's tone and strategy also run the risk of leaving the Tories stuck in the same rut they had been in before she took over the party. Post-Brexit, they are in many respects standing up for English – or at least Westminster – interests. Scottish Labour's Kezia Dugdale summed up the Tories' predicament best, speaking after Ruth in the first Holyrood debate on Brexit. 'I struggle to put into words the anger I feel towards [Ruth's] party at the moment,' Dugdale began, before ridiculing the Tories over their election pledges to protect the Union and provide strong opposition. She added: 'All that [the Tories] stand opposed to today is giving the First Minister some support to speak to EU institutions about our future. The Tories have put the future of the UK in danger at every turn and it is high time that they shouldered responsibility for that.'

Certainly, the Scottish Conservatives' position on Brexit is increasingly precarious. This is particularly the case when you consider their refusal to countenance any form of Scotland-specific Brexit deal. Of course, it could be argued that such a deal – if it were even possible – would only further cement a feeling that Scotland and the rest of the UK are heading in different political directions. It could, in short, strengthen the case for independence.

There is, however, the point that Scotland voted to Remain in the EU and, while the vote was a UK-wide one, an effort should be made to respect how Scotland voted too. Sturgeon sees this as a chance to secure Scottish membership of an organisation like the European Free Trade Area or European Economic Area. It is thought that such EU-lite options might be more palatable at home and abroad, given the reluctance among some member states – such as Spain and Belgium – to accommodate separatists. Such a scenario might also serve to placate Leave voters in Scotland to an extent, but without returning to the status quo they voted against. Indeed, while it is unclear if such an arrangement would even be possible, there is a danger Ruth's Tories will gain a negative image from refusing even to contemplate it. As we have noted, much of Ruth's success as Tory leader has been predicated on detoxifying the Conservative brand and making it appear less 'anti-Scottish'. Actions such as supporting devolution and standing up to her Westminster party – rarely but effectively – have helped the Tory resurgence. By toeing the party line on Brexit, however, this revival is undoubtedly put in danger. Ruth now runs the risk of being perceived as yet another Tory lackey, concerned more about the views of her London bosses than about the economic future and security of Scotland. Worse still, she could be viewed as being without influence among an increasingly right-wing Tory cabal she is unable to moderate.

The situation is compounded by Ruth's personal views. Not only is she avidly pro-European, she also actively and prominently campaigned for a Remain vote. She can, of course, justify her immediate switch to delivering Brexit as simply respecting the outcome of the democratic process. But the transition is yet another example of Ruth's ideological malleability. She will support something she believes is right, but only until the point it becomes advantageous to change course. One can argue over whether this trait displays pragmatism or cynicism – or perhaps both. But it certainly leaves Ruth open to attacks over her switch from the Remain camp to solidly hard Brexit.

Yet as the initial situation calmed, the Tories have regained some ground. The Liberal Democrats, for example, while initially supporting the First Minister, have since come to share Ruth's view that her efforts are merely a feint in the drive for independence. The First Minister herself has begun to lay the groundwork more overtly for a second ballot. Not only has the draft legislation for another plebiscite been published, but she has launched a 'national conversation', which she says is an attempt to understand Scots' views post-Brexit. 'Our activists will be hitting the doorsteps as well, asking people to take part and delivering a new leaflet explaining why,' Sturgeon explained in a speech in Stirling in September 2016. 'All in all, we plan to talk to at least two million people across Scotland between now and 30 November. The wealth of information and insight we gather will then inform the next stage of our campaign.'

Such rhetoric – and action – is of course deeply concerning to Unionist parties, and not least Ruth herself. She responded in typically robust terms to Sturgeon's announcement of the 'national conversation'. 'Nicola Sturgeon said that she wants to listen to people who voted No in the hope of meeting their concerns,' Ruth declared, the day after the First Minister had made her speech.

> Well, let me tell her how many of us feel. We do not look back at the referendum on independence with much in the way of nostalgia. It wasn't 'civic' or 'joyous', as the SNP have claimed. Instead, we remember the division it caused, we remember the pain felt by many, and we remember the fear that our country was about to be split up.

Ruth, speaking before a backdrop of Edinburgh Castle, became increasingly fired up. 'So if the First Minister wants to know the feelings of thousands of Scots across the country – I can give it to her right now,' she said.

> It is anger at an SNP government which has both broken its word and decided to put its own narrow political interests before those of the wider country. And it is frustration that we have a nationalist

administration which is acting like a drag on Scotland's progress. Instead of a proper government using new and existing powers to drive the country forward, we instead have a nationalist adminis- tration dragging Scotland backwards – allowing the lead weight of separatism to threaten our ambitions and hopes.

However, it should be remembered that the threat of separation serves Ruth's political purposes – and it is in her interests to make it seem more real than, perhaps, it is. Sturgeon's 'national conversation', for instance, has somewhat sunk without trace, and may have been merely a move designed to placate her more militant independence supporters, rather than a real push for a second referendum.

BBC Scotland's political editor, Brian Taylor, would certainly describe it as such. 'I categorise [this] announcement as a man- oeuvre. It is emphatically not an immediate gung-ho propaganda push for independence,' he wrote for the broadcaster's website. 'It is not the starting pistol on a new referendum campaign. It is not the comprehensive rewriting of the independence White Paper. For one thing, this is a party initiative, not a government one. Rather, it is tentatively preparing the ground, should a ref- erendum be sought and attempted.'

There is no doubt that Sturgeon remains cautious about holding a second referendum, which she might lose, but Ruth's rhetoric suggests otherwise.

* * *

It is clear, however, that while the EU referendum campaign in many ways cemented Ruth's position – certainly nationally – the Brexit result threatened to break it.

For now, Ruth and the Scottish Conservatives seem content to push ahead with Brexit and support the May government. Electorally, this has already yielded some successes, with anti-European voters seemingly viewing the Tories as Scotland's Brexit party. In the north-east of Scotland, a traditionally SNP area, the Tories have won a number of impressive by-election victories. The region – heavily reliant on fishing, as well as oil and gas – is also, as noted earlier, one of the most Eurosceptic areas of Scotland. Post-Brexit, however, the Conservatives outpolled the SNP (and also another pro-European party traditionally strong in the area, the Liberal Democrats) in the region, building on their success there in the Holyrood election months earlier.

Ruth herself would hail the by-election results, but not mention Brexit, despite party strategists insisting the vote to leave the EU was a key factor. She said:

> This double win proves once again that the Scottish Conservatives are the party which can take on and beat the SNP, including in Alex Salmond's backyard.
>
> The message is clear: the SNP must start listening to the people of Scotland who want them to focus on the day job of governing – not obsess over a second referendum on independence.

Yet despite her buoyant mood, the EU referendum has certainly left Ruth's future – and her party's future – more uncertain than it was just after the Holyrood election in May. But if one thing is apparent from Ruth's life and career in politics, it is that she does not give up without a fight.

CHAPTER 14

PEAK TORY

In the May 2016 Holyrood elections, the Scottish Conservatives ended a long period of decline in Scotland. The 2017 general election confirmed that the result was not an aberration: the Tories' long-lost foothold in Scotland had been regained. They are now the second largest party by seats in Edinburgh and have the second highest number of Scottish seats in Westminster. They have eclipsed Labour as the main opposition in Scotland and are winning votes from the SNP, too. But it is also worth noting that the Tories secured less of the vote in Scotland in 2016 than they did in the 1992 general election, under John Major. And there remains a deep-seated anti-Tory sentiment in much of urban Scotland. The legacy of Thatcher might be fading, but it has yet to disappear completely. Such feelings have only been compounded by the fact that it was a Tory government that called – and ultimately lost – the EU referendum. Many Scottish voters feel that a future outside the single market would, in the words of Sturgeon, amount to 'economic vandalism'.

Ruth herself has now – rather remarkably, for the first time

– set her sights on beating the SNP in 2021 and becoming First Minister. Like her party's success between 2011 and 2017, the likelihood of this happening is greatly down to circumstances, some but not all of which are out of her control.

There is no doubt that the constitutional question was a significant factor in the 2016 Holyrood vote – and it clearly played a role in 2017 too. This was not the result of some latent desire among voters, however, to rerun the debates of 2014 or turn politics into an 'us and them' binary contest. It was led by a deliberate and cynical ploy from the Scottish Conservatives, who knew it was one of their great strengths. The reality of the Brexit vote – and the return of the independence question – could therefore be a gift to the Tories as they look to solidify their gains north of the border. The relative successes of the 2017 general election campaign – undertaken again under the spectre of another independence vote – strengthen that argument.

Whether consciously or not, Sturgeon has played into Ruth's hands by suggesting a second plebiscite is now 'highly likely'. Such rhetoric naturally pits politics between the Unionists and the Nationalists. Labour – or, for that matter, the Liberal Democrats – will, for the moment at least, struggle to have their voices heard in such an argument. The Tories too are unlikely to suffer some of the pitfalls of those two left-of-centre parties as they make the case for the Union. While it is considered a crime for other parties to 'get into bed with the Tories', it is never an issue for the Conservatives to sleep comfortably next to them. Given the events post-2014, there is unlikely to be a reboot of the cross-party Better Together campaign in the event of another referendum – but, if there were, the Tories would not be the ones punished by the electorate for joining it.

Nor is there any doubt that the Tories would lead the fight in a second plebiscite, which is probably a question of when, not if. It was the Labour Party that played the decisive role in 2014, harnessing its activists and databases to drive home the Better Together message. Party grandees such as Gordon Brown were also instrumental in delivering a No vote. Cameron – and other party leaders – played a part in delivering 'The Vow', but this was in truth a minimal intervention in a contest that had already been won by the Labour Party. In a second vote, Labour will not prove such a key player. Its resources are somewhat diminished north of the border – although its relatively strong performance in the 2017 general election campaign has done much to revitalise the party, as has the wider popularity of Jeremy Corbyn. Nevertheless, there is a sense that it would be tactically imprudent of Labour to lead the fight against the Nationalists again. Of course, it would campaign for the Union again – that is not in question. With the collapse in the price of oil – on which much of the already shaky economic foundations for independence were based – the case for the pooling and sharing of resources to deliver social justice and protect public services is even stronger than it was in 2014. But it would be the Tories who would be responsible for leading the campaign from the front and centre.

This has obvious advantages for Ruth's party, most notably that it plays into their message that they are the true defenders of the Union. While a portion of Labour members support independence, the Tories have no such difficulty. They could – and would – campaign hard. Independence supporters are unlikely, it goes without saying, to ever vote Tory, so they do not risk losing voters either. The increased prominence from a second referendum campaign would also boost their position both nationally and domestically.

However, there are also menaces that lie in wait for the Tories in a second ballot. Most obviously, if they were to lose, they would be finished. Scottish politics needs a centre-right party, but it is hard to see how the Tories could survive losing their overarching ideology. There would be a great deal at stake.

Victory would – perhaps ironically – potentially be more devastating. If the Tories' success during Ruth's tenure has been down to the constitutional question, would they continue to rise if it were removed? Evidence from abroad – specifically Quebec – suggests a second referendum defeat, even by the tiniest of margins, ends the question of independence. In the Canadian state, an initial ballot, held in 1975, was roundly defeated. But it was not until a second vote was called twenty years later that the question was settled. Despite the No side winning by the slimmest of margins – they got 50.58 per cent – constitutional debate in Quebec has all but disappeared. It is likely that a similar scenario would take place after a second defeat in Scotland, something Sturgeon – in her hesitation – realises. If a second independence referendum were held and defeated in Scotland – as polls suggest it would be – the Tories' *raison d'être* of Unionism would become somewhat redundant. Of course, they would continue to enjoy support from small and big 'c' conservative quarters, but the removal of that dichotomy would surely hurt Ruth's party and the SNP, benefiting Labour and the Liberal Democrats.

But there is a subtler point too. Much of the Tories' success in 2016 was based around *opposing* a second referendum. Voters who had backed the party on this basis might move their support elsewhere if Sturgeon were to be allowed to hold one, especially if the move was not opposed by the Conservatives. Circumstances had already changed so radically since the Brexit vote that Ruth herself had suggested a second plebiscite should not be blocked if the Scottish Parliament asked for one. In July 2016, Ruth seemed almost resigned to that fact, saying: 'I would argue as strong as I could that we should stay part of our biggest market and closest friend. Constitutionally the UK government shouldn't block it, no.' Fundamentally, as a question of democracy, that is the correct response – but when Sturgeon actually brought forward plans for a second independence referendum, and secured support for one in the Scottish Parliament, this commitment was swiftly dropped. 'Now is not the time,' argued an – at that time – emboldened Theresa May, after Nicola Sturgeon called the vote in March. Indeed, simply blocking another referendum – a tactic Ruth now wholeheartedly endorsed – appeared popular with Unionist voters and, with a majority of the country still opposed to another ballot, could prove effective. Yet this strategy remains high-risk. Any attempt to stop a democratic vote – particularly if Brexit proves the calamity many are predicting – could swiftly prove untenable. The Nationalist backlash could be immense.

The ultimate result of all this is that much of the Tories' future success actually rests on what the SNP do and do not do. Clearly, the constitutional question has benefited Ruth and her party. If independence continues to be a matter of flirtation – rather than action – the Tories will benefit. If, however, a ballot does take place before 2021, there are at least as many risks as rewards for the Scottish Conservatives.

But Scottish politics – and the success of Ruth's party – is not just a question of the constitution. While that will continue to be a factor for many voters, there are equal numbers or more who are interested in issues of government. Even with the Brexit vote, at least 50 per cent of Scots do not want to hold another referendum, compared to around 36 per cent who do. These numbers fluctuate, of course, but there is a general consensus that Scots are not interested in a quick sequel to 2014. Such numbers should stand as a warning to those who believe the Tories can continue to achieve success simply by opposing independence. Sturgeon herself realises this. While she continues to throw red meat to those of her supporters driven solely by the question of separation, she makes a strong effort to put competent administration at the front and centre of her image. She insists that reforming education, for instance, remains the 'defining mission' of her government, despite the Brexit vote. The SNP's poll numbers are often significantly higher than the numbers who describe themselves as supporting independence, suggesting there are voters who back the party because of its broadly populist agenda in spite of the possibility of another constitutional vote.

The Tories too, despite much of their rhetoric, are keenly aware of this. As we have seen, their mantra for the 2016 election was 'Strong Opposition'. This was a bid to cast Labour as shambolic and ineffective, but also to emphasise their own competence. Much of this strategy is based around Ruth, who always tries to use reasoned and evidential arguments amid the often-scrappy scenes between Labour and the SNP. Their actual effectiveness since becoming Scotland's second party has, in truth, yet to be tested. Between 2007 and 2011, the Tories enjoyed success by drilling concessions out of the SNP minority government. Such a situation has now returned and there is a possibility that the Scottish Conservatives could push their agenda in Holyrood once again.

It will not, however, be easy. In contrast to 2007, when the general perception was that the Tories were going nowhere, they are now a party on the up. The SNP will be unlikely to want to give them any tangible successes for fear of boosting their enemy. Conversely, Labour will be reluctant – or perhaps too bitter – to offer any real support to the Tories to defeat the SNP. In a debate on the future of fracking, for instance, Labour was actually able to score a victory over the Tories with the help of SNP abstentions. There is, however, opportunity for cooperation. On issues such as healthcare, there is a cross-party consensus among the opposition that the SNP is not effectively managing the NHS. Harnessing such opportunities as and when they come will be crucial if the Tories are to be perceived as successful.

With Brexit and devolution too, a trap awaits the Scottish Conservatives. The massive devolution of powers under the post-2014 referendum Scotland Act yields new problems. Ruth has once again positioned the Tories as a party opposed to further devolution – in her words, it is 'devolution delivered'. This policy has its strengths given that, unlike Labour for example, it now commands the support, publicly at least, of her entire party. Yet the Scottish Conservatives once again run the risk of appearing to care more about Westminster than about Scotland – the very image that allowed their electoral hegemony to slip after 1955.

Such difficulties are further compounded by the imminent advent of Brexit. Sturgeon and the SNP have, as a way of avoiding a second independence vote, advocated more powers over areas like immigration and international trade, as well as agriculture. Control over these areas, the argument goes, would better allow Scotland to mitigate the effects of Brexit and better represent the will of the Scottish people in the vote. There is logic here, but the Tories' loyalty towards their government in Westminster could prove dangerous. Theresa May will be anxious to not let the SNP score a victory, nor deliver a Brexit deal that could artificially benefit Scotland, such as single market membership north of the border. Pressure will be applied to the Scottish Conservatives to follow suit. It will be very difficult for Ruth and her party to represent Scotland's interests, albeit within the Union, in such a scenario.

Merely opposing is easy as an opposition – actually getting things done is much harder. And getting things done for both Scotland and the Union is almost impossible.

Competence and the constitution therefore have a key role to play in any future success – or failure – for the Scottish Conservatives. Perhaps their greatest potential obstacle, however, remains Scottish Labour.

Once Scotland's dominant electoral force, Scottish Labour, led by Richard Leonard since November 2017, has been bruised and battered over recent years. Despite its success in 2014 in the referendum campaign, it has suffered as an electoral force at the hands of the SNP. Even after the 2016 vote, it remains a party going through a process of renewal and, increasingly necessarily, reinvention. The effect of those changes was shown in the 2017 general election, when the party won an additional six seats, and was in touching distance of winning at least fifteen more.

But it is no coincidence that the Tories' rise has come at the same time as Labour's fall. As they approached the Holyrood election, Labour was low on confidence and struggling to remain relevant. Their efforts to shift the political debate on to how to use new tax-and-spend powers – valiant though it was – failed. Ruth and the Tories, in contrast, had a better handle on what voters wanted to talk about.

The issue now for the Scottish Conservatives is whether things will continue in that vein. Jeremy Corbyn's re-election as Labour leader should have been a help to Ruth and the Scottish Conservatives. Questions over a lack of support from his parliamentary party means he is a gift to the Scottish Conservatives as much as the SNP. After a wave of resignations, for example, his then newly appointed shadow Scottish Secretary Dave Anderson touted a possible Labour alliance with the Nationalists. Such casual shifts in policy – seemingly made without consideration or coherence – are easy hits for Ruth's party.

Of course, there are few Labour/Tory marginal seats in Scotland, meaning that in the first-past-the-post system, the Tories' fight remains primarily against the SNP. Following Ruth's success at Holyrood in 2016, it is the Nationalists she is competing against in Westminster elections now, more than Labour.

A marker of how seriously the Scottish Tories are taking the next general election, anticipated in 2022, is that they have already put many candidates in place across the country, particularly in target seats. Across Aberdeenshire, for instance, where the Tories did well in the Holyrood elections, Westminster hopefuls are currently working towards the next House of Commons campaign. By having candidates who live in and know the local area, Tory strategists hope they will be able to better campaign on local issues, as well as raise their profile in the constituency.

As Ruth's own constituency vote in the Scottish election showed, it is also possible for the Tories to come from behind and into contention. A number of seats covering Edinburgh's more affluent areas would be likely targets. Council elections – which use the Alternative Vote system – also offer an opportunity for the Tories to gather strength at Labour's expense.

The Westminster election system does not naturally favour a Tory resurgence in 2022 – if that is when the vote is to be held. Yet if Labour continue to show no sign of recovery, that can only help the Scottish Conservatives rebuild. Scottish Labour could, however, undergo something of a resurgence over the next few months and years. Over the two years of her leadership, Kezia Dugdale reorganised the party's backroom staff and professionalised the operation. More tangibly, she completed a long-awaited autonomy plan for the Scottish party, which suffered from allegations of being a 'branch office' of the Westminster party when Dugdale's predecessor, Johann Lamont, stood down.

The truth remains that, at best, around 25 per cent of Scots seem to be willing to vote Conservative regularly. In the months following the Holyrood election, opinion polls have shown the Tories have continued to retain around 24 per cent of support – roughly the same amount they got in the election. Labour, in contrast, can appeal to a far wider portion of the population – and, despite winning fewer seats than the Tories in 2017, it is better placed to make further gains at the next general election. In 2017, Labour were just 100 votes behind the SNP in two seats and 1,000 votes behind in another six – with several more also viewed as winnable. A resurgent Labour could cause a real difficulty for Ruth and the Tories in their aim of unseating the SNP. Certainly, there is little precedent for swift recoveries in Scottish politics, despite the availability of the list system. The Liberal Democrats, for example, lost twelve seats in 2011, leaving them with just five – and that number would not increase in 2016. Should Labour buck that trend, however, it could create difficulties for the Tories and their ambitions to improve.

There is one final aspect worth considering: to what extent has the Scottish Conservatives' resurgence been the result of Ruth's leadership?

The best way to address this is through the counterfactual. Had Murdo Fraser won the leadership election in 2011, would the outcome have been different?

Clearly, the Holyrood election in 2016 shows, contrary to popular belief, that there is still an appetite for centre-right politics in Scotland. The 2017 general election reaffirms that suggestion. Ruth's modernisation programme sought to break the Tories from the legacy of Thatcher while, in many ways, returning it to the ideals of the original Unionist party. Fraser, in contrast, considered the Tory brand in Scotland finished, with the only solution being to form a new party north of the border, albeit taking the Conservative whip at Westminster. The evidence suggests that he was wrong to believe the Conservative Party did not have a future in Scotland, but that it needed a modern leader such as Ruth to revitalise it. Yet it has only resurged because it has been modernised.

If a new party had been formed, making a clean break from the past, Ruth's reinvention might not have been necessary. Fraser could have been free to present his centre-right agenda afresh, espousing policies that clearly find favour with a portion of the electorate.

In truth, while this would have stopped the centre-right disappearing altogether in Scotland, it would almost certainly not have led the Tories to the heights they have now reached. Voters are not – generally speaking – fools. Ruth's victory, inexperienced though she was, caused the public to reimagine the Conservative Party, more so than any rebranding could have done. Success at the 2017 general election also reflects that the Conservative brand still has some cachet in Scotland.

There are few major policy differences between Fraser and Ruth – except on devolution – although he is more of a small 'c' Conservative. But demands for lower taxes, for example, would have fallen on deaf ears without voters being inspired to re-evaluate their perceptions of who the Tories in Scotland are. Other supporters of Fraser's plan to form a breakaway party have recognised this. Former MSP Brian Monteith, writing in *The Scotsman*, said:

> Being a moderniser has meant that Davidson could redefine what being a Conservative in Scotland means – and this is the key point, for she has redefined the party as the leading proponent of Unionism. Her party is now not so much the Scottish Conservative and Unionist Party as simply the Unionist Party.
>
> Ironically, this particular branding was being considered for the possible launch of a new Scottish party, but Davidson has done it herself by simply changing perceptions about what her party stands for.

Professor James Mitchell has gone further, suggesting that now, following Ruth's significant rebranding work, would actually be the best time to form a new party, although he is cautions about how effective such a move would be:

> A bold move would be to go the whole hog and embrace Murdo Fraser's idea and wind up the party and create a new centre-right party but the results make it an unlikely course of action despite evidence from this election that there may be merit in this idea.
>
> Her record suggests she would unhesitatingly make the

change if she is convinced it would boost her support. But this might play into the impression that Tories under Davidson will say or do anything to win votes. A name change alone might backfire and certainly would not be enough.

Given the success of the Tories at the 2017 general election, this seems a logical argument. Ruth traversed difficulty and obscurity during the initial stages of her leadership, but has since proved herself an adept and popular leader. The Conservative Party does, of course, carry significant baggage, not least in that it is her party that is responsible for the seemingly impossible task of delivering Brexit.

But what is clear is that, whether at the helm of the current or a new party, Ruth herself remains the Scottish Conservatives' greatest electoral asset.

And, if they were to lose her, it would be their greatest loss.

CHAPTER 15

'NOW IS NOT THE TIME'

Nicola Sturgeon's call for a second independence referendum was delivered with typically extravagant pomp and ceremony. From Bute House – in the same room where her predecessor had resigned after failing to win the 2014 contest – the SNP leader declared that another vote should be rerun by 2019.

Her catalyst was Brexit and her speech, delivered in March 2017, on the eve of the triggering of Article 50, was particularly scathing of the Tories. Her efforts to 'compromise' with Theresa May had, the SNP leader said, 'been met with a brick wall of intransigence'. In the face of such chaos, Sturgeon said, Scotland needed to make a choice between the UK and a hard Brexit. She concluded: 'By taking the steps I have set out today, I am ensuring that Scotland's future will be decided not just by me, the Scottish government or the SNP. It will be decided by the people of Scotland. It will be Scotland's choice.'

That Sturgeon decided to press ahead with a vote came as no great surprise. Apart from independence being her political calling, she had been steadily agitating for another referendum ever since the Brexit vote, using the process to sow grievance – sometimes justified – and stoke resentment towards both the Tories and Westminster.

Despite no noticeable shift towards independence in polling (a few hasty polls in the aftermath of the Brexit vote showing increased support for Yes proved outliers), Sturgeon knew she would not get a better chance than this. The Brexit process, she judged, would most likely be shambolic and push up support for separation. Holyrood elections – and the prospect of losing her pro-independence majority in the Scottish Parliament – were also on the horizon. In short, Sturgeon thought it might not be just the best chance, but also her only chance.

The timing of the announcement was, however, unexpected and took many politicians – including Ruth – by surprise. There had been no trail of the speech and, despite the efforts of Holy-rood's press pack, no leaks or even hints as to its contents had emerged. Every opposition party had to scramble to respond – and the decisiveness of Sturgeon's announcement was generally praised as a masterstroke that gained the initiative for the SNP.

Sturgeon's speech was accompanied by an organised fundrais-ing drive and coordinated social media push, which led to the general impression that the Nationalists were on the front foot. The SNP was keen to rebrand the contest 'ScotRef', as opposed to the more ubiquitous 'indyref2', which was viewed negatively by party strategists. This was not to be a rerun of 2014, but a new, fresh contest for different reasons.

For Ruth, the prospect of a second independence referendum was both tantalising and terrifying. Sturgeon's decision to try to press ahead with the vote offered a number of clear benefits both to Ruth and the Scottish Conservatives. Most obviously, the tangible prospect of a second independence referendum would ensure the constitution was kept at the forefront of Scottish politics. As we have seen, this was a key part of Ruth's strategy and message post-2014 and it had resonated well with voters. The continuing emphasis on constitutional politics would help stop voters focusing on the delivery of public services. While the SNP had a poor, bordering on atrocious, record of managing public services, the Scottish Conservatives also suffered from a policy void. The 'Strong Opposition' strategy was clearly effective, but had left the Tories with embarrassingly little that they could suggest they would do differently. As well as being short on ideas, Ruth's party was – unsurprisingly – determined to cut taxes or, at the very least, not raise them, meaning it couldn't credibly advocate for greater investment, either. But the prospect of a second independence ballot meant Scottish politics would remain firmly focused on the constitution.

More personally, the prospect of a second referendum was an individual challenge for Ruth. Not only did she care passionately for the UK and want to fight to protect it, but a second referendum offered her the perfect opportunity to renew the case for the Union on her terms. There was little doubt she would play a far more prominent role in this campaign than she did in 2014, given her increased profile and improved political position. It was a chance for her to take centre stage and re-cement the Conservatives in the Scottish political lexicon. It was Nationalists versus Unionists, which fitted Ruth perfectly.

Despite being taken aback by Sturgeon's independence ambush, the Conservatives quickly recovered the initiative, largely under the guidance of Ruth. The Tories had campaigned as the party of the Union – now they had to prove it.

As it happened, Theresa May – having consulted extensively with Ruth and her team – struck on a simple but effective strategy. The Conservative government would just block any attempt to hold another referendum until at least 2021. Theresa May took to the nation's television screens to say 'now is not the time' – an effective sound bite.

Despite the Prime Minister initially taking the lead, it fell to Ruth to articulate the policy. Speaking after Sturgeon's announcement, in the shadow of the impregnable Edinburgh Castle, Ruth outlined her opposition to a second independence referendum. 'We reject conclusively the timetable for a referendum set out by the Scottish government,' she told assembled journalists, alongside a slightly redundant Secretary of State for Scotland, David Mundell. 'For a key reason – because it is unfair to Scottish voters.' In a subtle swipe at the Leave campaign, she said voters in the EU referendum complained they did not have the necessary information to make an informed decision. She added:

If we were to keep to the First Minister's timetable, this is exactly what would happen in Scotland, too. On the most important political decision a country can make, we would be voting blind. I believe that it is only right that people have the opportunity to examine the UK's new relationship with the European Union once it is up and running.

This, Ruth argued, should be after 2021, when the full benefits – or, more likely, costs – of Brexit were fully known. There should be no vote before then.

Undoubtedly, this was a risky strategy. In the coming weeks, the SNP would bring forward a Section 30 order to the Scottish

Parliament, the formal process to ask Westminster for another referendum. With the support of the Greens, such an order would pass. Rejecting it out of hand would, in effect, be rejecting the will of Holyrood and, by extension, the people of Scotland. As the strategy was outlined, Sturgeon already railed that such a move would be 'undemocratic' and, less convincingly, that Unionists were running scared of another ballot. This baton was picked up by pro-SNP politicians and commentators – reflecting, perhaps, their fear of a referendum being delayed. Indeed, in her letter to May formally asking to begin discussions about a second referendum being held, Sturgeon presented a thinly veiled threat to the Prime Minister if she continued to block a ballot.

'There appears to be no rational reason for you to stand in the way of the will of the Scottish Parliament and I hope you will not do so,' Sturgeon wrote in the letter, which was released alongside a carefully choreographed photo of the First Minister relaxing on a sofa in Bute House as she finalised the document.

> However, in anticipation of your refusal to enter into discussions at this stage, it is important for me to be clear about my position.
>
> It is my firm view that the mandate of the Scottish Parliament must be respected and progressed. The question is not if, but how.
>
> I hope that will be by constructive discussion between our governments. However, if that is not yet possible, I will set out to the Scottish Parliament the steps I intend to take to ensure that progress is made towards a referendum.

The threat, of course, was unspecified, but could have included attempting to frustrate the Brexit process (Holyrood may have held a vote, for instance, on the so-called Great Repeal Bill) or – less likely – proceeding with a vote anyway.

Nevertheless, Ruth felt confident this was the right course. Polling – even in these unreliable days – consistently showed that most Scots, including many who voted Yes, did not want another ballot. Ruth, therefore, was positioning herself on the side of the majority by blocking another vote.

More importantly, blocking a vote until after the 2021 election would serve Ruth's ambition to become First Minister. As Ruth persistently said, the SNP must 'earn' the right to hold another ballot and, with an ongoing constitutional battle, that Holyrood election would effectively be a vote on whether or not another referendum should be held. Ruth hoped the 2021 contest would in effect be a rerun of the 2016 election – a vote along constitutional lines that had served her so well previously.

With strong Unionist credentials, Ruth would be the natural home for all those who oppose another ballot – and she hoped that would be enough to push her over the line. This may be wishful thinking, but it is difficult – even among Tories themselves – to find any prospect of an easier path to Bute House.

* * *

Sturgeon's bid for a second referendum got off to an inauspicious start. In the middle of two days of debate on whether or not to vote for a Section 30 order – it would eventually pass with the support of the Greens – Khalid Masood conducted his vicious terror attack on Westminster Bridge.

The vote, after some unpleasant wrangling and taunting from the SNP, had to be postponed. In her speech, Ruth, as expected, stood firm with a combative and defiant display. 'Last week, in what was a disgraceful episode, we were shouted at from the SNP benches and told we were frightened to debate independence,' she told MSPs.

> We're not. But we are sick of it. And most people in Scotland have had enough too. Because this Parliament needs to and must focus on the priorities of the people of this country. This is not the time to be side-tracked by yet more unnecessary division. It is time for a government that focuses on the job we pay it to do.

It was a staunch and robust speech that held firm to her commitment to oppose another referendum at all costs.

As she left the Scottish Parliament chamber, Ruth steeled herself for a lengthy bout of constitutional wrangling as the Tory majority at Westminster readied itself to reject Sturgeon's demands for a second ballot. It was her aim to stop another vote before 2021 – but, in fact, one would be only weeks away, and it would halt Sturgeon's demands for another ballot almost completely.

CHAPTER 16

SNAP ELECTION

Ruth was the first elected politician in the UK the Prime Minister told of her intention to hold an early general election. This distinction represents an overwhelming transformation for Ruth. In just six years, she had turned the Scottish Conservatives – and by extension herself – from a political afterthought into the heart of the Tory decision-making process. When the Cabinet – the most senior Tories in the country – were told of the decision, Ruth had already known for several hours – and wasted no time in starting the campaign. As she hung up the phone with the Prime Minister, she was imbued with a confidence no previous Scottish Tory leader would have felt at an election being called. She told party staff: 'Bring it on.'

Ruth greeted the early election in the same way that many – though not all – Tory supporters did: she was excited and boisterous about her party's chances. Ever the fighter, she enjoyed the scrap of an election campaign, treating it as an army officer would treat going to war. For her, this was a chance to once again show off the progress she was making in Scotland to the UK media and commentators. But conversely – and unlike many of her colleagues in London – it carried fewer risks. Ruth herself had no seat to lose – she did not contemplate standing – while the general view of most observers was the Tories would do well to pick up any seats at all in Scotland. Anything other than losing their one Tory seat under David Mundell – a fairly unthinkable prospect, given the circumstances – could be spun as progress.

Ruth was confident. The Tories had continued to enjoy improved poll ratings in Scotland since 2016 and Ruth was certain that – finally – the party would be able to expand beyond its solitary MP in Scotland. The same was true in Scottish Conservative Central Office. While the Tories' surge in Holyrood had been based almost entirely on the proportional representation list vote, their support in constituencies had slowly been growing. Old Tory heartlands, such as the north-east of Scotland and the Borders, were now in play. The combination of Ruth's popularity, May's (seeming) appeal and the reigniting of the constitutional debate could put the Tories over the line in as many as ten constituencies, party strategists hoped.

This optimism was borne out by the local government elections, which took place just eight weeks before the Westminster election. Despite being overshadowed by the national campaign, the polls appeared to provide a good bellwether for the Tories in Scotland. Ruth's party gained over 100 council seats and consolidated the gains made in 2016. Particularly encouraging were the number of first-preference votes for Tory candidates in target seats for the general election. As Ruth herself stated:

If you look right across the Borders, in Dumfries and Galloway, East Renfrewshire, in places like Perthshire, Aberdeenshire

and in Moray – so in Angus Robertson's seat, the [SNP] group
leader ... in Westminster – you see it's the Scottish Conservatives who have topped that vote. So we need to use this as
a platform to take this fight to the SNP and lead Scotland's
fightback against the SNP.

This was not mere hubris – this was the general consensus
among political commentators too. As Professor James Mitchell,
co-director of the Academy of Government at the University of
Edinburgh, told *The Observer*: 'The Tories have the resources to
target effectively, as seen in [the 2016] Holyrood elections, so we
should expect a significant boost to parliamentary representation.
What they may lack in activists on the ground, they make up for
in money.'

It is of course difficult to compare like for like with Scottish
council and UK election results, given the different electoral systems
employed, but it was nevertheless an encouraging sign for Ruth.

Another key strength was Ruth's preparedness for a snap
election that many believed would never happen. Over the
previous six months the Scottish Tories had, extremely quietly,
begun selecting and placing candidates in their key target seats.
Around a dozen were in place by the time of Theresa May's announcement, according to party sources, and had already begun
a *piano* campaign, preparing literature and getting to know their
constituencies.

After the election was announced, the Scottish Tories were the
first party to put up posters and begin leafleting in their target
seats. In contrast, other parties were left scrambling to respond to
Theresa May's announcement, which almost universally came as
a surprise. In a hastily prepared statement, Nicola Sturgeon could

only describe the early general election as a 'political miscalculation' (she would of course be proved right), before adding: '[It will] once again give people the opportunity to reject the Tories' narrow, divisive agenda, as well as reinforcing the democratic mandate which already exists for giving the people of Scotland a choice on their future.' While the SNP only had to select candidates for five seats – the three it did not win in 2015, and two that had had the whip withdrawn – Sturgeon's party clearly lagged behind in terms of both planning and preparedness for a snap election.

It is unclear whether Ruth was told by May or her team of her intention to call a snap general election. Certainly, Ruth cannot have known the specifics of the Prime Minister's intentions – the fateful decision to call an election was, of course, made after her walking holiday during the Easter recess. Yet, despite her public denials, the prospect of an early ballot was clearly in May's thoughts for some time. It seems highly unlikely – given a lack of intimacy in their relationship – that May would have sought Ruth's counsel. On the contrary, the Prime Minister is frequently criticised for keeping decision making among a small selection of intimates. Yet Ruth clearly understood – at the very least intuitively – that an early general election was *possible* – and it is a tribute to her skill as a leader that she ensured her troops, as she would see them, were the best prepared.

* * *

The campaign itself began in earnest almost immediately after Theresa May's speech on the steps of Downing Street on 18 April 2017 – and it was a sign of how seriously the Tories were contemplating gains in Scotland that the Prime Minister chose Scotland among her first campaign stops.

The West Aberdeenshire and Kincardine seat – generally referred to by the acronym WAK – is a wealthy, traditionally Tory seat that had nevertheless backed the Nationalists at recent polls. *The Sun*, for instance, described it as 'a foray into enemy heartlands' for May. But in truth it was a natural target for the Scottish Conservatives and that was reflected in their candidate, the able Andrew Bowie.

May's visit, however, was something of a disaster that, with hindsight, would foreshadow the campaign ahead. The Prime Minister gave her standard, straightforward campaign stump speech, with a reference to Scotland added in. 'My message to the people of Scotland today is clear: if you vote for me it will strengthen my hand in the Brexit negotiations,' she told a rally of party members in the constituency. 'It will strengthen the Union, strengthen the economy and together the UK and Scotland will flourish. Because when Scotland is flourishing, the rest of the United Kingdom is flourishing too.'

The speech received the same manufactured and rather weary applause it would when it was repeated again and again across the country over the course of the following month. Yet it was an impromptu door-knocking session afterwards that proved particularly awkward.

After being shooed away at the first doorstep, May and Bowie – with the nation's media in tow – went to more than half a dozen doors without finding anyone in or willing to speak to them. After that, she swiftly fled in a motorcade. The footage made for the sort of cringeworthy viewing that would come to characterise May's media appearances.

Apart from the occasional constituency visit by May, however, Ruth's campaign remained largely immune to the increasing chaos of the Conservative campaign nationally. The UK Tory leader gradually struggled more and more as polling day neared. Her manifesto launch – particularly her policy on social care, which was not shared with either Cabinet colleagues or Ruth – resulted in a swift and humiliating U-turn. As it emerged that Labour leader Jeremy Corbyn was proving more popular with the public than the polls had predicted, May's performances become more jittery. The campaign's tag line – strong and stable – became a focus of ridicule as May and the Tories were quickly revealed to be anything but.

In contrast, Ruth enjoyed a fine campaign. It is, of course, one of the peculiarities of general elections in Scotland that policy agendas actually matter little, because so much is devolved and dealt with at a Holyrood level. Sturgeon, for instance, made her name by arguing against austerity at UK-wide level, despite having no ability to actually change it (and, indeed, despite positively implementing austerity in Scotland). As such, May's controversial manifesto had less of an impact in Scotland than it did across the rest of the country. The prominence of regional broadcast bulletins – and regional print media – also allowed Ruth to be the public face of the campaign in Scotland, ahead of May.

Ruth's strategy was not new or refreshing, but it was finely honed. Sturgeon's announcement that she intended to pursue a second independence referendum had focused the constitutional issue, in comparison to the 2016 Holyrood election, where it remained more hypothetical.

The rhetoric remained very much in the 2016 vein. Launching her general election campaign, for instance, Ruth said: 'Across

Scotland, we know people are looking for somebody to stand up to the SNP. So our challenge is this. It's to bring the SNP down to size. To show they can't take Scotland for granted.'

Yet she continued to moderate ambitions, saying it would take a 'Herculean' effort to defeat Nationalist MPs. Here, she was perhaps wary of promising too much, given historic Tory failures to make inroads in Scotland despite expectations. The volatile political climate – the Brexit vote, the election of Donald Trump – would only reinforce Ruth's caution. Again, as in 2016, she did not try to suggest the Tories would defeat the SNP across the country or strive to become the largest party. The 'Strong Opposition' script of 2016 remained.

'We have a massive fight on our hands against an all-powerful SNP,' she said at the same event.

> We go into this election with one seat. They go into it with fifty-four – and most of them with large majorities. Even to challenge the Nationalists in some of these seats is going to take a Herculean effort. Make no mistake, we are the underdogs.
>
> But we also know this. The SNP is not Scotland. And people across this country don't take kindly to Nicola Sturgeon pretending the opposite is true.

This strategy was borne out by the polling – Sturgeon was pursuing a second independence referendum with little sign that a majority of Scots wanted one, or that she would win one if it were held. As we have seen in the previous chapter, despite her efforts, support for independence remained at almost exactly the same level as in 2014. By reiterating her opposition to a second independence referendum, Ruth was positioning herself among the majority of Scots. But by doing so, she was also subtly infer-ring that Sturgeon was out of touch, separated from reality and hell-bent on pursuing separation regardless of public opinion.

This intonation provided an ideal segue into the second strand of Ruth's campaign: domestic politics. Of course, devolved issues were – technically speaking at least – irrelevant to the UK gen-eral election campaign. But there was an opportunity to develop a narrative that the SNP was failing to govern Scotland because of its obsession with a second independence referendum. This made the 2017 general election less about what government Scots wanted to see in Westminster and as much, if not more, about how they wanted to see decisions taken at Holyrood.

This line of attack – which was not just employed by the Tories but also by Labour and the Liberal Democrats – was particular-ly resonant given a number of disastrous recent reports on the state of public services under the SNP. 'This SNP government's handling of our education system over the last decade in power has been shameful – and change needs to happen,' Ruth told her party's conference in March, in what would become a running theme over the next three months. In March 2017, for instance, the PISA international education rankings were announced, with Scotland recording its worst results on record amid declin-ing standards in reading, writing and maths.

Such reports put Sturgeon and the SNP in a real bind. Having been in power for a decade, Nationalist ministers could hardly blame previous administrations for the failings – and nor could they blame Westminster without inevitably at least touching on independence. As Alex Massie would write for *The Spectator*:

A generous soul might conclude that this just goes to show

that Nicola Sturgeon is right to make education her 'top priority'. And it is true that she has, unlike her predecessor, at least
identified the problem.

Ms Sturgeon makes a virtue of her concern but this takes
some chutzpah, given that her party has been in power for a
decade now.

He goes on to conclude that the SNP's management of education is 'muddled'.

Such commentary had been endemic among the Scottish press
for much of the previous twelve months, with regular criticism of
the SNP's supervision of public services. Ruth's campaign narrative therefore fitted well into a growing suspicion that the SNP
was more interested in grievance than government.

That is not to suggest that she was entirely on the front foot
throughout the entire campaign, however. Ruth had seven years
of Tory government at Westminster to defend, and welfare
reform – particularly changes to tax credits – was especially
controversial.

Ruth came under fire for the so-called 'rape clause', a Tory
change that forced a woman to prove she had been raped in
order to receive child tax credits for more than two children. This
particular policy, widely regarded as abhorrent, was used as a bat-
tering ram by other parties to hammer Ruth, with the SNP using
Scottish Parliament time to force a debate on the policy. Ruth,
to her credit, stood up and defended the policy herself – but it
was a bruising debate in which she was repeatedly heckled and
refused to take interventions. In truth, she was only saved from
more damning coverage by an excellent speech from Scottish
Labour leader Kezia Dugdale, who grabbed the vast majority of

headlines by reporting the experiences of one of her constituents who had had to go through the 'rape clause' process.

Nevertheless, Ruth was largely able to set the agenda and keep to her key themes in the weeks leading up to 8 June.

* * *

While she had a confident, if not entirely new, campaign narrative, Ruth was realistic about her party's chances.

Polling in the run-up to the election suggested the Tories were in the running for a remarkable resurgence in Scotland. A high of 33 per cent in the polls would have given them – on a universal swing – a dozen seats. Most of these gains would be concentrated in areas where the Tories would traditionally expect to perform strongly: rural, farming communities and wealthy suburbs.

Party staff, wary of overconfidence, briefed that they thought seven seats was a likely estimate. Behind the scenes they ploughed resources into little more than thirteen key seats; all but one they would win. Many of these were in the north-east of Scotland, such as Aberdeen South, West Aberdeenshire and Kincardine, and Banff and Buchan. Not only had the Tories performed well here under Ruth in the 2016 Holyrood elections, but they were also strong Leave areas in the EU referendum. Ruth – showing once again the malleability of her beliefs – was careful to make clear she now supported Brexit, albeit in a softer form than the Prime Minister, in order to attract these voters. In contrast, the SNP's strong pro-EU stance, particularly in fishing communities devastated by the Common Fisheries Policy, was expected to hurt its support.

More ambitious targets – but ones where Ruth was equally

determined to succeed – were Moray and Gordon. The seats of Angus Robertson, SNP Westminster leader, and Alex Salmond, the former SNP leader, respectively, offered a tantalising chance for Ruth's Tories to defeat two SNP big beasts. Elsewhere, the Tories intended to make significant gains in the Borders, where Scottish Secretary David Mundell already had his seat, as well as Perthshire, another strong Leave area which was a historic area of Tory support.

Ruth would spend the vast majority of the campaign visiting these areas in support of her prospective candidates. Despite this being a UK-wide election, the vast majority of the candidates were Ruth allies. A number were already MSPs at Holyrood – some had been elected there only in 2016 – while others were Scottish Tory staff. In Moray, Douglas Ross – who won a list seat under Ruth at the Holyrood election – was selected to stand, while in Aberdeen South another Ruth loyalist, Ross Thomson, who was again elected only in 2016, was picked. In Berwick-shire, Roxburgh and Selkirk, one of Ruth's earliest supporters, John Lamont, was selected. In West Aberdeenshire and Kincar-dine, Andrew Bowie, a long-term party staffer under Ruth, was selected.

This is not particularly unusual, especially given the abrupt-ness with which the election was called. Parties regularly para-chute backroom figures into seats, while it was not uncommon for MSPs to run for Westminster. But the trend would take on a greater significance after Theresa May lost her majority. The new Scottish Tory MPs were categorically Ruth's people – loyal to her, rather than May. As we will see, this would give Ruth unprecedented power and relevance after 8 June.

Ruth supported these candidates with her usual bonhomie

and enthusiasm during the campaign. She tried her best to interject some serious policy points on the stump, although this is not her strong point. In the Borders, for instance, there were plenty of warm words but little substance. 'We're ... talking about the Borderland Growth Deal today, not just in the south of Scotland but we want to work with the north of England and make sure we have the economic development that this part of the country really needs,' she said.

Her efforts to appear more serious did not stretch too far, however. While she had little need of the press-attracting stunts of her early years – she was now too significant not to get attention – she still injected some fun into the campaign. At one photo call, she appeared with her pet cocker spaniel, Wilson, to the delight of the press pack. (The dog itself has a disconcerting similarity to its owner, having been hit by a car as a youngster, resulting in multiple operations, metal pins and even skin grafts.)

As polling day approached, and in another echo of the 2016 campaign, Ruth also took to the skies in a helicopter to conduct a whistle-stop tour of target seats – but on the whole it was a more serious campaign than those previously conducted.

* * *

When Scotland went to the polls, voters would elevate Ruth to be one of the most powerful politicians in the country. She enjoyed a stunning election night, with her party returning thirteen MPs – twelve more than the Scottish Conservatives had returned just two years earlier. As results trickled in throughout the early morning on 9 June, it became increasingly clear that Ruth had not just stalled the Tory decline in Scotland, but reversed it.

Party strategists had feared that bad weather – there was tor-
rential rain across Scotland throughout polling day – might affect
turnout in key areas and hurt their chances. Panicked messages
flew across Scotland, but they proved premature as the ballots
were counted. Several seats – such as West Aberdeenshire and
Kincardine – had wafer-thin SNP majorities and were early, and
expected, Tory gains. But as the hours wore on further unexpected victories came in. The two biggest – in Moray and Gordon
– completed Ruth's rout of the SNP in the historic Tory heartlands. It was an emphatic victory that reaffirmed Ruth's position
as a rising star of UK politics.

For the Tories as a whole across the UK, it was a night of con-
trasts – and it is easy to compare Ruth's night with that of Theresa May. The Prime Minister endured one of the most humiliating
of political humblings in history. Her snap election gamble had
categorically failed. In contrast to Ruth's heroics, May had not
only failed to expand her majority but lost it altogether. In terms
of image, the contrasting fortunes of the Tory leaders north and
south of the border could not be starker. The young, energetic
Ruth romped home, while the ageing, nervous May achieved
nothing but disaster.

But it is also worth contrasting Ruth's position with that of
Nicola Sturgeon, who endured a torrid night. Amid the Tory
surge and a more modest but nonetheless notable Labour effort,
the Nationalists lost twenty-one seats and could easily have lost
far more.

The vote was widely seen as a rejection of Sturgeon's renewed
drive for independence. Of course, it was always unlikely that the
SNP would retain all fifty-four seats it had held going into the
election. But the scale of the defeat was remarkable. Those who

backed the SNP in 2015 simply did not turn up and vote for them in 2017, while support for the pro-UK Tory and Labour parties held up. 'Indyref2 is dead – that's what's happened tonight,' Ruth declared, as the results flooded in.

May had held the election on the premise of gaining a strengthened majority to drive through Brexit. In this respect, she categorically failed. But the decision to hold an early ballot had the effect of inflicting early losses on the SNP and halting Sturgeon's momentum. In this respect, the early election was a triumphant success for the Tories.

Indeed, following her electoral humbling, Sturgeon was forced to rethink her plans for a second referendum, promising to 'reset' the debate. The half-hearted U-turn still leaves the door to another referendum open, but the margin of the SNP's defeat makes a second ballot highly unlikely.

However, the election was even more fundamental for Ruth than a mere rejection of independence, which had arguably taken place at every vote since 2014. The Scottish Conservatives' victory radically changed the dynamic of the relationship between it and its UK counterpart. As we have seen, the thirteen candidates elected in Scotland were very much Ruth's people – they owe their candidacy, position and indeed election to Ruth, not May. They won their seats because of Ruth and, arguably, in spite of May. Ruth therefore now has considerable political muscle in Westminster, as well as at Holyrood. While she enjoyed some influence under Cameron and Osborne, under May she now has tangible political power.

Her position of strength is further accentuated by the Tories losing their majority across the UK. On its own, thirteen MPs loyal to Ruth is noteworthy but not hugely significant. But May would have lost the election without Ruth's MPs. Indeed, the Prime Minister now has to rely on Ruth's MPs to maintain her parliamentary majority. The Prime Minister's coalition deal with Democratic Unionist Party (DUP) – at a cost of £1 billion for ten MPs – would be worthless if Ruth – or rather the MPs loyal to her – decided to vote against the whip. The fact that May sees DUP MPs as worth £100 million each gives a flavour of the power Ruth's thirteen Scottish Tories hold.

On minor political matters, a rebellion seems unlikely. Ruth, generally speaking, is a party loyalist, her military training keeping her comfortably disciplined to a particular line, even if she privately disagrees with it. Ruth rarely, for instance, spoke out against Cameron or Osborne. When she did dissent, it was carefully coordinated – she owed too much and had too much personal loyalty to Cameron in particular to fully rebel. This is not the case with May, whom Ruth reluctantly backed for leader after her preferred candidate – Stephen Crabb – pulled out. Indeed, while both Ruth and May were supporters of the Remain campaign, they do not agree on Britain's future outside the EU – the essential political debate of the next five years.

Ruth has a huge opportunity in this parliament to shape and influence the debate. She is capable, despite not being in the House of Commons herself, of being a major thorn in the side of Brexiteers hoping to sever all ties with Europe. Ruth may judge, of course, that she is better off staying quiet – but this seems unlikely. May is terminally weak and will surely not fight the next election, due in 2022. There is thus little benefit to Ruth from remaining loyal. As a passionate pro-European, it is therefore unlikely that she will acquiesce to a hard Brexit.

Regardless of whether or not she chooses to rebel, the 2017

election confirmed Ruth's and the Scottish Conservatives' remarkable resurgence. In just six years, Ruth has gone from being the novice leader of a declining party considered largely irrelevant to one of the most important politicians in the UK, at the head of growing political movement. When she became leader, the Scottish Conservatives were all but dead. Now, they are very much alive.

CHAPTER 17

PRIME MINISTER RUTH?

R uth Davidson's star has risen at an even greater pace than her party's. Despite her rocky start, the consensus is that she is a formidable leader with a bright political future ahead of her – if she wants it. She has achieved what no other leader of the Conservatives has managed for decades, taking the party out of the doldrums at Holyrood and regaining them a Scottish foothold in Westminster. But she has also boosted the Tory brand. Although she was first elected in only 2011, she is already being mentioned as a potential Conservative Cabinet minister – or Prime Minister. The question now for Ruth is whether she has achieved all she can with the Scottish Conservatives. And what, if any, future would she have outside of devolved politics?

Only Ruth herself can answer for her feelings and decisions, whatever they may be in the future. But we can draw firm inferences from her character and previous actions, as well as the political situation, to chart the possible courses for her future. There is no doubt that, objectively, Ruth has been a highly successful leader of the Scottish Conservatives. And the most remarkable thing about her career to date is how short it has been. Ruth entered politics proper as recently as 2009, which perhaps accounts for her perceived normality in the eyes of many voters. After two unsuccessful attempts to get a seat at Westminster, she was eventually elected to the Scottish Parliament on the Glasgow list. A relative unknown, she was thrust – amid Machiavellian intrigue – into a leadership bid, which she eventually won. Her grit and determination shone through in her early years, but in truth between 2011 and 2013 she struggled to get to grips with her new role. This is understandable, as too is the fact that it was the referendum that really made her. Ruth is best when she is at her most passionate. Yet there remained bumps in the road – most notably, the 2015 general election – before she could reap the rewards of her modernisation project at the Holyrood elections. Her performance in the 2016 EU referendum cemented her status as a rising star of the Conservative Party. In the 2017 general election, her success in Scotland was perhaps the only silver lining for the Tories in an otherwise disastrous election campaign.

The foundation of this success has been her ability to bring Scotland back onto the Tory agenda. Ruth has rekindled that dying ember in the Conservatives – the notion, ultimately, that you can represent both Scottish and UK interests. This factor, coupled with the continuing constitutional aspect to politics north of the border, has allowed her to drive her party forward. With such success behind – and, seemingly ahead – of her, it is understandable that many are anxious that she take on a greater role in the UK party. But Ruth does not want to head to Westminster – not yet, anyway. One friend said that Ruth remarked that she 'can't wait to get out of Holyrood' – but such an overly frank statement should be treated with caution. Ruth knows herself that her work with the Scottish Conservatives is not finished. While she has achieved two remarkable results in a short space of time, there is nothing to stop the party falling back. The Liberal Democrats were once just a seat behind the Conservatives in Holyrood, but have now collapsed and show little sign of recovery. There but for careful management might go the Tories.

It will take time to ensure the re-establishment of the Tory brand in Scotland is on solid foundations. Ruth is key to this. She is, according to recent polls, the most popular politician among Scottish voters. Even Sturgeon – who held the crown for so long – has been eclipsed. Ruth's net approval rating is around 15 per cent, no mean feat for a Tory in Scotland. Sturgeon, meanwhile, had a net approval rating of 0 per cent in January 2018, with equal numbers of voters rating and slating her performance. If Ruth were to desert the Scottish Conservatives, it would be a major loss. Even hypothetically, there is no clear successor who could take her place. Many of her MSPs are new to Holyrood – although so was she – while the relationship between the new and those who are more experienced is often tense. Even if the party could drum up someone, it is highly unlikely they would be as popular or successful.

There is also the issue of a Westminster seat, namely that there is not one. It would be unpalatable for Ruth to jump ship to a safe seat in England, despite the hopes of some. When David Cameron resigned, bookmakers were instantly taking bets – often on short odds – that Ruth would succeed him in Witney. Dramatic though it would have been, it was never going to happen.

Ruth could, if needed, fight a by-election in Scotland in a bid to get a Westminster seat. Here, the risks of losing would prob-ably be too great. While the Tories are enjoying a bump – and have now proved beyond doubt they can win Westminster seats in Scotland – by-elections are hugely unpredictable, stuffed with wild-card candidates and generally not a sure bet.

Ruth has also been, in this case, something of a victim of her own success. While winning the Edinburgh Central Scottish Parliament constituency in 2016 was a triumph, it has left her somewhat hamstrung. To fight a Westminster seat she would most likely have to resign, triggering a Scottish Parliament by-election. Former First Minister Alex Salmond served briefly as both Gordon MP and Aberdeenshire East MSP, but he was fortunate in that both constituencies covered a similar area. Such a seat is more difficult to find in Edinburgh, where there is no direct Westminster comparison to Ruth's Central constituency – and certainly not one currently held by a Tory who could make way. Ironically, had she lost Edinburgh Central and been elected on the list PR system, it would be easier for her to resign to contest another seat. The next Tory candidate on the list would simply replace her, ensuring a smooth transition rather than an ugly mess of an off-diary election.

Of course, all of this is not to suggest that Ruth is not hugely popular – or welcome – in the Westminster bubble. Ruth, as her post-Brexit speech showed, is something of a darling of the House of Commons lobby reporters, many of whom view her as a refreshing and unusual Tory. The Scottish Conservative leader has helped build this brand to ingratiate herself beyond the normal realms of Holyrood politicians. Her performances on the hit BBC show *Have I Got News For You* – as well as *Celebrity Bake Off* – are a good example of this strategy. She has used such high-profile performances to reinforce her image as a funny, self-effacing Conservative. In her first performance, at the end of 2015, she sat on the panel with Paul Merton and took jokes about her Scottish background with typically good grace, despite admitting she was terrified of appearing on the show beforehand. Host Michael Sheen joked that her hobbies included hiking, before adding: 'In fact, she's never happier than when she's walking 500 miles' – a reference to the famous song by Scottish band the Proclaimers. She joked about Scotland's recent exit from the Rugby World Cup amid a controversial refereeing decision, as well as her fondness for Scots player Greg Laidlaw. Some critics commented unflatteringly on her reflex of often loud and uncontained laughter, but it was, on the whole, a well-received performance. She would return to the panel again in 2016, while she has also expressed a desire to appear on *Strictly Come Dancing*. Referencing the former shadow Chancellor Ed Ball's appearance on the show, she told BBC *Breakfast* with typical bonhomie: 'I tell you what, I might be a Scottish Tory but there's a bit of my household that is forever Balls, because I've been supporting him 100 per cent, I love to see him throwing himself into it.' She added:

I bumped into Yvette Cooper [Ed Balls's MP wife and former shadow Home Secretary] when I was down in the House of Commons a couple of weeks ago and apparently he's really pleased with all the support he's had. So I think it's brilliant and I tell you something: if the BBC came asking, I would be there in a heartbeat, I would be spangled, I would make sure that I am spray-tanned, the frock, the heels, everything, I would love it.

Such comments are an absolute delight to journalists across the country – but particularly at Westminster. They have not only helped Ruth cultivate an image as a 'normal' person but have also reinforced the sense that she is a different type of politician. A politician, in short, who is fun, gregarious and who people want to be around. While this might not be an overt attempt to lay the groundwork for a move to Westminster, it has done nothing to dampen speculation – perhaps hopeful speculation – that she may one day make the move south.

The greater issue, however, is that Ruth wants to be First Minister of Scotland – a job you cannot do as an MP. Some columnists find this view bizarre, but Ruth is truly ambitious for the Scottish party. Speaking at the Tory Party conference after the EU referendum, Ruth said: 'I think that anybody would be in the wrong job if they were leading a political party in a legislature and they did not wish to be the party of government in that legislature. Of course that's the aim.'

She recognises, however, that this will take time. The next Scottish election is not due until 2021. Given the SNP currently have more than double the number of seats as the Tories in Holyrood, it will most likely take even longer, although the prospect of a coalition should not be ruled out. 'Just as it was fanciful five years ago to say we were going to overtake Labour and be the opposition, I understand there is a lot of work to do to be able to move from being a strong opposition to being an alternative party of government,' she admitted.

Such ambitions, of course, are unsurprising. Having run on the ticket of a 'Strong Opposition' in 2016, she could hardly do so again in 2021. Arguing that Ruth should be the next First Minister is, in truth, the only logical suggestion she could make.

It is telling, however, that she is willing to publicly share that ambition. Ruth has shown throughout her career that she is ready to jettison commitments when they no longer serve their purpose. But to abandon the Scottish Conservatives, with the momentum in their favour, while that was the stated objective would only leave the impression that she viewed making the Tories a party of government in Scotland impossible.

Alex Massie, writing for *The Spectator*, suggests there is a further reason for her to stay on in Scotland, particularly post-Brexit. 'Davidson, as leader of the largest opposition party at Holyrood, is tasked with leading Scottish Unionism and that too is a larger, more important, job than almost anything available at Westminster,' he wrote. 'Reviving Unionism is a ten-year project too. That's about more than just maintaining its current, though still provisional, numerical supremacy over nationalism but, just as importantly, about rethinking what Unionism *means* in 2016 and beyond.' There is doubtless great truth in this. As we have seen, Ruth's primary political motivator is the Union. Given her background in the army – and that other British institution, the BBC – it is unsurprising that she would be reluctant to ditch Scottish politics just as the UK faced perhaps its biggest challenge. That is simply not Ruth's style.

A prominent – indeed, leading – role in any future independence campaign would also be deeply attractive to her. Ruth is now – more so than in 2014 – a seasoned political operator. Her debating has vastly improved from her early days as leader, as has her grasp of policy and political nuance. There are still improvements to be made – as there is with anyone – but the prospect of going head-to-head with Sturgeon is a tantalising one for her. It can also only boost her profile further. Assuming the pro-Union side wins a future contest, which seems probable at the moment, Ruth would be an even more noteworthy figure, nationally and domestically.

While Ruth would never desert a campaign to save the Union, there is her personal life to consider. Now engaged to be married, there is certainly a part of Ruth that values the quiet life, away from the public eye. As this book was going to press, she had just announced she was pregnant with her first child, expected in October 2018. The Tory leader plans to take a few months off for maternity leave before returning to the Scottish Parliament in spring 2019, telling reporters, 'You can have a family and combine that with a career, and I don't think we should ever send a message to women that they can't have both.' Yet her family life may influence her decisions on the kind of political career she chooses to pursue – in Holyrood or Westminster, in the limelight or on the back benches.

There is a precedent, too, for Ruth resigning the Scottish Tory leadership. No previous incumbent has lasted more than around six years in the post. Ruth has already done five years and, by historical precedent, should not have long left.

It remains highly likely, however, that Ruth will lead the Scottish Conservatives into the beginning of the next decade and its elections. In that role, she will be, more likely than not, called upon to lead the campaign in favour of the Union. And she will also be tasked with convincing the public that her party – once the pariahs of Scottish politics – can now be a party of government. Neither of these tasks will be easy, but Ruth likes a challenge. Her qualities of leadership and determination have served her well in the past. There is no reason to think they will not do so in the future.

INDEX

Goldie, Annabel *cont.*
  and Calman Commission 84
  RD works for 90–91
  and 2011 Scottish parliamentary
    election 100, 101–2
  support for RD's leadership bid 124–5
  attacks RD's critics 145, 146
Goodman, Paul 156
Gove, Michael 117, 145–6, 251, 252
Gray, Iain 76, 99–100, 101, 102, 107

Hague, William 66, 70, 73–4
Harper, Robin 82
Harvie, Sir Jack 122–3
Harvie, Patrick 48, 262
Heath, Edward 21–4, 25
Hewitt, Gavin 265
Hood, Lorna 47
Hosie, Stewart 194

independence referendum (2014)
  and RD during campaign 8–10,
    163–72, 173–8
  and Scottish Conservative Party 9, 10
  signing of Edinburgh Agreement
    159–61, 173, 176
  Labour Party dominance in Better
    Together 162–3
  after result 178–82
  and Smith Commission 205–7

Jenkins, Roy 103
Johnson, Boris 12, 240, 243, 249–50, 251
Jones, Ramsay 7, 120, 228

Kerr, Aidan 5
Kerr, David 93
Kerr, Liam 231
Kettle, Martin 205
Khan, Sadiq 243, 245
Kidd, Colin 30
Kilgour, Robert 123
Kingdom FM 57

Lamont, Johann 128, 162, 168
Lamont, John
  and leadership of Scottish
    Conservative Party 7, 110, 111,
    112–14

and 2007 Scottish parliamentary
    election 79
  attack on Murdo Fraser 121
  and 2015 general election 193
  and 2017 general election 303
Lawson, Nigel 27
Leadsom, Andrea 12, 240, 243–4, 249,
    251, 252, 253, 254
Lennon, Neil 112
Letwin, Oliver 27

Macaskill, Malcolm 89–90, 96, 97
McColm, Euan 108, 109, 111
Macdonald, Catriona 29
McDougall, Blair 162
McFarlane, Ross 120
McLeish, Henry 74–5
McLetchie, David
  on autonomy for Scottish
    Conservatives 66
  becomes leader of Scottish
    Conservatives 70
  after 1999 Scottish parliamentary
    election 71–2
  support from William Hague 74
  and resignation of Henry McLeish
    74–5
  after 2003 Scottish parliamentary
    election 75–6
  resignation of 77
  in 2011 Scottish parliamentary
    election 105
Macmillan, Harold 20, 21
McMillan, Sir Iain 265
Mandela, Nelson 156–7
Marr, Andrew 175
Martin, Iain 196
Martin, Michael 92
Massie, Alex 151–2, 164, 195, 300–301, 315
May, Theresa
  becomes leader of Conservative
    Party 13, 251
  and 2017 general election 13–14, 293,
    296, 297, 298, 305, 306–7
  support from RD for leadership 252–3
  relationship with RD 253–7, 307–8
  and Donald Trump 260–61
  and possible second independence
    referendum 288

Strathclyde Commission 8, 136–7, 141,
147, 148, 149–53, 177
Stuart, Gisela 240
Sturgeon, Nicola
and 2016 Scottish parliamentary
election 3–4
and possible second independence
referendum 11, 13, 235, 246–8,
262–3, 267–8, 272, 285–6, 289, 290
during independence referendum
campaign 170, 171–2
appointed First Minister 179, 183–4
and 2015 general election 196–7
on increasing support for Scottish
Conservative Party 212–13
and Donald Trump 259–60
and Brexit negotiations 262–3
Summerskill, Ben 131
Sutherland, Colin 21
Swanson, Ian 226
Swinney, John 81

Taylor, Brian 81, 269
Terras, Jim 214
Thatcher, Margaret
and decline of Conservative Party in
Scotland 6–7, 25–6, 27–30
opposition to devolution 24–5, 67
and poll tax 27–9
RD's view of 30–32
comparison to RD 185–6
Thomson, Alice 152
Thomson, Ross 223–4, 303
Tomkins, Adam 141
Torrance, David 5, 65–6, 72, 73, 82, 184,
221
Trump, Donald 258–61

Unionist Party 17–21

Wallace, Jim 71
Wallace, Mark 167, 237–8
Warsi, Baroness 104
Watt, Nicholas 195
Wells, Annie 142, 223–4
Welsh, Ian 72
Whatever Happened to Tory Scotland?
(Torrance, ed.) 29–30
Whitaker, Andrew 109

Wilson, Jen
and 2016 Scottish parliamentary
election 3, 227
engagement to RD 47
and 2015 general election 188

Younger, George 23